ANCIENT INDIAN CITIES

ANCIENT INDIAN CITIES

Editor-in-Chief

Swami Chidatman Jee Maharaj

ANMOL PUBLICATIONS PVT. LTD.

NEW DELHI - 110 002 (INDIA)

ANMOL PUBLICATIONS PVT. LTD.
H.O.: 4374/4B, Ansari Road, Daryaganj,
New Delhi-110 002 (India)
Ph.: 23278000, 23261597
B.O.: No. 1015, Ist Main Road, BSK IIIrd Stage
IIIrd Phase, IIIrd Block,
Bangalore - 560 085 (India)
Visit us at: www.anmolpublications.com

Ancient Indian Cities

First Published, 2009
ISBN 978-81-261-3606-3

PRINTED IN INDIA
Printed at Mehra Offset Press, Delhi.

Contents

Preface

India colourful and vibrant, a land as diverse as its people. A mosaic of faiths, cultures, customs and languages that blend harmoniously to form a composite whole. One of the world's oldest living civilizations—which gave to the world—the concept of zero, the primordial sound Aum..., Yoga and Buddhism.

She is old. She is young. The two diametrically opposite, different yet unique and dynamic faces of India coexist even at this turn of the millennium. With a history of heritage, learning and civilisation dating back to almost 5000 years or perhaps even more, the modern India presents itself as an ideal country. From snow clad mountains to breezy sparkling blue sea side. From arid deserts with shifting sand dunes to lush green country sides. From ancient relics and architectural ruins dating back into antiquity to modern cities, India has it all.

To the north it is bordered by the world's highest mountain chain, where foothill valleys cover the northernmost of the country's maximum states. Further south, plateaus, tropical rain forests and sandy deserts are bordered by palm fringed beaches. Its southernmost tip is the meeting point of three Oceans.

India is a land of staggering contrast with a mingling of the tradition and modernity that is an unique experience to be in India. One will forever remember the stay in this wonderful Homeland-a land truly of mystery and enchantment. Only India can offer such an astonishing variety of contrasts.

She has given birth to numerous spiritual leaders and founders of some of the popular religions of the present day world. India probably has the most religious diversity in any country. It's the birthplace of Hinduism, Buddhism, Sikhism and Jainism and is among the few places to have a resident

Zoroastrian population. India with her veritable treasure trove of culture, mysticism, philosophy, art, music and architecture to name a few. Much of India's classical music is devotional and the North Indian Hindustani and South Indian Carnatic streams are distinct and both have a complex 'raga' framework. The legacy of dance in India is tremendous. The classical dances of India are numerous such as Kathakali of Kerala, Bharatnatyam of Tamil Nadu, Kuchipudi of Andhra Pradesh, Manipuri and Odissi from Orissa are the prominent dance forms in this country that sways to an altogether novel beat. The Yakshagana, nautanki and puppetry are ancient folk forms that live on till date. The earliest specimens of Indian painting are the ones on the walls of the Ajanta Caves dating back to 2nd century BC. The Mughals had a huge impact on Indian art. The influence of Persian art brought placid garden scenes, illustrations from myths, legends and history into Indian art. Word craft, handicrafts, architecture and sculpture all contribute to this rich and varied domain. Indian literature, both in English and in the vernacular, is ever more popular around the world.

The book aims at presenting perspectives of different aspects of Indian culture. It has topics on Indian classical music and dance, painting, ayurveda and yoga which are traditional and indigenous system of physical and mental wellbeing, language, philosophy and excellence achievements by Indian in the different branches of science and social sciences. It also includes our ancient religious and classic literature.

It is hoped that this book will be welcomed by the general readers as also scholars who are interested in the Indian heritage.

—Editors

1

Cities of Ancient India

Aror

The medieval city of Aror is the original homeplace of the Arora community in the Punjab region of South Asia. It was the ancient capital of Sindh, which is now in Sukkur, Pakistan. In 711 AD Aror was captured by Islamic invaders and in 962 AD it was hit by a massive earthquake that changed the course of the Indus river. After this, the Arora community left Aror and spread through other parts of the Punjab region.

In modern times, the once vibrant metropolis has been reduced to a small village. It used to be home to the popular Kalka Devi Mandir, one of the few temples in Pakistan, but this Hindu temple was burned in 1992 by Muslims in retaliation for the destruction of Babri Masjid in India.

Arab historians used the words Alor, Al-rur, Al-ruhr and similar variations to describe Aror.

Kannauj

Kannauj also spelt *Kanauj*, is a city and a municipal board or Nagar Palika Parishad in Kannauj district in the Indian state of Uttar Pradesh. The city's name is traditionally derived from the term *Kanyakubja* (maiden's womb). Kannauj is an ancient city, in earlier times the capital of a great Hindu kingdom. Kannauj is known for the distilling of scents and is a market centre for tobacco, perfume, and rose water.

Kannauj is the administrative headquarters of Kannauj District. The population was 58,932 in 1991. It has given its name to a distinct dialect of the Hindi language known as Kanauji.

History

Formerly known as Kanyakubja (called Kanogiza by Ptolemy), the town is known to have been an important centre during the Gupta empire. It was a centre of Brahmanical influence for centuries. Kannauj is frequently referred to in the epic *Mahabharata* and is alluded to by Patanjali in the second century B.C. In the year 405 A.D. when great Chinese pilgrim Fa-hien visited the city it had only two Buddhist monasteries and it was not a very large. When Hiuen Tsang visited the city in 636 A.D., however, Kannauj had grown large. Hiuen Tsang stayed here for seven years.

Kannauj reached the pinnacle of its glory in the 7th century under emperor Harshavardhana (606-647 A.D.) Harshavardhana made Kannauj his capital. At that time it had earned the name of Mahodaya Sree due to its grandeur and prosperity.

Kannauj then had a teeming population, with hundreds of Hindu and Buddhist temples and monasteries, extending along the east bank of the Ganges for about four miles. It had beautiful gardens and tanks, and was strongly fortified. Harshavardhana, however, was greatly weakened after being defeated by the Chalukya emperor Pulakesin II; his empire fell apart soon after his death.

By the end of the 8th century, Kannauj became the focus of a three-way contest by the three dominant dynasties of the time, the Pratiharas of Malwa, the Rashtrakutas of the Deccan, and the Palas of Bengal. The Pala king Dharmapala installed a proxy king at the end of the 8th century. However, when the Pratihara king Nagabhata II conquered Kannauj in the 9th century Kannauj became the Pratihara capital for nearly 200 years.

During this period, it became known as a centre for poetry. The Pratiharas ruled much of northern India in the latter half of the 8th century, but they had weakened by the early 10th century. The Rashtrakuta king Indra III captured Kannauj in

916, and by the end of that century, the Pratihara domains had been reduced to a small kingdom around the town of Kannauj.

In 1019, the town was sacked by Mahmud of Ghazni, beginning a chaotic period for the city. After this sacking of Kannauj, the area came to be dominated by the Chandela Rajput clan of Bundelkhand. The Gahadvala dynasty, descended from former vassals of the Pratiharas, established themselves as rulers of Kannauj at the end of the 11th century. Kannauj recovered some of its former prosperity under the Gahadvalas, but the respite was brief, for the city was sacked again in 1194 by Mohammed of Ghori, and by the early years of the 13th century it was incorporated into the Delhi Sultanate. Kannauj has never since recovered its importance.

Monuments

The size and scale of the ancient town can be gauged from the fact that existing ruins extend over the lands of five villages, occupying a semicircle fully 4 miles in diameter. While no historic Hindu structures remain intact, the "great mosque", constructed by Ibrahim Shah of Jaunpur in 1406 out of the remains of demolished Hindu temples, is still known to Hindus as "Sita's Kitchen". Brahminism in lower Bengal also dates its origin from a migration southwards from this city in the 9th and 10th centuries.

Geography

Kannauj is located at 27.07° N 79.92° E. It has an average elevation of 139 metres (456 feet).

Demographics

As of 2001 India census, Kannauj had a population of 71,530. Males constitute 53% of the population and females 47%. Kannauj has an average literacy rate of 58%, lower than the national average of 59.5%: male literacy is 64%, and female literacy is 52%. In Kannauj, 15% of the population is under 6 years of age.

Places of Interest in and around Kannauj

- *Kannauj Museum* : This museum depicts an

archeologically significant variety of clay idols. In ancient times Kannauj was best known for its art and culture like Mathura, Kashi and Koshambi. During the Maurya period it was a fully developed place. The clay models found here show that this was a very progressive district in that period. The great Chinese visitor Hiuen Tsang praised Kannauj during his visit to India. The sculptures from antiquity can be categorized as follows: i. Ancient Period (exact time period not available) ii. Maurya Period (325 BC) iii. Shudag period (184 BC) iv. Kushar Period (100 AD) v. Gupta period (319 AD to 450 AD) vi. Post Gupta period (450 to 650 AD) and Harsh Period

- *Lakh Bahosi Bird Sanctuary :* The Bird Sanctuary at Lakh Bahosi is a major tourist attraction for bird watchers. Bird watching can be done from month of November to the end of March in this sanctuary. December, January, and February are the months when one can see the greatest variety of birds in the 3 sq. km. sanctuary area. A total of approximately 97 bird families are found in India, according to surveys; birds from 49 families have been seen at Lakh Bhosi Bird Sanctuary.
- Gauri Shankar Temple in Kannauj city.
- Annapurna Templeat Tirwa, Kannauj.
- Dargah of Haji Sharif in Kannauj city.

Bairat

Bairat is a town in northern Jaipur District of Rajasthan, India located 52 km north of Jaipur, and 66 km west of Alwar.

History

The ancient name of the town was Viratnagar, and its history goes back to the time of the Mahabharata. Viratnagar was the capital of the ancient Indian kingdom (Mahajanapada) of Machcha or Matsya. The kingdom came under the control of the neighbouring Chedi Kingdom in the 5th century, and was later part of the Mauryan Empire. The ruins of the *Bijak-*

ki-pahadi, a Buddhist Chaitya (chapel) from the 3rd century BC, is the oldest free standing Buddhist structure in India. The town also has the ruins of a Buddhist monastery, a wood and timber shrine, and rock-cut edict from Emperor Ashoka that date from the Mauryan period.

In 634 Xuanzang had visited the Bairat and Mathura towns. He went east to Jalandhar in eastern Punjab, before climbing up to visit predominantly Theravada monasteries in the Kulu valley and turning southward again to Bairat and then Mathura, on the Yamuna river.

The town has a number of Mughal structures, including a *Chhatri* (cenotaph) with some of the earliest surviving murals in Rajasthan, and a lodge where the Mughal emperor Akbar hunted and stayed overnight on his yearly pilgrimage to Ajmer.

The town's Viratnagar Museum houses artifacts from Bairat's long history, including sculptures, coins, pottery, seals and metal objects the banganga river originates from nearby village mair.

Demographics

As of 2001 India census, Viratnagar had a population of 17,237. Males constitute 53% of the population and females 47%. Viratnagar has an average literacy rate of 50%, lower than the national average of 59.5%: male literacy is 65%, and female literacy is 34%. In Viratnagar, 20% of the population is under 6 years of age.

Kalibangan

Kalibangan is a town located at 29.47° N 74.13° E on the left or southern banks of the Ghaggar (Ghaggar-Hakra River), identified by some scholars with Saraswati River in Tehsil Pilibangan, between Suratgarh and Hanumangarh in Hanumangarh district, Rajasthan, India 205 km. from Bikaner. The prehistoric and pre-Mauryan character of Indus Valley Civilization was first identified by Luigi Tessitori at this site. Kalibangan's excavation report was largely unpublished, until, in Jan 2003, ASI (Archaeological Survey of India) brought out a detailed report, 34 years after the completion of excavations, which justified the previously held view of Kalibangan being a major provincial capital of the Indus Valley Civilization. Kalibangan is distinguished by its unique fire altars and *world's earliest attested ploughed field.*

Indus Valley Civilization

The identity of Kalibangan as a pre-historic site was discovered by Luigi Pio Tessitori, an Italian Indologist (1887-1919). He was doing some research in ancient Indian texts. He was surprised by the character of ruins in that area, and he sought help from Sir John Marshall of the Archaeological Survey of India.

At that time ASI had some excavations done on Harappa, but they never had any idea about the character of the ruins. In fact, Tessitori is the first person to recognise that the ruins are 'Prehistoric' and pre-Mauryan. Luigi Pio Tessitori also pointed out the nature of the culture, but at that time it was not possible to guess that Indus Valley Civilisation lied in the ruins of Kalibangan, and he died five years before Harappan culture was duly recognized.

After India's independence, both the major Harappan cities together with the Indus went into Pakistan and Indian archaeologists were compelled to intensify the search for Harappan sites in India. Amlanand Ghosh (Ex. Director General, Archaeological Survey of India, or ASI) was the first person to recognise this site as Harappan and marked it out for excavations.. Under the leadership of B.B. Lal (then Director General, ASI), Balkrishna (B.K.) Thapar, M. D. Khare, K. M. Shrivastava and S. P. Jain carried out excavations for 9 years (1960-9) in 9 successive excavation sessions. Two ancient mounds were excavated, spread over half kilometre (area quarter square kilometer). On western side is the smaller mound (KLB1), 9 metres high and known as citadel. Eastern mound is higher (12 metres) and bigger, known as lower city (KLB2).

The excavation unexpectedly brought to light a twofold sequence of cultures, of which the upper one (Kalibangan I) belongs to the Harappan, showing the characteristic grid layout of a metropolis and the lower one (Kalibangan II) was formerly called pre-Harappan but now it is called "Early Harappan or antecedent Harappan".

Proto-Harappan Phase

Traces of pre-Harappan culture have been found only at the lower levels of the western mound. According to archaeological evidence, the Indus Valley culture existed at the site from the proto-Harappan age (3500 BC-2500 BC) to the Harappan age (2500 BC-1750 BC). This earlier phase is labelled Kalibangan-I (KLB-I) or Period-I.Similarity of pottery relates Kalibangan-I with the Sothi culture because this type of pottery was first discovered at Sothi village in Afghanistan.

Fort and Houses

In this phase, the settlement was fortified, using dried mud bricks, from the beginning of occupation. This *fort* had been built twice in different periods. Earlier, fort wall had a thickness of 1.9 metres, which was raised to 3.7-4.1 metres during reconstruction in this phase. Brick size was 20 x 20 x 10 cm in both construction-phases. The citadel mound (smaller mound) is a parallelogram about 130 metres on the east-west axis and 260 metres on the north-south. Town planning was like that of Mohanjodaro or Harappa. The direction of houses and brick sizes was markedly different from that used in the Harappan phase (KLB-II).

Within the walled area, the *houses* were also built of mud bricks of the same size as used in the fort wall; the use of burnt bricks is attested by a drain within the houses, remains of ovens and cylindrical pits, lined with lime plaster. Some burnt wedge shaped bricks also have been found.

Earliest Ploughed Field

B. B. Lal, former DG of ASI, said : "Kalibangan in Rajasthan has given the evidence of the earliest (ca. 2800 BC) ploughed agricultural field ever revealed through an excavation." It has been found south east of the pre-Harappan settlement, outside the fort. "Kalibangan excavations in present western Rajasthan shows a ploughed field, the first site of this nature in the world. It shows a grid pattern of furrows, placed about 30 cm apart running east-west and other spaced about 190 cm apart running north-south, a pattern remarkably similar to the one practised even now." Even today, similar ploughing is used for two simultaneous crops in this region, esp. of mustard and gram. For preservation, this excavated ploughed field area was refilled after excavation and the area was marked by concrete pillar posts.

Pottery

The distinguishing mark of this early phase is pottery, characterized by six fabrics labelled A, B, C, D, E anf F, which were first identified at *Sothi* in Afganistan.

Fabrics A, B, and D can be clubbed together. They are red painted. Fabric-A is carelessly potted in spite of use of potter's wheel. It contains designs in light-black, often decorated with white lines. Lines, semicircles, grids, insects, flowers, leaves, trees and squares were favourite motifs. Fabric-B shows marked improvement in finishing, but the lower half was deliberately roughened. Flowers, animals and flowers were painted in black on red background.

Fabric-D contained designs of slanted lines or semicircles in some, while most pots were plain. But Fabric-C pottery was thicker and stronger. Fabric-C was distinguished by violet tinge and fine polish, with designs in black; it is the best proto-Harappan pottery in finishing. Fabric-E was light coloured and Fabric-F was grey..

Other Finds

Among the other finds of this Period are: small blades of chalcedony and agate, sometimes serrated or backed; beads of steatite, shell, carnelian, terracota and copper; bangles of copper, shell and terracota; terracota objects like a toy-cart, wheel and a broken bull; quem with mullers, a bone point, and copper celts, including an unusual axe, etc. Toy carts suggest carts were used for transportation in early phase of Kalibangan.

Earliest Earthquakes & End of Phase-I

B.B.Lal, former DG of ASI, said : "Kalibangan in Rajasthan... has also shown that there occurred an earthquake around

2600 BC, which brought to an end the Early Indus settlement at the site." This is perhaps the earliest archaeologically recorded earthquake At least three pre-historic earthquakes affecting the Indus Valley Civilization at Dholavira in Khadir have been identified during (2800 or) 2900–1800 BC.

KLB-I phase has left 1.6 metres of continuous deposits during five distinct structural strata, the last of which was destroyed perhaps by an earthquake and the site was abandoned around 2600 BC, soon to be settled again by Harappans.

Harappan Phase

The most distinctive feature of KLB-II or Harappan phase was settlements in two parts, one citadel and another lower town, as in other Harappan towns, which was absent in KLB-I.

Citadel

In KLB-I, all the inhabitants lived within the fortified town on western mound. But in KLB-II, the citadel was built atop the ruined citadel of KLB-I on the western mound, with a lower town at some distance in the east. The citadel comples was roughly a parallelogram, consisting of two equal halves (northern and southern), both squares but differently designed. Both parts were within a fort whose wall was 3-7 metres wide with bastions at some distances, made of 40 x 20 x 10 cm bricks in first phase of Harappan period, and of 30 x 15 x 7.5 cm in second structural phase.

The fort had four entrances from the outside, three in the eastern-northern half. The southern gate is in a dilapidated state, but stairs outside the southern gate have been identified. There was a narrow corridor beside the stairs. This southern gate was for the public, while northern gate was for the aristocracy living in the northern half of the citadel. The main northern gate was between two bastions. There were two other gates in the north-eastern side.

Fire Altars

At Kalibangan fire Vedi (altar)s have been discovered, similar to those found at Lothal which S.R. Rao thinks could have served no other purpose than a ritualistic one. These altars suggest fire worship or worship of Agni, the Hindu god of fire. It is the only Indus Valley Civilization site where there is no evidence to suggest the worship of the "mother goddess".

Within the fortified citadel complex, the southern half contained many (five or six) raised platforms of mud bricks, mutually separated by corridors. Stairs were attached to these platforms. Vandalisation of these platforms by brick robbers makes it difficult to reconstruct the original shape of structures above them but unmistakable remnants of rectangular or oval *kundas* or fire-pits of burnt bricks for *Vedi (altars)* have been found, with a *yupa* or sacrificial post (cylindrical or with rectangular cross-section, sometimes bricks were laid upon each other to construct such a post) in the middle of each kunda and sacrificial terracota cakes (pinda) in all these fire-pits. Houses in the lower town also contain similar altars. Burnt charcoals have been found in these fire-pits.

The structure of these fire-altars is reminiscent of (Vedic) fire-altars, but the analogy may be coincidental, and these altars are perhaps intended for some specific (perpaps religious) purpose by the community as a whole. In some fire-altars remnants of animals have been found, which suggest a possibility of animal-sacrifice.

"Besides the above two principle parts of the metropolis there was also a third one-a moderate structure situated upwards of 8O m e. of the lower town containing four to five fire altars. This lonely structure may perhaps have been used for ritual purposes." Thus, fire-altars have been found in three groups : public altars in the citadel, household altars in lower town, and public altars in a third separate group.

Lower Town

The lower town was also a fortified parallelogram, although only traces are now left. The fort was made of mud bricks (40 x 20 x 10 cm) and three or four structural phases have been recognised. It had gates in north and west.

B. B. Lal wrote :"Well-regulated streets (were) oriented almost invariably along with the cardinal directions, thus forming a gridiron pattern. (At Kalibangan) even the widths of these streets were in a set ratio, *i.e.* if the narrowest lane was one unit in width, the other streets were twice, thrice and so on. (...) Such a town-planning was unknown in contemporary West Asia.".

The lower town was 239 metres east to west, but north-south extent cannot be determined. 8 main roads have been recognised, 5 north-south and 3 east-west. Few more east-west roads are expected to be buried within the unexccavated remains. Second east-west road ran in a curved outline to meet the first at the north-eastern end (towards the river), where a gateway was provided. This road was an anomaly in the grid-pattern of straight roads. There were many lanes connected to specific housing complexes. Roads and lanes had widths in accurately determined proportions, like in other Harappan cities, ranging from 7.2 metres for main roads to 1.8 metres for narrow lanes. Fender posts were installed at street corners to prevent accidents. In second structural lavel, roads were laid with mud tiles. Drains from houses emptied into pits (soakage jars) beneath the roads. Some central authority must be there to plan and regulate all this.

Housing

Like town planning, housing also followed the common pattern of other Harappan cities. Due to grid-pattern of town planning like a chess board, all houses opened out to at least two or three roads or lanes. Each house had a courtyard and 6-7 rooms on three sides, with a well in some houses. One house had stairs for going to the roof. Houses were built of 30 x 15 x 7.5 cm mud bricks (same as those used in second structural phase of fort wall). Burnt bricks were used in drains, wells, bathing platforms and door-sills, besides fire-altar. Floors of rooms were built of thrashed fine mud, sometimes laid with mud bricks or terracota cakes. One house had floors built of burnt tiles decorated with geometrical designs.

Pottery

Some early Kalibangan pottery has close resemblance to the pottery of the Hakra ware in Cholistan, to other Early

Harappan pottery from the Indus Valley Civilization and to the pottery of the Integration Era. Functionally, pottery can be classified into household pots, religious and burial purposes. Structurally, we have classes like plain and decorated wares. Some pots had Harappan inscriptions (undeciphered) on them.

Terracota

The best terracota figure from Kalibangan is that a charging bull which is considered to signify the "realistic and powerful folk art of Harappan Age".

Seals

Harappan seals have been found in this phase. Most noteworthy is a cylindrical seal.

Other Finds

A cylindrical graduated measuring rod and a clay ball with human figures are other notable findsa.

Burial Systems

Three systems of burial have been attested in the burial gound ~300 yards south-west of the citadel, where ~34 graves have been found :

1. Burial in rectangular or oval pit, with corpse laid down straight (extended), head northwards amidst pottery. In one pit a copper mirror was found among these objects. Pits were mud filled after burying. One grave was enclosed with a mud brick wall plastered from inside. One child had six holes in the skull. Many paleopathological evidences have been gathered from these graves.
2. Burial in pot (urn) in a circular pit, with no corpse. Four to 29 pots and utensils were placed around the main pot (urn). In some graves beads, shell, etc. have been found.
3. Rectanglliar or oval grave-pit, containing only pottery and other funerary objects. Like the first type, the length of this type of graves was also along north-south. The latter two methods were not associated with

any skeletal remains and may be related to symbolic burial, not found at other Harappan towns. The third type of graves contained objects as in the second type, like beads, shells, etc., but no corpse.

End of Civilisation

Robert Raikes has argued that Kalibangan was abandoned because the river dried up. Prof. B. B. Lal (retd. Director General of Archaeological Survey of India) supports this view by asserting: "Radiocarbon dates indicate that the Mature Harappan settlement at Kalibangan had to be abandoned around 2000-1900 BC. And, as the hydrological evidence indicates, this abandonment took place on account of the drying up of the Saraswati (Ghaggar). This latter part is duly established by the work of Raikes, an Italian hydrologist, and of his Indian collaborators".

Modern Kalibangan

Kalibangan is also known for its bangle industry. Its name translates to "black bangles" ("Kala", in Hindi, means black and "bangan" means bangles). Few miles downstream is the railway station and township named Pilibanga, which means *Yellow Bangles*.

ASI set up a *Archaeological Museum* at Kalibangan in 1983 to store the excavated materials excavated here during 1961-69. In one gallery, Pre-Harappan finds are displayed, while Harappan finds are displayed in the other two galleries.

Sravasti

Sravasti or Savatthi a city of ancient India, was one of the six largest cities in India during Gautama Buddha's lifetime. The city was located in the fertile Gangetic plains in the present day's Gonda district of Uttar Pradesh. Jetavana monastery was a famous monastery close to Savatthi.

Origin of Sravasti

According to the epic Ramayana, Sravasti was a new city created for Lava (the son of Raghava Rama). Rama divided his Kosala Kingdom into two parts and installed his son Lava at

Sravasti and another son Kusha at Kushavati, another town in Kosala. According to the Mahabharata, the origin of Sravasti lies with the legendary king Shravasta. According to Buddhist tradition, the city was called Savatthi because the sage Savattha lived there. Another tradition says there was a caravanserai there, and people meeting there asked each other what they had ("Kim bhandam atthi?"), then replied "Sabbam atthi" (meaning "we have all things", as in everything). And the name of the city was based on the reply.

Sravasti in the Buddha's Time

Savatthi was located on the banks of the river Aciravati (now called the Rapti river). It was the capital city of the kingdom of Kosala, and its king was called Pasenadi, who was a disciple of Buddha. Buddhaghosa says that, in the Buddha's day, there were fifty seven thousand families in Savatthi, and that it was the chief city in the country of Kasi Kosala, which was three hundred leagues in extent and had eighty thousand villages. He stated the population of Savatthi to have been 180 million.

The road from Rajagaha to Savatthi passed through Vaishali, and the Parayanavagga gives as the resting places between the two cities: Setavya, Kapilavatthu, Kusinara, Pava and Bhoganagara. Further on, there was a road running southwards from Savatthi through Saketa to Koshambi. Between Saketa and Savatthi was located Toranavatthu.

The Buddha passed the greater part of his monastic life in Savatthi. His first visit to Savatthi was at the invitation of Anathapindika, whom he met in Rajagaha. The main monasteries in Sravasti were the Jetavana and the Pubbarama. Savatthi also contained the monastery of Rajakarama, built by Pasenadi, opposite Jetavana. Not far from the city was a dark forest called the Andhavana, where some monks and nun went to live. Outside the city gate of Savatthi was a fisherman's village of five hundred families.

The chief patrons of the Buddha in Savatthi were Anathapindika, Vishakha, Suppavasa and Pasenadi. When Bandhula left Vaishali he came to live in Savatthi.

Woodward states that, of the four Nikayas, 871 suttas are said to have been preached in Savatthi; 844 of which are in Jetavana, 23 in the Pubbarama, and 4 in the suburbs of Savatthi. These suttas are made up of 6 in the Digha Nikaya, 75 in the Majjhima Nikaya, 736 in the Samyutta Nikaya, and 54 in the Anguttara Nikaya.

The Commentaries state that the Buddha spent twenty five rainy seasons in Savatthi, this leaving only twenty to be spent elsewhere. Of the 25 rainy seasons Buddha lived in Sravasti, he spent 19 in the monastery named Jetavana, and 6 in the monastery called Pubbarama. Thus, Sravasti is the place where Buddha lived the longest amount of time, and it is the place where he gave the largest amount of discourses and instructions.

Savatthi is the place where the Twin Miracle (Pali:Yamaka Patihara) took place, in which Buddha made a demonstration of his supernatural powers for the purpose of silencing certain believers of other faiths who proclaimed that the Buddha was incapable of performing supernatural miracles. The Buddhist commentarial tradition says that Savatthi is the scene of each Buddha's Yamaka patihariya; Gotama Buddha performed this miracle under the Gandamba tree.

The Chinese Pilgrim Hiouen Thsang found the old city in ruins, but recorded the sites of various buildings.

Current Sravasti

Of the ancient Savatthi the city walls are still standing. Within these, the remains of 3 ancient buildings can be visited: Angulimala's stupa, Anathapindika's stupa, and an old temple dedicated to a Jain Tirthankara. Outside of Savatthi is located the stupa where the Twin Miracle (Pali:Yamaka Patihara) took place.

The site of Jetavana monastery is the main pilgrim destination, with meditation and chanting mainly done at the Gandhakuti (Buddha's hut) and the Anandabodhi tree. Buddhist monasteries from the following countries have been constructed at Sravasti: Thailand, South Korea, Sri Lanka, Myanmar, Tibet and China.

Sagala

Sagala, believed to be modern Sialkot, was a city of located in northern Punjab, Pakistan. Sagala (alias Sakala) is mentioned as the capital of the successor Greek kingdom when it was made capital of King Menander I empire.

References in Mahabharata

There is a town of the name of Sakala, a river of the name of Apaga, and a clan of the Vahikas known by the name of the Jarttikas (Mbh 8:44). Nakula, proceeding to Sakala, the city of the Madras, made his uncle Shalya accept from affection the sway of the Pandavas (Mbh 2:31).

Destruction by Alexander

The city appears in the accounts of Alexander the Great's conquests of Persia's eastern provinces in Asia. After crossing the Hydraotes, Alexander, joined by Porus with elephants and 5,000 local troops, laid siege to Sagala, where the Cathaeans had entrenched themselves. The city was razed to the ground, and many of its inhabitants killed:

"The Cathaeans... had a strong city near which they proposed to make their stand, named Sagala. The next day Alexander rested his troops, and on the third advanced on Sangala, where the Cathaeans and their neighbours who had joined them were drawn up in front of the city. At this point too, Porus arrived, bringing with him the rest of the elephants and some five thousand of his troops. Alexander returned to Sangala, razed the city to the ground, and annexed its territory". Sagala was rebuilt and established as an outpost and incorporated into Alexander's vast empire. I was the most easternmost outpost established by Alexander and remained a centre of Hellenistic influence for quite some time after. Arrian, Anabasis of Alexander, V.22-24

Sunga Period

Following his overthrowing of the Mauryan Empire, Pusyamitra Sunga is believed in tradition to have expanded northwest as far as Sagala. According to the 2nd century Ashokavadana:

"Then King Pusyamitra equipped a fourfold army, and intending to destroy the Buddhist religion, he went to the Kukkutarama. Pusyamitra therefore destroyed the sangharama, killed the monks there, and departed.

After some time, he arrived in Sakala, and proclaimed that he would give a hundred dinara reward to whomever brought him the head of a Buddhist monk" (*Shramanas*) Ashokavadana, 133, trans. John Strong.

Indo-Greek Period

The Indo-Greeks apparently repelled the Sungas and Sagala was used as a capital by the Greco-Bactrian (alternatively Indo-Greek or Graeco-Indian) king Menander during his reign between 160 and 135 BC.

Though many Graeco-Bactrian, and even some Indo-Greek cities were designed along Greek architectural lines. In contrast to other imperialist governments elsewhere, literary accounts suggests the Greeks and the local population of cities like Sagala lived in relative harmony, with some of the local residents adopting the responsibilities of Greek citizenship-and more astonishingly, Greeks converting to Buddhism and adopting local traditions.

The best descriptions of Sagala however, come from the Milinda Panha, a dialogue between king Menander and the Buddhist monk Nagasena. Historians like Sir Tarn believe this document was written around 100 years after Menander's rule, which is one of the best enduring testimonies of the productiveness and benevolance of his rule, which has made the more modern theory that he was regarded as a Chakravartin-King of the Wheel or literally Wheel-Turner in Sansrkit-generally accepted.

In the Milindapanha, the city is described in the following terms:

"There is in the country of the Yonakas a great centre of trade, a city that is called Sagala, situate in a delightful country well watered and hilly, abounding in parks and gardens and groves and lakes and tanks, a paradise of rivers and mountains and woods. Wise

architects have laid it out, and its people know of no oppression, since all their enemies and adversaries have been put down.

Brave is its defence, with many and various strong towers and ramparts, with superb gates and entrance archways; and with the royal citadel in its midst, white walled and deeply moated. Well laid out are its streets, squares, cross roads, and market places. Well displayed are the innumerable sorts of costly merchandise with which its shops are filled.

It is richly adorned with hundreds of alms-halls of various kinds; and splendid with hundreds of thousands of magnificent mansions, which rise aloft like the mountain peaks of the Himalayas. Its streets are filled with elephants, horses, carriages, and foot-passengers, frequented by groups of handsome men and beautiful women, and crowded by men of all sorts and conditions, Brahmans, nobles, artificers, and servants.

They resound with cries of welcome to the teachers of every creed, and the city is the resort of the leading men of each of the differing sects. Shops are there for the sale of Benares muslin, of Kotumbara stuffs, and of other cloths of various kinds; and sweet odours are exhaled from the bazaars, where all sorts of flowers and perfumes are tastefully set out. Jewels are there in plenty, such as men's hearts desire, and guilds of traders in all sorts of finery display their goods in the bazaars that face all quarters of the sky.

So full is the city of money, and of gold and silver ware, of copper and stone ware, that it is a very mine of dazzling treasures. And there is laid up there much store of property and corn and things of value in warehouses-foods and drinks of every sort, syrups and sweetmeats of every kind. In wealth it rivals Uttara-kuru, and in glory it is as Alakamanda, the city of the gods". (The Questions of King Milinda, Translation by T. W. Rhys Davids, 1890)

Later Times

Sagala was described as "Sagala or Euthydemia" in the Geography of Ptolemy in the 1st century CE.

Incidentally, Sagala was also the capital of the Indo-Hepthalite King Mihirakula.

Sirkap

Sirkap is the name of an archaeological site on the bank opposite to the city of Taxila, Punjab, Pakistan.

The city of Sirkap was built by the Greco-Bactrian king Demetrius after he invaded India around 180 BC. Demetrius founded in the northern and northwestern Indian subcontinent an Indo-Greek kingdom that was to last until around 10 BC. Sirkap is also said to have been rebuilt by king Menander I.

A Greek City

- Fluted vase with bead and reel design (Bhir Mound, stratum 1)
- Cup with rosace and decoratice scroll (Bhir Mound, stratum 1)
- Stone palette with individual on a couch being crowned by standing woman, and served (Sirkap, stratum 5)
- Handle with double depiction of a philosopher (Sirkap, stratum 5/4)
- Woman with smile (Sirkap, stratum 5)
- Man with moustache (Sirkap, stratum 5)

The site of Sirkap was built according to the "Hippodamian" grid-plan characteristic of Greek cities (See: Sky view of Sirkap). It is organized around one main avenue and fifteen perpendicular streets, covering a surface of around 1200x400 meters, with a surrounding wall 5-7 meters wide and 4.8 kilometers long. The ruins are Greek in character, similar to those of Olynthus in Macedonia.

Numerous Hellenistic artifacts have been found, in particular coins of Greco-Bactrian kings and stone palettes representing Greek mythological scenes. Some of them are purely Hellenistic, others indicate an evolution of the Greco-

Bactrian styles found at Ai-Khanoum towards more indianized styles. For example, accessories such as Indian ankle bracelets can be found on some representations of Greek mythological figures such as Artemis. Following its construction by the Greeks, the city was further rebuilt during the incursions of the Indo-Scythians, and later by the Indo-Parthians after an earthquake in 30 CE.

Religious Buildings

Buddhist stupas with strong Hellenistic decorative elements can be found throughout the Sirkap site (Stupa of the two eagles), as well as a Hindu temple, indicating a close interaction of religious cultures. A Greek religious temple of the Ionic order is also visible at the nearby site of Jandial (650 meters from Sirkap), but there is a possibility that it may have been dedicated to a Zoroastrian cult. The site of Sirkap bears witness to the city-building activity of the Indo-Greeks during their occupation of the Indian territory for close to two centuries, as well as their integration of other faiths, especially Buddhism.

Visit by Apollonius of Tyana

The Greek philosopher Apollonius of Tyana is related to have visited India, and specifically the city of Taxila in the 1st century CE. He describes constructions of the Greek type, probably referring to Sirkap:

"Taxila, they tell us, is about as big as Nineveh, and was fortified fairly well after the manner of Greek cities"

"I have already described the way in which the city is walled, but they say that it was divided up into narrow streets in the same irregular manner as in Athens, and that the houses were built in such a way that if you look at them from outside they had only one story, while if you went into one of them, you at once found subterranean chambers extending as far below the level of the earth as did the chambers above."

Taxila

Taxila is an important archaeological site in Pakistan containing the ruins of the Gandharan city of Takshashila (also

Takkasila or Taxila) an important Vedic/Hindu and Buddhist centre of learning from the 6th century BC to the 5th century CE. In 1980, Taxila was declared a UNESCO World Heritage Site with multiple locations.

Historically, Taxila lay at the crossroads of three major trade routes: the royal highway from Pamaliputra; the north-western route through Bactria, Kapiua, and Puckalavati (Peshawar); and the route from Kashmir and Central Asia, via Srinigar, Mansehra, and the Haripur valley across the Khunjerab pass to the Silk Road.

Today, Taxila is situated at the western region of the Islamabad Capital Territory—to the northwest of Rawalpindi and on the border of the Punjab and North West Frontier Provinces—about 30 kilometres west-northwest of Islamabad, just off the Grand Trunk Road.

History

Legend has it that Taksha, an ancient Indian king who ruled in a kingdom called Taksha Khanda (Tashkent) founded the city of Takshashila. The word Takshashila, in Sanskrit means "belonging to the King Taksha". Taksha was the son of Bharata and Mandavi, historical characters who appear in the Indian epic Ramayana.

In the Indian epic *Mahabharata*, the Kuru heir Parikcit was enthroned at Taxila.

Ahmad Hasan Dani and Saifur Rahman Dar trace the etymology of Taxila to a tribe called the Takka. According to Damodar Dharmanand Koshambi, "Taxila" is related to "Takcaka," which means "carpenter" and is an alternative name for the Naga.

- 9th Century BC-Sushrutha compiles his medical treatise "Sushrutha Samahita". The first plastic surgery and cataract surgery procedures are described.
- 6th Century BC-Panini's Sanskrit grammatical classic, Ashtadyayi is compiled.
- *c.* 518 BC – Darius the Great annexes the North-West of the Indian-Subcontinent (modern day Pakistan),

including Taxila, to the Persian Achaemenid Empire.

- *c.* 450 BC, Herodotus makes reference to Greek influences in this area. The language used in the area is bilingual for the better part of a 1000 years, with Greek being the second language. See coins that reflect this bilingual function.
- 326 BC – Alexander the Great receives submission of Ambhi, king of Taxila, and afterwards defeats Porus at the Jhelum River.
- *c.* 317 BC – In quick succession, Alexander's general Eudemus and then the satrap Peithon withdraw from India. Candragupta, founder of the Mauryan empire in eastern India, then makes himself master of the northern and northwestern India, including Punjab. Chandragupta Maurya's advisor Kautilya (also known as Chanakya) was a teacher at Taxila.
- During the reign of Chandragupta's grandson Ashoka, Taxila became a great Buddhist centre of learning. Nonetheless, Taxila was briefly the centre of a minor local rebellion, subdued only a few years after its onset.
- 185 BC – The last Maurya emperor, Bhadratha, is assassinated by his general, Pucyamitra Shunga, during a parade of his troops.
- 183 BC – Demetrios conquers Gandhara, the Punjab and the Indus valley. He builds his new capital, Sirkap, on the opposite bank of the river from Taxila. During this new period of Bactrian Greek rule, several dynasties (like Antialcidas) likely ruled from the city as their capital. During lulls in Greek rule, the city managed profitably on its own, managed independently and controlled by several local trade guilds, who also minted most of the city's autonomous coinage.
- *c.* 90 BC – The Indo-Scythian chief Maues overthrows the last Greek king of Taxila.
- *c.* 25 CE – Gondophares, founder of the Indo-Parthian Kingdom, conquers Taxila and makes it his capital.
- 76 – The date of and inscription found at Taxila of

'Great King, King of Kings, Son of God, the Kushana' (*maharaja rajatiraja devaputra Kushana*).

- *c*. 460–470 – The Ephthalites sweep over Gandhara and the Punjab; wholesale destruction of Buddhist monasteries and stupas at Taxila, which never again recovers.

Before the fall of these invader-kings, Taxila had been variously a capital for many dynasties, and a centre of Vedic and Buddhist learning, with a population of Buddhists, Classical Hindus, and possibly Greeks that may have endured for centuries.

The British archaeologist Sir John Marshall conducted excavations over a period of twenty years in Taxila.

Ancient Centre of Learning

Takshashila was an early centre of learning dating back to at least the 5th century BC. There is some disagreement about whether Takshashila can be considered a university. While some consider Taxila to be an early university or centre of higher education, others do not consider it a university in the modern sense, in contrast to the later Nalanda University. Takshashila is described in some detail in later Jataka tales, written in Sri Lanka around the 5th century CE.

Takshashila is considered a place of religious and historical sanctity by Hindus and Buddhists. The former do so not only because, in its time, Takshashila was the seat of Vedic learning, but also because the strategist, Chanakya, who later helped consolidate the empire of Emperor Chandragupta Maurya, was a senior teacher there. The institution is very significant in Buddhist tradition since it is believed that the Mahayana sect of Buddhism took shape there.

Some scholars date Takshashila's existence back to the 6th century BC or 7th century BC. It became a noted centre of learning at least several centuries before Christ, and continued to attract students from around the old world until the destruction of the city in the 5th century CE. Takshashila is perhaps best known because of its association with Chanakya.

The famous treatise Arthashastra (Sanskrit for The knowledge of Economics) by Chanakya, is said to have been composed in Takshashila itself. Chanakya (or Kautilya), the Maurya Emperor Chandragupta and the Ayurvedic healer Charaka studied at Taxila.

Generally, a student entered Takshashila at the age of sixteen. The Vedas and the Eighteen Arts, which included skills such as archery, hunting, and elephant lore, were taught, in addition to its law school, medical school, and school of military science.

Taxila Today

Present day Taxila is one of the seven Tehsils (sub-district) of Rawalpindi District. It is spread over an undulating land in the periphery of the Pothohar Plateau of the Punjab. Situated just outside the capital Islamabad's territory and communicating with it through Tarnol pass of Margalla Hills, Taxila is a mix of posh urban and rustic rural environs. Urban residential areas are in the form of small neat and clean colonies populated by the workers of heavy industries, educational institutes and hospitals that are located in the area.

The industries include heavy machine factories and industrial complex, ordnance factories of Wah Cantt and cement factory. Heavy Industries Taxila is also based here. Small, cottage and house hold industries include stone ware, pottery and foot wear. People try to relate the present day stone ware craft to the tradition of sculpture making that existed here before the advent of Islam.

In addition to the ruins of Gandhara civilization and ancient Buddhist/Hindu culture, relics of Mughal gardens and vestiges of historical Grand Trunk Road, which was built by Emperor Sher Shah Suri in 15th-16th centuries, are also found in Taxila region.

Taxila Museum, dedicated mainly to the remains of Gandhara civilization, is also worth visiting. A hotel of the tourism department offers reasonably good services and hospitality to the tourists.

Taxila has many educational institutes including University of Engineering and Technology (UET). Thomas is still honoured in Taxila in an annual festival in early July, attended by thousands, celebrating the passage of his bones through Taxila on their way to Edessa.

Some notable and famous people of Taxila are Khan Mohammad Younas Khan, Ghulam Sarwar Khan (minister for labour & Overseas Pakistanis) and Siddique Khan (town nazim).

Sitanagaram

Sitanagaram is a small town and an ancient site located in the District of Guntur in East-Coast part of India. It is 18 miles north of Guntur City on the bank of River Krishna near Vijayawada. The place is related to the ancient history of Ramayana during the last Treta Yuga (Traditional time scale: 1.6 million years ago).

Introduction

It is on the bank of River Krishna with a vast sandy beach for recreation and leisure. The famous Someswara Swamy temple is situated here according to the legend Lord Rama wept here for Sita when she was abducted by Ravana, hence the name Sitanagaram.

Rama Krishna Matt

Ramakrishna Mission High School (Govt. Aided-Telugu Medium) from VI to X Std.

- Free education for 350 children.
- Free coaching classes.
- Free distribution of uniforms to all students and books and stationery to deserving students.
- Student scholarships.
- Free distribution of Evening Snacks for 350 students daily.
- Silver Medals to 27 meritorious students of X Std-2004 batch.
- Furniture worth Rs.3.5 lakhs provided.

- Work on new school building with an estimated cost of Rs.1.2 crores is in progress with the funds collected so far.
- A primary school (English Medium) from Nursery to 4th Std newly started during the academic year 2004-05.
- Free Weekly Homoeo Dispensary.
- Occasional free medical camps for school children.
- Free eye checkup camps and prescription glasses for school children.

Spiritual and Cultural

- Daily morning worship
- Evening Aratrikam and devotional songs
- Ramanam Sankirtan on Ekadasi days
- Discourses in Telugu on festivals such as Guru Purnima, Sri Krishna Asthami, Vijaya Dasami, Shivaratri, Rama Navami etc.
- Birthday celebrations of Bhagavan Sri Ramakrishna, Holy Mother Sri Sarada Devi, Swami Vivekananda and other direct disciples
- Spiritual Retreats-Once in every three months
- Vivekananda Balala Sangham-a special programme for children on Sundays
- Annual conventions for youth and teachers

Vedic University

The town has an Vedic University. It is run by the Jeeyar Educational Trust of Sri. Chinna Jeeyar Swamy, ref.

Access: Sitanagram comes under the Tadepalli Mandal in the Guntur District of Andhra Pradesh State in India. It is on the Guntur Side of the Prakasham Barriage. It is accessible by Train and Bus from Guntur, Vijayawada.

Hansi

Hansi is a city and a municipal council in Hisar district in the Indian state of Haryana. Its 2005 population is estimated to be 82,984. It is located at a distance of 16 miles east of Hisar on National Highway 10. Geographically, it is semi-arid with around 46 cm of annual rainfall. It appears that at one time Hansi was larger, more prosperous and more important than Hisar. The town has several important buildings of archeological importance.

The Town

The city of Hansi has five gates of entry-Delhi Gate (East), Hisar Gate (West), Gosain Gate (North-west), Barsi Gate (South) and Umra Gate (South west). The peculiarity of this town is that its altitude increases after entry from any of the gates. Deserts guard this city towards its west (cities like Tosham, Devsar, Khanak).

Another prominent feature of this ancient city is its fort. Extended in an area of 30 acres, it is square in shape and has security posts in all the four corners. The fort is said to be that of Great King Prithvi Raj Chauhan. Later, son of King Anangpal, Drupad established sword manufacturing factory in this fort, hence it is also called "Asigarh". Swords from this fort were exported as far away as to Arab countries. As per *Talif-e-Tajkara-e-Hansi* by Qazi Sharif Husain in 1915, around 80 forts across the area were controlled from this centre "ASIGARH". During the period of Firoz Shan Tuglaq, an *underground tunnel* was constructed connecting the present Hansi to Hisar. Gate of fort has horrifying figures of gods, and pictures of gods, goddesses, birds can also be seen on the walls of the fort. The entry gate of the fort was built by George Thomas. This fort was declared a Protected Monument of National Importance in 1937 by the Archeological Survey, the present ASI, and is still in good condition, a must visit site for all archeologists.

Right in front of the Fort, ancient statues of "Jain Gods" like Mahavira and Gautama Buddha are placed. These statues are worth $1 million as calculated by the Archeologists.

History

As far as the history of this town is concerned, it find its mention in Panini's Mahabharat as *ASI/ASIKA*. Though the origin of this city is wrapped in controversies, some prominent names and documentary proof like "Majkura Hansi" describe it as being founded by ill daughter *Hansivati/Ambavati* of Prithvi Raj Chauhan. Others say it as being found by King Anangpal Tomar for his guru "*Hansakar*" (957AD). Even one Asaram Jat also projected as its founder.

Shahjahan also came to Hansi, met the famous Hindu saint Jagganath Puri and after his approval Hindus were allowed to settle in Hansi. Some, now prominent casts in this area *viz.* Jain, Saini, Brahmins, came here during this Mughal rule.

Guru Gobind Singh came to Hansi in 1705 and inspired Hindus to revolt. In 1707, Veer Lakshman Singh (Banda Bahadur) attacked Hansi and punished muslims. Hansi was under Maratha rule in 1736 and after 3rd battle of Panipat in 1761 was lost to Ahmed Shah Abdali.

George Thomas (soldier), an Irish adventurer who rose from an ordinary sailor to become an independent king, formed Hansi as his capital. Hansi came under British East India Company rule in 1802. From 1819-1832, Hansi was District HQ which was later shifted to Hisar in 1832.

Hansi is known for its famous sweet "Pera" which is made from milk and is sent to many other towns and cities for retail selling.

In 1947 when British India was divided into Pakistan and India, a large number of muslims from hansi including Syeds and Ranghars migrated to Pakistan from Hansi city and their villages (some of them are Balyalli, Khanig).

Geography

Hansi is located at 29.1° N 75.97° E. It has an average elevation of 207 metres (679 feet).

Demographics

As of 2001 India census, Hansi had a population of 75,730. Males constitute 54% of the population and females 46%. Hansi has an average literacy rate of 68%, higher than the national average of 59.5%: male literacy is 73%, and female literacy is 61%. In Hansi, 13% of the population is under 6 years of age.

Tamralipta

Tamralipta is the name of an ancient city on the Bay of Bengal corresponding with Tamluk in modern-day India. Tamralipti may have been one of the most important urban centres of trade and commerce of early historic India, trading along the Silk Road with China, by Uttarapatha, the northern high road, the main trade route into the Middle East and Europe; and by seafaring routes to Bali, Java and other areas of the Far East.

Background

Tamluk's strategic location as a sea port on the Bay of Bengal and at the crossroads of various trade routes to East Asia and South-East Asia like Sri Lanka, Myanmar, Java, Sumatra made it an important site for ancient commerce. In addition to the long northwestern land route to Central Asia, China and Europe, the cities in the Ganges valley had river outlets to the east through the ports of Tamluk and others. The famous Silk Road was offered attractive trading possibilities with Tamluk in its early dates. From the ports in Bengal a seafaring route covered Bali, Java and the Far East.

Tamralipti's ancient settlement is mentioned in early Indian literature, in Ceylonese texts, and in accounts of Greek geographers and Chinese pilgrims. These texts indicate that Tamralipti was located on the eastern coast near the confluence of the Bay of Bengal and River Ganga, or Ganges. They also indicate that Tamralipti was connected with trade routes and frequented by traders, travellers and pilgrims. From the texts, the chronology of this settlement will be roughly between fourth-third century BC to eighth century AD.

The Dudhpani rock inscription of Udaymana, of the eighth century AD, contains the last record of Tamralipti as a port of ancient South Asia. In the map of the Greek geographer Ptolemy, Tamralipti appears as Tamalities. Chinese pilgrim Hiuen Tsang (Xuanzang) calls the town Tan-mo-lih-ti (te). Other texts show the name as Tamalitti (Tamalitthi).

These textual references have led scholars to identify Tamralipti as one of the most important centres of trade and commerce of early historic India. It has also led to the belief that Tamralipti had emerged as a thriving urban settlement in this period and had multidirectional links with different geographical regions of South Asia.

Archaeological Excavations in Tamluk

Tamluk has been subjected to archaeological excavation at least twice and has been explored frequently. Gourdas Bysack, a friend of the renowned Bengali poet Michael Madhusudan Dutt, was the first person to write on the antiquarian remains of Tamluk in the last quarter of the eighteenth century. He published a note on his findings in the Jan-Dec 1888 issue of *Proceedings of the Asiatic Society of Bengal* (Calcutta, 1889). Around the same time Umacharan Adhikari, a leading personality of Tamluk, wrote an account of the antiquity of the town in a book.

In 1920-21 the Archaeological Survey of India (ASI) also produced a short report on Tamluk. Gurusaday Dutt, I.C.S was the first to carry out archaeological diggings. Subsequently, T. N. Ramachandran, and K. N. Dikshit also carried out archaeological diggings in 1940. Among the antiquities recovered through excavation were terracota objects, pottery and coins. Some of these antiquities belong to the third century BC. ASI undertook the next excavation in 1954-55 under the supervision of M. N. Deshpande. As a result, a four fold cultural sequence was established. However, no structures could be unearthed in the excavation; only rammed floor levels and ring wells were encountered.

ASI undertook further excavation of the site in 1973-74 under the supervision of S. K. Mukherjee. This excavation revealed four successive occupational periods, the first of which (Period I) yielded an assemblage of Neolithic celts, ill-fired pottery, a large number of microlithic tools, bone awls and a small number of copper objects. Period II, dated to third-second century BC, yielded a few fragments of NBPW, a good number of beads of semi-precious stones, and a large number of punch marked and cast copper coins. One may link this period to the so-called Maurya-Shunga times. Evidence of a brick built tank and a few terracota ring wells were also exposed. Period III, belonging to the Shunga-Kusana phase seems to have been the richest one and have yielded ceramics, and a very large collection of terracota figurines, some with a definite hellenistic affiliation. The assemblage indicates a sophisticated urban life where citizens indulged in art. Period IV stratigraphically represents the so-called Gupta period. The yield of antiquities from this occupational level has not been impressive, certainly they do not match the evidence furnished by Chinese pilgrims.

Between 1954-55 and 1973-74, explorations by individual scholars brought to light rich antiquities from different regions in and around Tamluk. Professor P. C. Dasgupta was a pioneer researcher in this field. He recovered beautiful terracota figurines from the site along with other important antiquities. After the 1973-74 season, the Tamralipta Research and Museum Centre has carried out independent research in the region. Explorations have brought to light early historic sites from the region.

The early historic period of Tamluk is marked by the occurrence of pottery such as roulleted ware, grey ware, red ware, black polished ware and northern black polished ware. In addition to pottery, the site has also revealed terracota objects of exceptional beauty. Terracota figurines of yaksis, animals, and plaques depicting life of ordinary men and women are found in the collections of the Tamluk Museum. The famous figurine of Yaksi at the Ashmolean Museum, Oxford was recovered from Tamluk. Although the question of chalcolithic origin has not been properly resolved, the occurrence of Black and Red ware along with numerous bone objects like harpoons have made the issue problematic.

Origin of the Name Tamluk

According to some scholars Tamluk derives its name from the Sanskrit word Tamra Lipta meaning "Full of Copper".

Tamralipta (Tamluk), lower down the river Hooghly and sea port, had been an important waterway for more than 3000 years. It gets its name from the copper which was mined, as it is even now, at Ghatsila, Jharkhand, Orissa areas which are not far from the city. Copper had been eclipsed by iron around 100 B.C., so the name must have originated during the Copper Age, when Tamralipti exported the ore and metal to peninsular India; the alternative was the less accessible Rajasthan area. The longer, original name of the port was in use till the third century B.C., when Ashoka's daughter and son sailed from it for Sri Lanka.

According to local folklore the name Tamralipta came from the King Tamradhwaja (which means The King with Copper Flag/symbol) of the Mayura-Dhwaja (Peacock) dynasty. If you go according to Mahabharat's description the ruling period of the King Tamradhwaja is nearer to the end of the Copper Age. Probably this ancient king had a huge base of copper, and the metal brought prosperity to the region at his time. Thus both of the names — Tamralipta and Raja Tamradhawja — might have been originated from it.

Some early Vaishnava religious texts tell a facinating story about the origin of the name of Tamralipta. Once, when Lord Krishna was playing Maharaas in Vraj at Vrindavan Surya (Sun God) Dev rose from the east and accidentally saw Lord Krishna in intimate situation with his Gopis and Sri Radhika. Immediately Surya Dev had felt ashamed, became embarrassed and blushed a reddish copper colour like Tamra. And then Surya Dev again returned to the same corner of the east coast of Bharata and did hide (Lipta) himself in the Bay of Bengal. Where Surya Dev went back and hid himself is the place called Tamralipti.

History of Tamluk

This ancient port city and kingdom was bounded by the Bay of Bengal in the south, river Rupnarayana in the east and Subarnarekha in the west. The Rupnarayana is the joint flow of the river Dwarkeshwar and the river Shilai. The Bay of Bengal and these great rivers and their numerous branches created a prosperous and easy water navigational system fostering commerce, culture and early contacts with the people outside the region. At the same time, these rivers helped to develop the agriculture in this region.

History tells us that the rivers have been central to urban settlement and development in the subcontinent from the ancient period. The Indus and the Ganges were cradles of ancient civilization. Tamluk was a civilisation based on Bay of Bengal and river Rupnarayana. And the most important natural resource of this area was water from the rivers and sea.

Archaeological remains show continuous settlement from about 3rd century BC. It was known as Tramralipti (in the Purans and the Mahabharata) or Tamralipta (in Mahabharata) or Tamalika (in historical documents) or Tamalitti (in foreigners' descriptions) or Tamoluk (in the British Raj). It was a seaport, now buried under river silt. For this reason, Tamluk has many ponds and lakes remaining today.

In the Mahabharata (Bhishma Parba/Nabam Adhyay) while describing the names of the holiest rivers and kingdoms of India, Sanjay took the name of "Tramralipta" to Dhritarashtra.

Tamluk was also known as Bhivas (in religious texts) and Madhya Desh (as the Middle State of Utkal/Kalinga and Banga).

According to Jain sources, Tamralipti was the capital of the kingdom of Venga and was long known as a port.

Kumbhoj

Kumbhoj (pronounced as *kam'bho'j*) is the name of an ancient town located in Kolhapur district in Maharashtra. The town is about six kilometers from Hataklangada, about twenty seven kilometers from Kolhapur and currently, also is the Taluka or Tehsil Headquarters. The famous Jain Tirtha (pilgrom place) *Kumbhojgiri*, also known as *Kumbhoj Bahubali*, is just two kilometers away from the Kumbhoj city. The Vidyapeeth's Degree College of Engineering and Technology is also located in Kumbhoj.

Geographically, Kumbhoj is located at a latitude (DMS) of 16° 49' 60 N and longitude (DMS) of 74° 25' 60 E.

As the name itself suggests, Kumbhoj seems to be connected with well known ancient term Kamboja of Sanskrit/Pali literature.

Alternative name of Kumbhoj is *Kumboj* (=Kamboj). The former name is apparently free from Iranian or *Paisaci* influence since Maharashtra location was far removed from the north-west division of ancient India. Kamboj is the standard name found in numerous ancient Sanskrit and Pali texts.

Padma Vibhushan Dr. Karmaveer Bhaurao Patil, a renowned social worker and philanthropist was born at Kumbhoj.

The cult figure of Bahubali at Kumbhoj is identical to the Bahubali of Shravanbelgola known as Gomateshwar to the south in Karnataka.

Epilogue

During second century BC, a section of Kambojas from Central Asia had joined the great tribal movement from Central Asia, and in alliance with the Sakas, Pahlavas, Abhiras etc., they are known to have spread into western and south-western parts of India. One section of those Kambojas appears to have given their name to this coastal town of south-west India. There still is said to be a microscopic Jain community, predominantly agrarian, called Kambhoj living near Nanded in Maharashtra.

There is a reference to sage Kumbhoja (q.v.) who finds reference in southern Indian recensions of Ramayana. He seems to have lived somewhere on the banks of river Godavari, in south-west India during Ramayana times. Seems like sage Kambhoja originally belonged to north-west and had migrated to south of Vindhya on river Godawri.

Kalpi

Kalpi is a city and a municipal board in Jalaun district in the Indian state of Uttar Pradesh. It is on the right bank of the Yamuna.

History

The city of Kalpi is believed to be known as Kalpriya Nagari in the ancient times. Over the period of time the name of the city got abbreviated to Kalpi. Kalpi is said to have been founded by King Vasudeva at the end of the 4th century. In 1196 it fell to Qutb-ud-din Aybak, the viceroy of Mohammed Ghori, and during the subsequent Muslim period it played a significant part in the history of central India. During Akbar's reign, Kalpi was a governor's seat and had a mint for copper coinage. Kalpi is also considered by some as the birth place of Ved Vyas, the author of Mahabharata.

About the middle of the 18th century it passed into the hands of the Marathas. It was captured by the British in 1803, and after 1806 remained in British possession until India's independence in 1947. In May 1858 Sir Hugh Rose (Lord Strathnairn) defeated here a force of about 10,000 freedom fighters under the Rani of Jhansi. The British East India Company made it one of their principal stations for providing "commercial investment".

Archaeology of Kalpi

Kalpi has many historical as well as archaeological sites. Few of them are enlisted below:

- Kalpi Fort
- Lanka Tower

Most recently the archaeological department of Uttar Pradesh has discovered a prehistoric site that has been dated back 45000 years. Excavation work is in progress on this site.

Geography

Kalpi is located at 26.12° N 79.73° E. It has an average elevation of 112 metres (367 feet).

Location and Industry

The old town, which is on the Yamuna river, has the ruin of a fort, and several temples of interest, while in the neighbourhood are many ancient tombs. Away from the river to the south-east is a lofty modern town ornamented with representations of the battles of the Ramayana. Kalpi is still a centre of local trade (principally in grain, ghee and cotton) with a station on the railway line from Jhansi to Kanpur, which crosses the Yamuna here.

In late 1970s and early 1980s Kalpi was one of the areas in central India affected by dacoits, and was frequented by the much dreaded Phoolan Devi gang. It has been declared an Industrial belt by the Government of India and is known for the hand-made paper produced here.

Bhinmal

Bhinmal also known as Shrimal, is a town in the Jalore District of Rajasthan, India. It is 72 km south of Jalore town. The name Bhinmal is derived from the word Shrimal. Bhinmal was the capital of ancient Gujarat. According to some historical accounts, the kingdom with capital at Bhinmal (or Srimal) was established by the Gujjars. A minor kingdom of Bharuch was the offshoot of this Kingdom. In 640-41 CE, the Chinese traveller Xuanzang (Hieun Tsang) described the kingdoms Kiu-che-lo (identified with Gurjara) in his writings. He stated that the Gurjaras ruled a rich and populous kingdom with capital at Bhinmal (Pilo-mo-lo). According to his expositor, M. Vivien de St. Martin, Su-la-cha represents the modern Gujarat, and Kiu-che-lo (Gurjjara), "the country of the Gujars", represents the region between Anhilwara and the Indus River.

The town is the birth place of the Sanskrit poet Mahakavi Magh (poet) | and mathematician and astronomer Brahmagupta.

History of Bhinmal

Bhinmal was the capital of ancient Gujarat. The further earlier name of the town was Bhillamala. Hiuen Tsang visited Bhillamala (bhinmal) in about 641 A.D. According to Hiuen Tsang Bhillamala was capital of Gurjara kingdom. The King of the place was a Kshatriya, celebrated for his wisdom and virtue, a believer in Buddhism and a man of exceptional abilities. He was just twenty years old. The people of the place were flourishing. Brahmanism dominated the city. There was only one Buddhist monastery with 100 brothers.

Ala-ud-din Khilji also destroyed Srimala when he conquered Jalore in 1310 A.D. Before that Srimala was a premier city of northern India. The city was laid out in the shape of a square. It has 84 gates. The mid-15th century chronicle Kanhadade

Prabandha provide description of many islamic attacks on Bhinmal.

There were several temples of Jain Tirthankar and Hindu god-Ganapatis, Kshetrapalas, Chandikadevis, Shivalingas and others. The temple of Bhinmal known as Jagatsvami was one of the earliest and most famous temples of Rajasthan. The temple had beautiful torana (archway). The temple was perhaps built during the reign of Gurjara Pratiharas who were sun worshippers. A festival was held at temple in the Hindu calendar month of Asvin.

There were a number of Jain temples too, temple of Mahavira being the most famous. In ancient time this temple was built by king Kumarpal and established by Acharya Hemachandra, dedicated to 1st Jain Tirthankar Lord Rishabhadev, currently this is dedicated to 24th Jain Tirthankar Lord *Bhagwan* Mahavira.

Bhinmal was a great centre of learning. The scholars of Srimala were known far and wide for their scholarship and learning. The well known Sanskrit poet Magha, the author of Sisupalavadha also lived here in 680 A.D. Brahmagupta was born in 598 A.D. in Bhinmal. He is likely to have lived most of his life in Bhillamala (modern Bhinmal) in the empire of Harsha. As a result Brahmagupta is often referred to as Bhillamalacarya, the teacher from Bhillamala (Bhinmal). He was the head of the astronomical observatory at Ujjain, and during his tenure he wrote two texts on mathematics and astronomy: The Brahma Sphuta Siddhanta in 628, and the Khandakhadyaka in 665.

The well known Jain scholar Siddharshi Gani, a resident of Bhinmal wrote *Upmitibahava prapancha katha* in 905 A.D. The Jain Ramayana was written by Jain monk Vijayagani in 1595 A.D.Jain Acharya Udyotan Suri wrote *kuvyalmala* the well known sanskrit story book) here.

The city of Bhinmal had four gates. At a distance of 8 kilometers in the north, there was the Jalori gate, in the south Laxmi gate, in the east the Sun gate and in the west Sanchori gate.

Jainism in Bhinmal

This city has witnessed many risings and falls. Stone inscriptions of the year 1333 of the Vikrama Samvat (1277 A.D.) are found among ruins of temples. There are signs here and there showing that Lord Mahavira Swami, the 24th Jain Tirthankar wandered about here. They can provide historical evidences to researches.

There was a time when this city had a circumference of 64 kilometers and the fort had 84 gates. This city looked beautiful with hundreds of pinnacled temples. From the seventh to the tenth century, talented Jain monk/wiritter Acharya Haribhadra, Mundas Gani, Udayprabhsuri and many more created here valuable Jain literature and sanctified and beautified this place. The temple of 23rd jain Tirthankar Parshvanatha in Hathi pole area is regarded to be ancient. This temple has great archeological importance. Golden-coloured idol of Shri Parshvanatha *Bhagwan* in *padmasana* posture is the presiding deity.

On the image of the main deity, On the idol, there is an inscription of the year 1011 of the Vikram era (954 A.D.). It is believed that the idol was found from a hollow of the ground. Many other idols were also found. Eight hundred years ago Bhinmal as the *tirth* is described in the *'Sakal Tirth Stotra'* composed by Jain monk Acharya Siddhasen Diwakar surisvarji. The writer of Abhidhan Rajendra Kosh (Dictionary of Prakrit, Sanskrit & Pali Language Jain words) & famous Jain monk of 20th century Acharya Rajendrasuri made his chaturmas here in 1880 A.D.

The Shrimal and Porwad Jain communities have originated from Bhinmal and its vicinity.

With emergence of Patan, Gujarat (ancient Anahilavada), a large fraction of the Jain population moved from Bhinmal and Patan emerged as the major Jain centre.

Geography

Bhinmal is located at 25.0° N 72.25° E. It has an average elevation of 146 metres (479 feet).

Economy

The economy of the town and surrounding area is mainly based on agriculture and animal husbandary. The oilseeds specially mustard oilseeds is predominant crop. Jeera, wheat, bajra, kharif pulses, barley, jowar and seasmum are other produces.

Bhinmal is main Mandi (market) for agricultural produce of the area. The town has Krishi Upaj Mandi Samiti (Agricultural Produce Market Committee). Food Corporation of India has its warehouses here. The town is main supply point for various agricultural inputs like fertilisers, seeds and pesticides and for agricultural implements, motors, tractors and spare parts.

Bhinmal is known for fine quality of *Mojari* (embroided lather shoes).

There is no large and medium size industry in the Bhinmal industrial area. The main small scale industries are: granite slabs and tiles, marble cutting and polishing, mustard seed crushing, skimmed milk powder, butter and ghee, handloom cloth, leather shoes (mojari).

Infrastructure

Transport: Bhinmal is on Samadari-Bhildi section of North Western Railway. The name of railway station is Marwar Bhinmal. The railway tracks are meter gauge. There are plans to convert these to broad gauge. Bhinmal is connected to all major cities by all weather roads.

Electricity: There is one sub grid station of 220 KV at Bhinmal. The town receives power from Power Grid Corporation of India's grid station in Kota District. Almost all villages of the Bhinmal sub division are electrified. The Power Grid Corporation of India has plans to construct one more 400 KV power substation at Bhinmal to supply electricity to whole Marwar area.

Water: The town gets drinking water from Savidar, Dhanwara & Rajpura. The town area drinking water supply is managed by PHED (water dept. of Govt. of Rajasthan). The main source of irrigation for farmers continues to be wells.

Accommodation: There are many hotels in the town. Some well known hotels are: Hotel Samarat, Hotel Neelkamal, Hotel Rajdeep, Hotel Surya-kiran and Hotel Sagar. The heritage hotel known as Castle Durjan Niwas is at village Daspan 25 km from Bhinmal. There is a Government Rest house too run by Public Works Department (PWD).

Education: The town has a graduate/degree College called G K Gowani Government College affiliated to Maharshi Dayanand Saraswati University, Ajmer and accredited by National Assessment and Accreditation Council (NAAC). There are three higher secondary and about forty five primary and middle schools in Bhinmal.

Telecommunications: All the basic phone and cellphone service provider companies have their network in Bhinmal. Internet and fax services is available at main Tel. exchange building of BSNL.

Hospitals: Bhinmal town has good medical facilities. The town has a government referral hospital and many private hospitals. There is an Ayurvedic hospital too.

Sports: The town has a stadium by name of Shivaraj Stadium. It was inaugurated by staging Ranji trophy match in December 1985 between Rajasthan and Madhya Pradesh. It has indoor & outdoor games facilities. The yearly state level badminton tournament held here.

Banking: Two nationalised Banks State Bank of Bikaner & Jaipur and Punjab National Bank have their brances here. Some cooperative and local banks also have their branches in the town. They are: Jalore Nagrik Sahakari Bank ltd., Madhav Cooperative bank, Marwar Gramin Bank, Jalore Central Cooperative Bank and Bhumi Vikas Bank.

Library: The town has two public libraries one is managed by the municipality and other one by Saraswati Temple Trust.

Administrative Set-up

- The town is one of two sub-divisions in Jalore district.
- The Bhinmal sub division covers three tehsils namely Bhinmal, Sanchore and Raniwara and four panchayat

(block) samitis namely Bhinmal, Sanchore, Raniwara and Jaswantpura.

- The civic affairs are administered by the Bhinmal Municipal Council (BMC) (Nagarpalika Mandal Bhinmal), with executive power vested in the Municipal excutive officer. The Council comprises 25 directly elected councillors representing the twenty five municipal wards. Three nominated Councillors and a local MLA also have a rights of councillor.
- The Bhinmal sub-division area is under the jurisdiction of a Deputy District Collector/Sub divisional Officer (SDO)
- Bhinmal Tehsildar is in charge of property records and revenue collection of Bhinmal tehsil
- The Bhinmal Police is headed by a Deputy Superintendent of Police who is an IPS officer.
- Bhinmal also has a Lower court, the Small Causes Court for civil matters and the Sessions Court for criminal cases.
- Bhinmal constituency elects one member to the Vidhan Sabha(Rajasthan State Assembly)

Demography

As of 2001 India census, Bhinmal had a population of 39,278. Males constitute 53% of the population and females 47%. Bhinmal has an average literacy rate of 52%, lower than the national average of 59.5%; with male literacy of 67% and female literacy of 36%. 18% of the population is under 6 years of age.

The Bafna, Vardhan, seth, Jogani, Nahar, Mehta, Gowani, Raysoni, Sanghvi, Vanigota, Shrimali Brahmins, Bohra, Dhokad, Hundiya, Palgota, Kothari, Haran are the some of the surnames of the people from the town. Bhinmal is an important town in the history of oswal Jain community.

Many people from Bhinmal are now settled in Mumbai and are engaged in trade, building, construction and export-import and other businesses. Some well known business houese are

Vardhan group, Nahar group, Bafna business houses, Jogani constructions, Govani group, Veetarga Developers, and Nahar & Seth group. Some people from Bhinmal presently reside in Bangalore, Chitradurga and Ahmedabad too. They keep regular contact with Bhinmal through social and religious functions.

Temples in Bhinmal

Jain Temples

- Mahavira Swami Jain temple
- Parshvanatha Jain temple (Hathi pole)
- Shantinath Jain temple (Ganesh chowk)
- Ganthi Mehata vaas (4 Jain temple complex)
- Nakoda Parshvanatha Jain temple
- Riddhi-Siddhi Parshvanatha Jain Temple
- Chomukhji Jain temple (viju bai Temple)
- Manmohan Parshvanatha Jain temple'
- Jagawallabh Parshvanatha Jain temple (station road)
- Padmaprabhu Jain temple (magh colony)
- Jeerawalla Parshvanatha Jain temple (magh colony)
- Seemandhar swami Jain temple (Rath Mandir)
- Shankheshwar Parshvanatha Jain temple complex.
- Gaudi Parshvanatha Jain temple.
- Kirti Stambh Jain Temple (Tower Temple).
- Bafna Wadi Jain Temple (Three Temple complex).
- Shankheshwar Parshvanatha Temple, Dhora-Dhal.
- Kunthunathji Jain Temple, Hundia vas.

Hindu Temples

- Varaha Shyam temple
- Chandinath temple
- Neel Kantha Mahadev temple
- Kshemekari mata (Mataji ki Bhakri temple)
- Mahalaxmi temple, Mahalaxmi road
- Mahalaxmi temple, Dhora-dhal
- Gayatri temple

- Fafariya Hanuman temple
- Baba Ramdevji temple
- Vishwakarma temple
- Saraswati temple

Monuments

- Chandinath Bavadi
- Jeevdaya Gaushala
- Jakoba Talab
- Bal samundra pond
- Trayamkeshwer pond

Distances

Nearest Airports:

- Jodhpur 200 km; Udaipur 230 km.; Ahmedabad: 315 km

Nearest Airstrips:

- Noon Jalore; Sirohi; Abu Road; Deesa.

By Road:

- Jodhpur: 200 km; Jalore: 72 km; Sirohi: 73 km; Mount Abu: 170 km; Palanpur: 120 km
- Ranakpur: 140 km; Jaisalmer: 335 km; Ahmedabad: 315 km; Abu Road: 125 km;

Bhinmal in News

- A 450 years old Jain temple was unearthed in year 2002 during construction work at the premises of Shri Parshwa Nath temple at Bhinmal. The temple has five images of Jain Tirthankars made in white marble.
- In September 1997, Naina Jogani, a Jain woman, was allegedly harassed by a Jain muni in Bhinmal. The muni later committed suicide. A judicial inquary later found the Jain muni innocent.
- Recently Bafna families of the Bhinmal town has built one temple complex of goddess Osiya Mata (Sachiya Mata Temple), 24th Jain Tirthankar Lord Mahavira

Swami and Jain monk Acharya Rajendrasuri. The temple complex is named as Bafna Wadi Jain Tirth and its situated in the south west of the Bhinmal town. All the temple were built on a small hill top. This is a three temples complex with vast ground, Dharmashala, Bhojanshala. It was declared open to public on 2 March 2006 after Paratistha Mahotsava by Jain monk Muni Jayanandvijay ji maharaj.

Ujjain

Ujjain pronunciation (also known as *Ujain*, *Ujjayini*, *Avanti*, *Avantikapuri*) is an ancient city of central India, in the Malwa region of the Indian state of Madhya Pradesh, on the eastern bank of the Kshipra River. It is the administrative centre of Ujjain District and Ujjain Division. In ancient times the city was called Ujjayini. As per epic Mahabharata Ujjayani was the capital of Avanti Kingdom. It has been the first meridian of longitude for Hindu geographers since the 4th century BC. It is one of the seven sacred cities of the Hindus, and the Kumbh Mela religious festival is held there every twelve years. It is also home to Mahakaleshwar Jyotirlinga, one of the twelve Jyotirlinga shrines to the god Shiva.

History

The earliest references to the city, as *Ujjaini*, are from the time of the Buddha, when it was the capital of the Avanti Kingdom. Since the 4th century BC the city has marked the first meridian of longitude in Hindu geography. It is also reputed to have been the residence of Ashoka (who subsequently became the emperor), when he was the viceroy of the western provinces of the Maurya empire.

In the Post-Mauryan period, the city was ruled by the Sungas and the Satavahanas consecutively. It was contested for a period between the Satavahanas and the Indo-Scythian Sakas, known as Western Satraps; however, following the end of the Satavahana dynasty, the city was retained by the Sakas from the 2nd to the 4th century CE. Following the conquest of the Sakas by the Guptas, the city soon became an important seat in the annals of that empire. Ujjain is considered to be the traditional capital of King Chandragupta II, also known as *Vikramaditya*, at whose court the nine poets known as the *navaratna* (nine jewels) of Sanskrit literature are said to have flourished.

In the 6th and 7th centuries, Ujjain was a major centre of mathematical and astronomical research. The famous mathematicians who worked there included: Brahmagupta, whose book *Brahmasphutasiddhanta* was responsible for spreading the use of zero, negative numbers and the positional number system to Arabia and Cambodia; Varahamihira, who was the first to discover many trigonometric identities; and Bhaskaracharya, or Bhaskara II, whose book *Lilavati* broke new ground in many areas of mathematics.

Ujjain was invaded by the forces of the Delhi Sultanate led by Iltutmish in 1235, suffering widespread destruction and systematic desecration of temples. Under the Mughal emperor Akbar it became the capital of Malwa.

During the last half of the 18th century Ujjain was the headquarters of the Maratha leader Sindhia. The Sindhias later established themselves at Gwalior, and Ujjain remained part of Gwalior state until Indian Independence in 1947. Gwalior state became a princely state of the British Raj after the Maratha defeat in the Third Anglo-Maratha War, and Gwalior, Ujjain, and the neighbouring princely states were made a part of the Central India Agency. After Indian independence, the Sindhia ruler of Gwalior acceded to India, and Ujjain became part of the Madhya Bharat state. In 1956 Madhya Bharat was merged into Madhya Pradesh state.

Names

Since Ujjain is one of the oldest cities in India, it has changed very many names, among which were:

- Avanitika
- Padmavati
- Kushasthali
- Bhagavati

- Haranyavati
- Kandakatringa
- Kumudvati
- Pratikalpa
- Vishala

Geography

Ujjain is situated on the Malwa Plateau in Central India. The soil is black and stony. The vegetation is the typical of arid regions with thorny trees like babul and acacia dominating the landscape. Soybean, wheat, jowar and bajra are the main crops grown.

Ujjain is located at 23.182778° N 75.777222° E. It has an average elevation of 491 metres (1610 feet).

Demographics

As of 2001 India census, Ujjain had a population of 429,933. Males constitute 52% of the population and females 48%. Ujjain has an average literacy rate of 72%, higher than the national average of 59.5%: male literacy is 79%, and female literacy is 66%. In Ujjain, 13% of the population is under 7 years of age.

Climate

Ujjain experiences typical climate conditions of the interior Indian subcontinent. The summer months (April–June) are harsh with temperatures reaching up to 45°C. In addition, hot winds (called loo) may blow in the afternoons, worsening the heat. The winter months (Nov.–Feb.) are pleasant and cool with daytime temperatures typically 20°C, though it may drop to 3°C in the night. The monsoon typically arrives in late June and the months of June till September receive moderate to heavy rainfall. There are periods of rainfall followed by long periods of bright sunshine and high humidity. The month of October generally is very warm and with high humidity.

Administrative

Ujjain city has two legislative assembly zones, known as Ujjain North and Ujjain South. For Parliamentary purposes it is treated as one seat: Akhat Kashyap.

Economy

The economy of Ujjain is mainly dependent on the agricultural activities of the nearby villages. Two main crops are grown each year: soybean as the major Rabi crop, wheat as the major Kharif crop. Ujjain agriculture is sensitive to changes in rainfall and failure of monsoon cycles can lay a devastating toll on agriculture and the local economy.

Ujjain was previously a centre of the textile industry with a number of textile mills in and around the city. These mills have since closed, unemploying hundreds. Religious tourism is also a contributor to the economy, especially during the Simhasta Mela.

Commercial Zones

One good thing about the old city is that the market is quite organized. For utensils you have the Patni Bazaar, for jewellery; Sarafa, for grocery; Daulat Ganj, for clothes; VD Cloth Market, Kanthal.

There are various shopping areas like Freeganj, Gopal Mandir, and Satigate.

Freeganj is a rapidly growing area, complete with relatively better modern amenities.

Transport

Ujjain is well-connected by rail and road. It is on the Western Railway and is connected by direct train to most major Indian cities (Mumbai, Delhi, Chennai, Kolkata, Bangalore, Ahmedabad, Pune, etc.).

The nearest airport is Indore, which has daily flights to Delhi, Mumbai, Kolkata, Ahemdabad & Bhopal.

The road network is developed with other parts of Madhya Pradesh. Private buses ply on these roads, though it is best to take your own vehicle for short distances.

An extensive network of old but inexpensive three-wheelers called tempoes serves the majority of the population. Three-wheeler auto-rickshaws are also quite popular. Recent years have seen an explosion of privately owned vehicles, especially two-wheelers unsuited for the traffic, that congest the narrow thoroughfares.

Railway Stations

There are three well-known railway stations:

1. Ujjain City Junction
2. Vikram Nagar
3. Chintaman (metre gauge)

Bus Stations

1. Dewas Gate
2. Nana Kheda

Major Roads

Indore Road, Dewas Road, Agar Road, Badnagar Road, Maksi Road etc.

Places to Visit

Ujjain is a holy city for Hindus and has many places to visit for the religiously inclined.

The Mahakal Temple, one of the twelve Jyotirlings, is the most famous and venerated Shiva temple. The Shivling in this temple is supposed to be the only Jyotirling which faces south and hence it is known as Dakshinmukhi or the south-facing ling. Other temples are Harsidhhi (Durga Temple), Chintaman Ganesh, Gadh Kalika, Kaal Bhairav, Sandipani Ashram, Triveni (Nav Graha/ Shani), ISKCON (The International Society for Krishna Consciousness) temple and Mangalnaath.

Ujjain, being an ancient city, is home to many monuments that have survived from the ancient period. The most stunning example is the Kaliyadeh Palace on the outskirts of the city, which is a fine piece of ancient Indian architecture, though in poor upkeep.

The Bhrathari Gufa is an ancient cave which has some interesting legends associated with it.

The Observatory (Veda Shala) built by a Rajput king, Raja Jai Singh II, is one of the five such observatories in India and features ancient astronomical devices.

The new ISKCON temple is a must for every tourist. Also Prashanti Dham (Sai Baba's Ashram) is a holy place to visit.

It is quite a soothing experience to sit on the coast of river Kshipra, relieving all you mental worries.

Also there are many Jain temples like-Jai Singh Pura Atishay Kshetra, Tapobhoomi, Avanti Parshwanath, Hanumant baag etc.

Kothi Palace presents a sight worth watching in the evening.

Hotels in Ujjain

Here is the list of some of the well known Hotels/Restaurents of ujjain.

1. Hotel Shanti Palace, Nanakheda
2. Hotel Anand Palace
3. Hotel Surana Palace
4. Hotel Ashray
5. Hotel Shipra
6. Meghdoot Restaurent

Education

Ujjain city is well known for its university Vikram University which is the main institution of higher education in the city. Besides the university, Ujjain also has different colleges and institutes where students can pursue various courses.

Schools in Ujjain

1. St. Paul's Higher Secondary School
2. Ujjain Public School
3. St. Mary's Convent School
    1. Kalidas School
    2. Lokmanya Tilak Higher Secondary School
    3. Model Higher Secondary School
    4. Aadivasi Chatra Seva Kalyaan Seva Higer Secondary International School
    5. Kendriya Vidyalaya Ujjain
    6. Oxford Junior college

7. Takshila Junior College
8. Christu Jyoti Senior Secondary School
9. Stanford International Girls School
10. Gyan Sagar Academy

Engineering Colleges in Ujjain

1. Government Engineering College, Ujjain (GECU)
2. Mahakal Institute of Technology (MIT)

Urayur

Urayur (Currently in Tiruchirappalli) was the capital of the early Cholas from before the first century CE until the dynasty was revived by Vijayalaya Chola c. 850CE. The Cholas were one of the three great Tamil dynasties (Cheras and Pandyas being the other two) who ruled over the Tamil country in South India from early antiquity. Urayur was located near the town of Tiruchirapalli in Tamil Nadu.

The word *Urayur* in Tamil literally means "the residence". Urayur was an ancient Chola city with a fortress and city wall on the southern banks of river Kaveri. The Imperial Cholas of the 9th century CE and later made Tanjavur as their capital. Urayur slowly lost its place in the Chola administration.

This place is also known as Thirukkozhi / Laapuri / Ranthai. The famous temples like Sri Azhagiya Manavala Perumal Temple, Panchaverneswara temple, Vekkaliamman temple are situated here.

Dwarka

Dwarka pronunciation is a city and a municipality in Jamnagar district in the state of Gujarat, India. Dwarka (Dvaraka in Sanskrit-this name shall be used in this article when referring to the city in a historical context) is rated as one of the seven most ancient cities in the country. The legendary city of Dvaraka in Hindu History was the dwelling place of Krishna. It is believed that, due to damage and destruction by the sea, Dvaraka has submerged six times and modern Dwarka is the 7th city to be built in the area

Geography

It is located in the Jamnagar District of Gujarat. It is on the mouth of the Gomti River into Gulf of Kutch. The city lies in the westernmost part of India.

Dwarka is located at 22.23° N 68.97° E. It has an average elevation of 0 metres (0 feet).

Demographics

As of 2001 India census, Dwarka had a population of 33,614. Males constitute 53% of the population and females 47%. Dwarka has an average literacy rate of 64%, higher than the national average of 59.5%: male literacy is 72% and, female literacy is 55%. In Dwarka, 13% of the population is under 6 years of age.

The temple

The temple has five storey tower which was built by Sambha, who is the grandson of Lord Shri Krishna. The city was built by Vishwakarma who is a celestial architect. The temple was made of limestone and sand. There is a flag hoisted in the temple tower everyday which waves in air beautifully welcoming the pilgrims.

The structure of the temple is quite complicated. Even in Tsunami or Earthquake the temple was not destroyed. There are two gateways namely Swarga Dwar where pilgrims enter and Moksha Dwar where pilgrims exit. From the temple one can view the Sangamam of River Gomati flowing towards the sea. There are shrines for Vasudeva, Devaki, Balarama and Revathy, Subhadra, Rukmini Devi, Jambavathi Devi and Sathybhama Devi.

There is a special temple for Rukmini Devi on the way to Bet Dwaraka. Bet Dwaraka can be reached through boat. It is also the temple which is like Palace where Lord Shri Krishna had ruled. It is the same idol of Lord Dwarakanath kept in Bet Dwaraka.

The temple looks like a Palace and has many Shrines for Lakshmi Narayana, Trivikrama, Jambavathi Devi, Sathybhama Devi and Rukmini Devi.

Holy City

The city derives its name from word "Dwar" meaning door in Sanskrit. Dwarka is one of the holiest cities in Hinduism and one of the 4 main "dhams" along with Badrinath, Puri, Rameshwaram.

The Jagatmandir temple which houses the Dwarkadhish, a form of Krishna.

Nageshwar Jyotirling, one of the 12 holy shrines of Lord Shiva, is located near Dwarka.

Dwarka is also the site of Dwaraka Pitha (also known as Kalika Pitha), one of the four cardinal mathas established by Sri Adi Shankaracharya, the others being those at Sringeri, Puri and Jyotirmath.

Legend

Dvaraka is mentioned in the Mahabharata, the Harivansha, the Bhagavata Purana, the Skanda Purana, and the Vishnu Purana.

Sri Krishna renounced war in Mathura for the greater good (and hence the name Ranchodrai) and founded (and settled in) Dvaraka. Sri Krishna killed Kansa (his maternal uncle) and made Ugrasen (his maternal grandfather) the king of Mathura. Enraged, the father-in-law of Kansa, Jarasandha (king of Magadha) with his friend Kalayavan attacked Mathura 17 times. For the safety of the people, Krishna and Yadavas decided to move the capital from Mathura to Dvaraka.

Land was reclaimed from the sea near the western shores of Saurashtra. A city was planned and built here. Dvaraka was a planned city, on the banks of Gomati River. This city was also known as Dvaramati, Dvaravati and Kushsthali. It had well organized six sectors, residential and commercial zones, wide roads, plazas, palaces and many public utilities. A hall called "Sudharma Sabha" was built to hold public meetings. The city also boasted a good harbour.

After Krishna left for the heavenly abode, and the major Yadava heads were killed in disputes among themselves; Arjuna went to Dvaraka to bring Krishna's grandsons and the Yadava wives to Hastinapur. After Arjuna left Dvaraka, it was submerged in the sea. Following is the account given by Arjuna, in Mahabharata:

"The sea, which had been beating against the shores, suddenly broke the boundary that was imposed on it by nature. The sea rushed into the city. It coursed through the streets of the beautiful city. The sea covered up everything in the city. I saw the beautiful buildings becoming submerged one by one. In a matter of a few moments it was all over. The sea had now become as placid as a lake. There was no trace of the city. Dwaraka was just a name; just a memory."

The Vishnu Purana states that "On the same day that Krishna departed from the earth the powerful dark-bodied Kali Age descended. The oceans rose and submerged the whole of Dvaraka."

Sri Dwaraknath Mahatyam

Adi Sankara had visited Dwarakdish Shrine and had established a Mutt. The Lord here is dressed in Kalyana Kolam where he appears to be a Royal Wedding costume. The place is so sacred as Lord Shri Krishna himself had resided and his successors had built the temple. It is one of the 108 Divya desam.

Prasadam

Prasadams vary from time to time at Dwarakadish temple. They are sugar candy, Kher, Dry Fruits, Paan, Delicious and Nutritious Food, Fruits, Meals and Saffron Sharbath.

Darshan, Sevas and Festivals

There are many Darshan and Sevas for Lord Dwaraknath. The dress is changed accordingly. The Darshan are

- Mangala
- Shringar
- Gval
- Rajbhoj

- Uthapan
- Bhog
- Sandhya Aarati
- Shayan
- Hindola

Recent Archeological Findings

The recent underwater studies conducted by the ASI (Archeological Survey of India) reveals the existence of city dated to the 2nd millennium BC.

The search for the lost city was going on since 1930's. The Marine Archaeology Unit (MAU) of the National Institute of Oceanography, took part in this search in 1983. This search was carried out in the coastal waters of Dwarka in Gujarat.

Explorations between 1983 and 1990 revealed the well-fortified township of Dvaraka, that extended more than half a mile from the shore. The township was built in six sectors along the banks of a river. The foundation of boulders on which the city's walls were erected proves that the land was reclaimed from the sea.

Dvaraka extended up to Bet Dwaraka (Sankhodhara) in the north and Okhamadhi in the south. Eastward it extended up to Pindara. The general layout of the city of Dvaraka described in ancient texts agrees with that of the submerged city discovered by MAU.

Bet Dwarka

A team of archeologists have carried out onshore and inter-tidal zone explorations and a few trial trenches were laid to trace a proper cultural sequence. The most potential sites, where a large number of antiquities were recovered are Bet Dwarka-I, II, VI, and IX.

The findings of Bet Dwarka may be divided into two broad periods: Protohistoric period which includes seal, two inscriptions, a copper fishhook and late Harappan pottery (circa 1700-1400 BC) and the Historical period consisting of coins and pottery. Onshore and intertidal zone explorations have indicated some kind of shoreline shifting around the Bet Dwarka island as a few sites get submerged during high tide.

Offshore explorations near present Bet Dwarka brought to light a number of stone anchors of different types that include triangular, grapnel and ring stones. They are made out of locally available rocks and their period may also be similar to those found at Dwarka and other places. Recently, Roman antiquities including sherds of amphorae and a lead ingot and lead anchors were found. There is also an indication of a shipwreck of Roman period in Bet Dwarka waters. The proposal for the Dvaraka museum, submitted by the MAU, involves laying a submarine acrylic tube through which visitors can view through glass windows the ruins of the city.

The State Government of Gujarat and the Travel & Tourism Department of Gujarat are working on this proposal (for over two decades). When completed, it will be the first museum to be built under the sea.

Compositions

Mirabai, Surdas had composed lot of songs on Dwarakdish. The Alwars like Tirumalisai Alvar, Nammalvar, Periyalvar, Andal, Thondaradippodi Alvar, Tirumangai Alvar have sung in praise of Dwarakanath in Tamil.

Places of Interest

- Nageshwar Temple, Dwarka-a famous Shiva temple and one among the 12 Jyotirlingas
- Shree Swaminarayan Temple-Dwarka
- Rukmini Hrid-collection of 7 ponds.
- Brahma kund.
- Bet Dwarka, a small island near Dwarka
- Somnath Temple famous Lord Shiva Temple

Osian

Osian (Osiyan) is an ancient town located in the Jodhpur District of Rajasthan state in western India. It is an oasis in the Thar Desert, 65 km north of the district headquarters at Jodhpur, on a diversion off the main Jodhpur–Bikaner Highway.

Osian is famous as home to the cluster of ruined Brahmanical and Jain temples dating from the 8th to 11th centuries. The city was a major religious centre of the kingdom of Marwar during the Pratihara dynasty. Of the 18 shrines in the group, the Surya or Sun Temple and the later Kali temple, Sachiya Mata Temple and the main Jain temple dedicated to Lord Mahavira stands out in their grace and architecture.

The nearest airport is at Jodhpur. National Highway 11 passes through Osian. Osian Railway Station is situated on the Jodhpur–Phalodi line of North Western Railway.

History of Osian

Osia is a small village sixty-five kilometers north-east of Jodhpur. It is an important Jain pilgrimage centre for Oswal Jain community. The temple built here in A. D. 783 is an important tirtha for Jain built by Pratihara King Vatsa raja. The Jain Harivamsa Purana refers to Vatsa raja's rule in Saka year 705 (A. D. 783). He must have held sway over Upakesapura, *i.e.,* Osian as an inscriptions of Vikram Samvat 1013 (A. D. 956) found from there refers to this place.

In "Nabhinandana-jirnodhara Prabandha"-:Upakesapura has been described as the 'Svastika' (a mystical mark denoting good luck) of the earth, an ornament of the desert endowed with natural beauty where the groves are full of trees and the noble ascetics are wifeless (adara), but amongst the citizens none are like that; where the beautiful damsels and the peacocks educate each other without formal instructions merely by observing each other's graceful gait; where the tanks are replete with fully blossomed lotuses and the nocturnal darkness is dispelled by the light emanating from the luminous gems and where the rays of moon entering during the night through latticed windows in the houses of fair ladies, separated from their spouses, appear like the silver-arrows hurled by Cupid. Shorn of its usual literary exaggerations, the description does indicate that Osian was an important flourishing town then. The derivation of the cast name Oswal from Osian-the place name also sounds acceptable as it is a common practice in India to derive the family names from place names.

Osian and Jainism

It is conjectured from several evidences that the people of Osian were converted to Jainism by Jain Acharya Ratnaprabhasuriji, who had impressed the populace of the region by his supernatural powers.

A niche in Mahavira Temple contains sculpture of interwined snakes which also is worshipped by Oswal Jain, as adhisthatyaka-devetas. This leads us to believe that a sizeable part of the populace in that period may have belonged to naga extraction. 'Nagabhatta' was a Pratihara ruler of Mandor near Jodhpur. It is said that the 'Nagabhatta' must have defeated the nagas and so he must have been given the name Nagabhatta which means 'master of nagas'. 'Nagabhatta' the son of 'Narbhatta' of Mandor line established his capital at Merta near Nagaur, whose old name as *Nagapura*. The Pratiharas may have conquered these areas from the nagas. *Nagapriyagachha* of Jain also indicates in the same direction.

The Nagas of Osian and surrounding region, thus seem to have continued serpent worship even after their conversion to Jainism and for this reason their parallel worship of Sachiya Mata by Oswal Jain community seems relevant. The Sachiya Mata Temple also equally old and important situated on a hill north-east of Mahavira Temple, enable us some clues to understand the social history of that period. This Temple was built by Upaldev who is the brother of Raja Punj the son of King 'Bheemsain' (king of Bhinmal).

This has many decorative features of a Jain Temple, however, it is dedicated to Sachiya Mata, though Jain also worship here, which also is a matter of interest to understand the emergence of Jain community in this city.

The Bafna clan of Jain community conduct their 'Mundan-Sanskar' in Sachiya Mata Temple

Bayana

Bayana is a historical town in Bharatpur district of Rajasthan in India. It is a historical city founded by Banasur, who was an "Asura". He lived during the time of Krishna. His daughter "Usha" was married to Aniruddh (grand son of Shri Krishna after a long battle).

Geography

Bayana is located in a small plain, between two hill ranges running more or less parallel to each other near the left bank of the Gambhir river, at a distance of 48 km to south west of Bharatpur.

Bayana is located at 26.9° N 77.28° E. It has an average elevation of 196 metres (643 feet).

Demographics

As of 2001 India census, Bayana had a population of 33,504. Males constitute 54% of the population and females 46%. Bayana has an average literacy rate of 64%, higher than the national average of 59.5%; with 63% of the males and 37% of females literate. 17% of the population is under 6 years of age.

History of Bayana

The ancient name of Bayana was Sripatha or Sriprashtha or Shantipura. A big hoard of the ancient Indian coins were discovered in 1946 at the distance of 11 kms from Bayana. In 372 A.D Vishnu Vardhana erected the sacrificial pillar in memory of pundarika sacrifice for propsperity. In 1046 AD Chittralekha, the queen of Mangalaraja (Mangalraja was Kachawaha king of Gwalior. He was son of Vazradama, who died in a battle with Mahmood of Gazni in 1000 AD.) built the temple of Vishnu.

It is a curious mixture of Hindu and Mohammad relics. Ruled by stalwarts like Muhammad Ghori, Sikandar Lodhi and Humayun, Bayana held a special place in history. According to Abul Fazal: "this town is the burial place of many illustrious men". It can be adjudged that various important battles were fought here. Akbarnama mention that in former times Bayana was the capital of a province of which Agra was merely a dependent village.

Before the main Battle of Khanua, in 1527. Rana Sanga and Hasan Khan Mewati had initial success here. Many generals and soldiers of Babur were killed here. The graves of these generals still present in Bayana. It was here that Babur renounced alcohal. A mosque named "Talaqani Masjid" is still present to commemorate this event. Babur also constructed "Jhajhri" here. Which is present till now. Bayana is about 35 kilometers from Khanwa and about 45 KM from Fatehpur Sikri.

Bayana is famous for Bijaigarh (Vijaygarh) fort which was built by Jadon Raja Bijai Pal in 1040 A.D. The Bijaigarh fort contains several old temples and a red sandstone pillar bearing an inscription of Vishnuvardhan, a feudatory of Samudragupta. The fort was described as one of the most famous forts in India by Babur himself. Besides this there is a monolithic sandstone pillar, a combination of Hindu and Muslim styles, which bears many inscriptions.

Another important place is Temple of Usha, which was built during the reign of Raja Laxman Sen, (Laxman was father of Vazradama the kachawaha king of Gwalior) by his wife. Usha loved and married Aniruddh after a long battle. This is the only temple in India dedicated to Usha.

Chunar

Chunar, located in Mirzapur District of Uttar Pradesh state, India, is an ancient town. The railway tracks passing through Chunar leads to major destinations of India, including Howrah, Delhi, Tatanagar and Varanasi. National Highway number 7 also passes through Chunar. It is connected to Varanasi, the ancient and pilgrimage city also well-known as Kashi or Benaras, by roads and rails. Chunar is well-known for its pottery work especially clay toys.

History

In spite of being a small town, Chunar has a great influence in history. The Chunar Fort was established by Maharaja Vikrmaditya, the King of Ujjain, in honour of the stay of his brother Raja Bhrithari. As per Puranas, Hindu book of preachings, the oldest name of Chunar was Charanadri as Lord Vishnu had taken his first step in his Vaman incarnation in the dynasty of Great king Bali in the age of Satyug. It was also well known as Nainagarh.

Chunargarh of 'Chandrakanta', the famous classic novel by Babu Devakinandan Khatri, is only 40 kms from the holy city of Varanasi. The Chunar Fort is situated on an extension of the Vindhyan range of mountains, with river Ganga, Ganges, flowing near its base. Various exotic waterfalls and religious worship places attract thousands of tourists and locals.

Chunar is very well known for its pottery industries.

Geography

Chunar is located at 25.13° N 82.9° E. It has an average elevation of 84 metres (275 feet).

Demographics

As of 2001 India census, Chunar had a population of 33,919. Males constitute 53% of the population and females 47%. Chunar has an average literacy rate of 57%, lower than the national average of 59.5%: male literacy is 66% and, female literacy is 47%. In Chunar, 16% of the population is under 6 years of age.

People and Place

People here are humble, simple and down to earth. Primary mode of earning livelihood is agriculture and agri-based business. Agriculture is primarily dependent on the moderate rainfall occurring between July to September, and the area is well connected with water sources by means of canals. Local dramas and melas (fun-fair and social gathering during off-time in agriculture primarily focused for entertainment), are favourites of the locals.

Chunar is also a place of tourist interest. A temple of Maa Durga is situated in a cave near in the midst of beautiful sceneries. Chunar is also known for its communal harmonies. People of all communities live together with peacefully and took part in the each other communal festivals.

Chunar and surrounding villages are majorly populated with Kurmi Kshatriyas, contributing more than 50% of the population.

Sopara

Sopara (identified by Hebrew texts as Ophir) was an ancient port town near the present day Mumbai exurb of Nala Sopara. During ancient times, the town was the largest on India's west coast, trading with Mesopotamia, Egypt, Cochin, Arabia and Eastern Africa.

Coins and artefacts can be found in the Asiatic Society of Bombay.

Agroha

Agroha, 29.20 N 75.38 E, is ancient town in Haryana, the "birthplace" of the Agrahari and Agrawal community. Ancient structures, pot-sherds, coins and seals have been found in archaeological excavations. Agroha was the capital of legendary Emperor Agrasen.

It is close to Hisar and Hansi on NH 10. During the last 20 years Agroha Vikas Trust has done a lot of development of this Holy town. Now a very fine staying facility with lodging and boarding is available. A no. of temples have been constructed in the Complex. A Medical and Engineering college is also in function at Agroha. In Aggarwals, there are 17 and half Gotras. They are very strict in marriage and do not marry between the Same Gotras.

Kurukshetra

Kurukshetra is the name of a city in the present-day Indian state of Haryana. The name literally means "Land of the Kaurava" after the Kuru clan. It is supposed to be the site of the Kurukshetra war, described in the Mahabharata. It is of great importance in Hinduism as this is where the Bhagavad Gita was taught to Arjuna on the battle field, just before the great battle. Rashtrakavi Ramdhari Singh 'Dinkar' had written a poem by the name of *Kurukshetra*.

Thanesar or Sthaneswar, a historical town is located adjacent to what is now newly created Kurukshetra city. Local hearsay identifies the legendary "Kurukshetra" with a nearby obscure hamlet, and with the active abetment of the state government, it is presently experiencing a tourist boom. A few kilometres from Kurukshetra is the village, Amin where there are remnants of a fort and it is said to be Abhimanyu's fort.

In some ancient Hindu texts, the boundaries of Kurukshetra correspond roughly to the state of Haryana. Thus according to the Taittiriya Aranyaka 5.1.1., the Kurukshetra region is south of Turghna (Srughna/Sugh in Sirhind, Punjab), north of Khandava (Delhi and Mewat region), east of Maru (=desert) and west of Parin.

Educational Institutes

- Kurukshetra University: Imparts various courses including professional courses like MCA, MBA.
- National Institute of Technology, Kurukshetra.
- Shri Krishana Institute of Engineering. & Technology, Kurukshetra.

Places of Interest

- Brahma Sarovar: Every year lakhs of people come to take holy bath at Brahma Sarovar on the occasion of "Somavati Amavasya" (Sacred No-Moon Day that happens on a Monday).
- Sannihit Sarovar.
- Jyotisar: The famous site where Bhagavad Gita was delivered to Arjuna.
- Krishna Museum: Have some historical artifacts, paintings depicting Mahabharata war.
- Science Museum: Nice science museum esp. for children. Also a 15 mins 3-D movie is shows there.
- Bhishma Kund at Naraktari: The place where Arjun shot an arrow towards earth to quench Bhisma Pitamah thirst.
- Saraswati Forest Reserve: It is a large reserved forest area with rich flora and fauna in Kurukshetra district.
- Sheikh-Chilli ka makbara (tomb): This monument is maintained by ASI. It's a nice and well maintained monument which was built during Mughal period in

remembrance of Sufi Saint Sheikh Chilli, believed to be spiritual teacher of Mughal Prince, Dara Shikoh.

- Sthaneshwar Mahadev
- Kamal Nabhi
- Bhadrakali Mandir
- Birla Mandir
- Chhati Path Shahi Gurudwara
- Pehowa
- Ban Ganga

District Administration

- The Deputy Commissioner, an officer belonging to the Indian Administrative Service, is the overall in-charge of the General Administration in the district. He is assisted by a number of officers belonging to Haryana Civil Service and other Haryana state services.
- The Superintendent of Police, an officer belonging to the Indian Police Service, is responsible for maintaining Law & Order and related issues in the district. He is assisted by the officers of the Haryana Police Service and other Haryana Police officials.
- The Deputy Conservator of Forests, an officer belonging to the Indian Forest Service, is responsible for the management of the Forests, Environment and Wild-Life in the district. He is assisted by the officers of the Haryana Forest Service and other Haryana Forest officials and Haryana Wild-Life officials.
- Sectoral development is looked after by the district head/officer of each development department such as PWD, Health, Education, Agriculture, Animal husbandry, etc. These officers are from various Haryana state services.
- Shahbad and Ladwa are other towns in the district with a significant population.

Paithan

Paithan, formerly Pratishthana, was the capital of the Satavahana empire of ancient India. It is located within 50 kilometres of present-day Aurangabad on the Godavari River in Maharashtra. Paithan was home of the great Maharashtrian saint Eknath, whose tomb can be found there. The town is mostly famous today for its sarees—the Paithani. Sant Dnyneshwar Udyan is famous garden developed based on Mysore Garden.

A major dam called Jaikwadi/Jayakwadi Dam is also located near Paithan. On August 9, 2006, Paithan experienced its worst flood in known history when floodgates of the Jayakwadi dam were opened near the town because of heavy rainfall in the region. Photography at this dam is banned and driving your vehicle up to the dam is not permitted. All notices are only in Marathi.

Vallabhi

Vallabhi (modern Vala) is an ancient city located in Saurashtra peninsula in Gujarat, in western India, near Bhavnagar. Also known as Vallabhipura, it was the capital of the ancient Maitraka dynasty.

Origins and History

Legend has it that a Kshatriya named Vijayasena founded the city around the 3rd century. The Maitrakas, descending from general Bhatarka, a military governor of Saurashtra peninsula during Gupta ruler Skanda Gupta (455-467), had ruled the peninsula and parts of southern Rajasthan from Vallabhi from the fifth to the eighth centuries.

Vallabhi has been a famous Jain centre, and there is a possibility that the Maitrakas (Sun-worshippers) may have embraced Jainism later on. But when Chinese traveller Xuanzang visited Vallabhi during second quarter of 7th century, he found its ruler to be a Buddhist follower. When Itsing, another Chinese traveller visited Vallabhi in the last quarter of 7th century, he found the city as a great centre of learning including Buddhism.

Gunamati and Sthiramati are stated to be two famous Buddhist scholars of Vallabhi at the middle of seventh century.

Vallabhi was famous for its catholicity and the students from all over the country, including the Brahmana boys, visited it to have higher education in secular and religious subjects. We are told that the graduates of Vallabhi were given higher executive posts.

Maitraka rule ended with the sacking of Vallabhi by the barbarians in 524, according to James Tod and in second or third quarter of the 8th century by various other scholars. There is no agreement among the scholars as to who these barbarians were.

Gajni or Gayni is one of the ancient names of port of Vallabhi (Cambay), the ruins of which are about three miles from the modern city. H. A. Rose and several other scholars have identified this Gajni with the Gajni referenced in the traditions of Karnal Kamboj (*Garh Gajni Nikaas, Lachhoti Ghaggar*). This and some other traditions of *Karnal Kamboj* seem to connect them with Vallabhi (Kambay) in Saurashtra.

One of the bardic chronicles of Sisodias of Mewar reads thus about the destruction of Gajni and the killing of Siladitya-VI and his defence forces:

"The barbarians had captured Gajni. The house of Siladitya was left desolate. In its defence, his hero fell; of his seed but the name remains ". This reference seems to connect the ancestors of the Sisodias to the same Gajni as of the Kamboj traditions.

Kalinjar

Kalinjar is a fortress-city in the Bundelkhand region of central India. Kalinjar is located in Banda District of Uttar Pradesh state, near the temple-city and World Heritage Site of Khajuraho. The fortress is strategically located on an isolated rock at the end the Vindhya Range, at an elevation of 1203 feet overlooking the plains of Bundelkhand. It served several of Bundelkhand's ruling dynasties, including the Chandela dynasty of Rajputs in the 10th century, and the Solankis of Rewa. The fortress contains several temples, dating as far back as the Gupta dynasty of the 3rd-5th centuries.

History

Kalinjar is one of the most characteristic specimens of the hill-fortresses, originally hill-shrines, of central India. Its antiquity is proved by its mention in the Mahabharata. It was besieged by Mahmud of Ghazni in 1023, and here the Afghan emperor Sher Shah Suri met his death in 1545. Kalinjar played a prominent part in history down to the time of the Revolt of 1857, when it was held by a small British garrison. Both the fort and the town, which stands at the foot of the hill, are of interest to the antiquary on account of the remains of temples, sculptures, inscriptions and caves.

Kalinjar means *the destroyer of time* in Sanskrit. 'Kal' is time and 'jar' destruction. It is therefore a common belief associated with the Kalinjar hill that Lord Shiva had slain the god of time on it. Since then, the hill has been considered a holy site, casting its shadow across the patches of grasslands as well as the densely forested valley. The natural splendour of the surroundings makes it an ideal place for penance and meditation and, surprisingly, a strange mystique still pervades all over the hill.

The scriptures state that the holy place had four different names in the four yugas, or epochs within a cycle of four ages:. In Satyuga it was known as Kirtinagar, in Treta it was Madhyagarh, in Dwapar it was Singhalgarh, and finally in Kalyuga it came to be known as Kalinjar. The hilly peak has several legends attached to it.

Its origin being shrouded in mystery, not much is known as to when and by whom the fort was built on this holy hill, though modern historians conjecture that a Chandela king, Kedar Burman, had it built in the 7th century. The fort was a unique monument of its time and had no parallel in any other part of the country in terms of sheer grandeur and artistry.

Its historical background is replete with numerous battles and invasions. The Hindu princes of different dynasties as well as the Muslim rulers fought hard to conquer it and the fort continued to pass from one ruler to another. But, except for the Chandelas, no other ruler could reign over it for long.

In 1812, the British troops marched into Bundelkhand. After a long battle they were able to annex the fort. The British seizure of Kalinjar proved to be a great watershed, transferring the legacy of the old aristocracy into the hands of the new bureaucracy of officials who showed their loyalty to British imperialism by damaging the captured fort. The damages caused to the fort can still be seen on its walls and open spaces.

Attractions

The majesty and grandeur witnessed within Kalinjar's precincts is due to the Chandela rulers' creative imagination, their highly developed aesthetic sense and religious fervour. Though they were great devotees of Lord Shiva, they evinced a great interest in the construction of temples of other deities, too. The massive rock cut sculptures include figures of various gods and goddesses from ancient mythological themes. Wherever the Chandelas had established their reign they left their mark by enriching them with fine works of art, stone images, and sculpture.

The western part of the fort rewards all who take the time to look inside the temple of Neelkanth Mahadev. Each time one peeps through a cavelike opening and glances at an imposing Shivlinga of around five feet, one is awestruck. The idea has been to use landscape and cave-isolation to set the solemnity of the mood for prayer. Its intrinsic feature is to reflect and refract light in the appropriate seasons, letting in light in winter and darkening to restrict its entry in summer.

Close to the Shivling cave, stand the idols of Bhairava and goddess Parvati, made of black stone. Images of numerous gods and goddesses are carved on both sides of the gateway. A number of broken pillars are seen at regular distances. On these pillars, it is said, six-storey constructions were raised, but they were demolished later.

There are numerous rock-cut sculptures showing neglect and ravages of time. The vagaries of nature and of man have taken their toll but the remnants indicate a synthesis of several ancient cultures and faiths, the legacy of a glorious past.

Another beautiful sight is the palace of prince Aman Singh. He was the descendant of King Chhatrasal. A number of legends are associated with this Mahal whose big lawns and walls unfold a long history of Chandela culture. Thousands of images made of granite and sandstone have been collected in a museum set up informally. Rich carvings on these images arrest the eye, even though they are broken and have been struck by the ravages of time.

Trimurti images are also many, showing the faces of Brahma, Vishnu and Mahesh (Shiva). Some distance away is a massive figure of Vishnu lying in the ocean of milk, enclosed within the coils of the Sheshnag. It presents a unique artistic charm. The presence of images of Lord Shiva the god of love Kamadev, Indrani the wife of Indra etc. speaks of influence from diverse cultures and religions. It also leads us to believe that the creation of the Chandela culture was not the handiwork of artists from one region.

The Chandela princes were influenced by the 'Shaiva' cult. Therefore, among the rock-cut and stone images are mostly those of Shiva, Parvati, Nandi and the Shivling. Shiva is seen at times in his dancing posture of tandava and at others in a close embrace with goddess Parvati.

There are numerous other attractions. The Venkat Bihari temple presents a majestic look from the outside though its interiors are decayed now. Persons suffering from skin diseases can take a dip in the 'pond of million tirthas'. The Sita-kund, Pandu-kund, Patal-ganga etc. speak for the Chandelas' taste for the aquatic resorts.

Cemented roads have been built all through the mountainous passage along which people can conveniently travel to reach the fort. But to discover the real charm and pleasure of adventure, one has to walk along the old beaten track, making way through the rough and rocky terrain of the seven magnificent gates falling in between. Seeing these gates, one truly appreciates the functional relevance of this invincible fort and its strategic defences.

Tirunelveli

Coordinates: 8°442 N 77°422 Tirunelveli district is the penultimate southern most district of Tamil Nadu in India. It is described as a microcosm of the state. The district has diverse geographical and physical features like lofty mountains, low plains, rivers and cascades, sea coast and thick inland and mountain forest, sandy soil and fertile alluvium, a variety of flora, fauna and protected wild life.

Tirunelveli is a Municipal Corporation, sixth largest city in Tamil Nadu and the district headquarters of Tirunelveli district. The city is considered as one of the oldest city in Indian subcontinent around 3,000 years old located on the west bank of the perennial Thamirabarani River in the state of Tamil Nadu in Southern India.

Brief History of Tirunelveli

Tirunelveli is culturally very old city. To add on evidence of its oldness, in the outskirts of the city in Adichanallur, the archaeologist unearthed urns containing human skull, skeleton and bones with some Tamil Brahmi script on it. Along with skeleton, they found husks, grains of rice, charred rice and Neolithic Celts. By this the archaeologists authentically confirmed it as 2800 years old of Neolithic period. The same has been published in The Hindu English daily on May 26, 2004. This assured that Tirunelvéli has been the abode for human habituation from Neolithic period around 3,000 years old. Now, Adhichanallur has been announced as an archaeological site for further excavation and studies.

This culturally old city is called in another name also "Nellai". In fact, the exact translation in Tamil for paddy is "Nell". So, both the name Tirunelveli or Nellai directly associates with paddy. Just in glance even on satellite pictures, it can be seen that the city is surrounded by fertile paddy fields enriched by a perennial river "Tamirabarani". It flows through out the year, which supplies water through various canals to agricultural field.

It has a deep rooted history on puranical perspective to get this name. It is said that a devotee was invited by God in his dream to settle with his family near the Tamirabarani River. He collected paddy from various other people as the way of begging due to famine. And he spread out the paddy to dry under the sunlight and went for ablution in Tamirabarani river. He prayed to Lord for rain. Suddenly a thunder strom broke out and rained heavily.

Although his prayer answered, he worried about the paddy he spread out to dry under the sun light. So he ran there and what he saw was a miracle. Despite the heavy rain, that the paddy he spread did not even get a drop of rain or even soaked. Since then the city is called as Tirunelveli, the meaning is like this-'TIRU' means Respectable, 'NEL' means paddy and 'VELI' means Fence. As having the rain become the fence for the paddy he spread out, it is called as Tirunelveli. In other words the city is having paddy fields as fence

In the period of the Pandian Empire, the city served as the south capital for them. The city was the chief commercial town in the period of Arcot Nawabs and Nayaks. They were one of the various ruling dynasties of Tamil Nadu. In fact, they called the city as "Nellai Chemmai", cheemai means foreign developed town. Tirunelveli first came into prominence under the Pandya kings, serving as their capital for some time. It was an important city of the Chola kingdom (c.900 – 1200) and of the Vijayanagar empire. Thereafter, it fell under the rule of local Nayaks and of the Nawab of Arcot, who in 1781 granted its revenues and local administration to the British. In 1801 it was annexed by the British, who governed it until India achieved independence in 1947.

On the event, the British acquired it from Arcot Nawab in 1801 and named it as Tinnevely district and Tinnevely city. They were comfortable calling it as Tinnevely due to the difficulty in pronouncing the original name. After coming under the British East India Company's administration, it served as the military headquarters for British during their operation against Palayakars. From that time, both Tirunelveli and Palayamkottai generally called as twin cities grew together.

Apart from the above, it has one more name "Halwa City". A wheat based sweet Halwa is very famous in Tirunelveli, which brought this nick name. The city has Swamy Nellaiappar and Sri Kandimathi Ambal temples, which are saivites. The city has been trifurcated in to three administrative provinces such as Tirunelveli, Palayamkottai and Melapalayam.

The city has become a corporation from 1999 and possesses the title of sixth largest city in the state of Tamil Nadu. Generally, the corporation status has been given to a city according to its income generation and the population. The city is well connected by roads. From Madurai it is 150 km south in NH7 and 80 km north of Kanyakumari or Cape Comerin in NH7. An NH7A connects Tirunelveli with Tutuicorin port in 50 km and a major highway connects to Quilon, Kerala in 150 km. Lakshmana Velu is one of the prominent leaders from this part of the South India.

Tiruneveli has two tier flyover named as Tiruvalluvar Flyover, which is the second longest double decked flyover in Asia.

Geography

Tirunelveli is located at 8°442 N 77°422. It has an average elevation of 47 metres (154 feet). It is in the southern most tip of the Deccan pleateu in the Indian peninsular. Tirunelveli is located in the National Highway 7 stretch. The nearest land mark are: Gangai kondan in the north, Vallanad in the east, Alangukulam in the west, Ambasamudram in the south west and nanguneri in the south. The perennial river Thamiraparani splits the city in to Tirunelveli and Palayamkottai. The major lake present in the city are Nainar lake and Udayarpetti lake.

Climate

The climate of Tirunelveli is usually tropical and unpredictable, *viz.*, hot and humid. The average temperature during the hot season (March to September) ranges from 23 to 36 °Celsius and during the mild season (October to February) ranges from 19 to 30 °C. The average annual rainfall is 680 mm, most of which occurs during the North-East monsoon (October-December). No earth quake has been reported in Tirunelveli city so far.

Demographics

As of 2001 India census, Tirunelveli had a population of 411,298. Males constitute 49% of the population and females 51%. Tirunelveli has an average literacy rate of 78%, higher than the national average of 59.5%: male literacy is 83%, and female literacy is 73%. In Tirunelveli, 10% of the population is under 6 years of age. Among the Municipal Corporations, Tirunelveli has returned the best sex ratio with 1024 females for every 1000 males.. The growth rate of Urban Agglomeration is 20.22%.

The Tirunelveli City spreads over an area of 108.65 sq.km. The population density of the Corporation had increased to 3781 persons per sq.km in 2001 from 2218 Persons per sq.km in 1971. The disabilites in the City as per Census 2001 are 1308246, out of which male 645142 and female 663104. Hindus are the most in urban population. Followed by Muslims and then Christians.

The language mainly spoken in the city is Tamil. The usage of English is common. Majority of office matters and teachings in Educational Institution are dealt in English. People here in the city are rooted to Dravidians.

Projected Population

Year	*Population*	*Type*	*Source*
1991	345,772	census	official
2001	431,603	census	official
2009	457,979	calculation	

Sl. No	*Domain*	*Rank in population*	*Rank in UA*
1	World	not-defined	not-defined
2	Asia	440	400
3	India	91	89
4	Tamil Nadu	6	7

Economy

The economy of Tirunelveli district is chiefly agrarian in nature and people are engaged in the cultivation of cumbu, ragi, pulses, groundnut, gingelly, coconut, chillies, indigo and cotton. It is rich in mineral resources of limestone, sulphides and ilmenite-garnet sands. The city of Tirunelveli has a quite a number of industries in its area like cement factories, cotton textile mills, spinning and weaving mills, beedi companies, steel products and so on. A large number of small scale industries supported by NELSIA (Nellai Small Scale Industries Association) are active. Tannery industries in small scale are also found in this town. In addition to these industries, a few smallscale units of brick kilns and oil mills exist in the industrial area of this town.

Recently Tata groups have signed a significant project of Titanium dioxide plant for Rs. 2,500 crore in Tirunelveli and Tuticorin districts. The project will create job opportunity for 1,000 person directly and 3,000 indirectly.

The living cost of the city is less when comparing with other cities. Many of the basic raw materials for food are available in afforable price.

Civic Administration

Total population in Tirunelveli Municipal Corporation as per 2001 census.

Tirunelveli City Voters

Number of Wards	55
Total population	411,832
Male population	203,232
Female population	208,599

Transport

Roads: Tirunelveli is well-connected by road. The city is located on NH 7, 150 km to the south of Madurai and 80 km to the north of Kanyakumari. NH 7A, an extension of NH 7, connects Palayamkottai with Tuticorin Port. Now 4 lane track has been under progress and NH 7A stretch is almost in finishing stage. Tirunelveli is accessible by road from Madurai (3 hours) or Nagercoil (1 1/2 hours). Tirunelveli is also connected by major highways to Kollam, Tiruchendur, Rajapalayam, Sankarankovil, Ambasamudram and Nazareth. Bus Stand The main mofussil busstand is located in Veinthaankulam. This bus stand was opened for public usage from 2003 onwards. Here buses from and to outside the city and state operates services. The other bus stand for local services (within the city) Junction (Nellai Santhippu Perunthu Nilayam) Palai Bus stand (Palai Perunthu Nilayam). Both Government and private buses are being operated for city travel round the clock.

The Tirunelveli sub-division of the TNSTC (Tamil Nadu State Transport Corporation), Madurai Division services the district's road transport needs with a string of local and mofussil (out-of-town) services. The State Express Bus Corporation (SETC) operates express services to Chennai, Bangalore, Salem, Coimbatore, Tirupur, Nagapattinam, Erode, Villupuram, and Tirupati.

Railways: A majestic looking structure with a high elevated facade, Tirunelveli Junction Railway Station is one of the busiest and most important ones in Tamil Nadu. It is connected to major cities in all four directions, Madurai/Sankarankovil to the north, Nagercoil to the south, Tenkasi/Kerala (kollam) to the west and Tiruchendur to the east. The segment Tirunelveli-Tiruchendur broad gauge conversion is under progress and is expected to complete December 2007. Train Engine maintenance service station in under construction at Tirunelveli Junction railway station. At present, the engine and coaches are being sent to Nagarcoil for maintenance. The railway station is facilated with computerized ticket booking and touch screen to know the train schedule and train running status. It is proposed computerized ticket booking centre at Palayamkottai to clear the extra rush at Junction station. Although Tirunelveli Junction station is one of the most important stations in the state, only two express trains having origination, one Nellai Express and Kollam Mail.

This railway station produces profit for the Madurai Railway division. The Nellai Express—a super-fast train connecting Tirunelveli and Chennai Egmore—runs packed almost throughout the year. The station has six platforms, three for metre gauge and three for broad gauge. Tirunelveli Junction is coded as TEN. Any train passing through the station halts in Tirunelveli Junction station.

The major trains at Tirunelveli Junction:

- Nellai Express
- Kanniyakumari Express
- Ananthapuri Express
- Guruvayur Express
- Nagarcoil-Mumbai Express
- Kollam Mail
- Thirukural Express
- Kanyakumari-Howrah Express
- Mysore Express

There are five local railway stations in the city:

- Palayamkottai
- Town
- Pettai
- Melapalayam
- Thalaiyoothu

Airport: The nearest airport is Vagaikulam airport, located at Vaagaikulam, about 24kms east of Tirunelveli city. Connections to Chennai are via Air Deccan, once a day. The Madurai Airport and Thiruvananthapuram International Airport are about 150 km away by road. An unused runway at Kayatar, which is 30 km from the heart of the city, will become operational once the IT park at Gangaikondan is set up.

Media

Print: Dina Thanthi, Dina Malar, Dinakaran, Dina Mani, Tamil sudar, Kathiravan, Tamil Murasu, Malai Malar, Malai Murasu (an evening paper) are the prominent Tamil news dailies currently printed in the city. The Hindu is the most widely read English daily.

Local Cable TV: Air Media Network, Karan TV, Sathya, Krishna TV are the local cable television networks.

Radio Stations: Tirunelveli is served on the FM dial by Suriyan FM, frequency 93.5 MHz, run by the Sun Network, and Tirunelveli Vanoli Nilayam (AIR), by the Government of India. Tirunelveli has been identified as one of 40 cities in India to have FM station. IGNOU has planned to air its distant education lecture (named *Gyan Vani*) soon via FM, Tirunelveli.

Pincodes

Pincode is the postal numbering system used in India.

Location	*Pincode*
Tirunelveli Junction	627 001
Palayamkottai	627 002
Vannarpettai	627 003
Pettai	627 004
Melapalayan	627 005
Nellai Nagarm	627 006
Perumalpuram	627 007
Gandhinagar	627 008
Kokkirakulam (Collectorate)	627 009
Industrial Estate, Pettai	627 010
Sankarnagar	627 357
Maharajanagar	627 011
Abisheikapatti	627 012

Temples

The Nellaiappar Temple with Kanthimathi is situated in the centre of town at a distance of two km from the railway station. This is a twin temple dedicated to Goddess Parvathi and Lord Shiva. Rare jewels, the Golden Lily Tank, Musical Pillars, the hall of a thousand pillars are worth seeing. From a distance one can have a view of the great gopurams (towers). Both the gopurams were built according to the rules laid down in the agamasastras by Rama Pandyan.

Nindrasir Nedumaran, who reigned in the seventh century CE, contributed by constructing and renovating important parts in this temple. A beautiful garden founded in 1756 CE, next to this chain mandapam, welcomes visitors with many colourful and fragrant flowers. This garden was designed by Thiruvengadakrishna Mudaliar. A square vasantha mandapam with 100 pillars is found in the midst of this garden.

The Nellaiappar Temple is bigger than the Madurai Meenakshi Amman Temple, though the latter is more famous owing to its historical importance.

Education

The Manonmaniam Sundaranar University is located in Nellai, on the Tenkasi road, about 11 km from junction. The university is named after a famed poet who was the author of *Tamil Thai Vazhthu* (Praise to Mother Tamil), which is the official state song.

In the view to improve the quality of Education in the southern parts of Tamil Nadu, the Finance ministry has stated in the budgetary note that one more Anna University is to be created in the city of Tirunelveli.

The city has many prestigious old government and private colleges in the medical, legal, engineering, arts, pharmacy, and physiotherapy fields. Tirunelveli Medical College and the Government College of Engineering Tirunelveli are professional colleges run by the government of Tamil Nadu. St. Xaviers College run by Jesuits, St. Johns College and Sarah Tucker College run by CSI Diocease, M.D.T. Hindu College and Sadakathulla Appa College are well-known arts colleges.

Students from the city's schools have been consistently performing well in the state examinations.

Sl No	*Educational Institutions*	*No of Institutions*
1	University	1
2	Arts and Science College	21
3	Medical College	2
4	Sidha Medical College	1
5	Engineering College	13
6	Law College	1
7	Pre Kindergarten School	201
8	Primary School	1521

9	Middle School	394
10	High School	114
11	Higher Secondary	148
12	Teacher Training Institute	6

Science Centre

The city has a District Science Centre, a satellite unit of Visvesvaraya Industrial & Technological Museum, Bangalore. The centre is committed to the cause of science education through fun and entertainment. The Centre has an evergreen science park in sylvan surroundings and is located adjacent to the perennial river Thamirabharani, along the highway to Kanyakumari. Permanent exhibitions, science shows, interactive guide tours, a mini-planetarium, sky observation through a telescope are some of the activities of the Centre *'Fun science gallery' inaugurated in Tirunelveli*—The Hindu.

Language

There is a tradition that the Tamil language originated from the *Pothigai Malai*, a hill situated in western Ghats near Papanasam, a small village in the Tirunelveli district. As per Brahminical legend, Lord Shiva sent the two saints Vyasa and Agatyar (in Sanskrit Agastya) to create the divine languages Sanskrit and Tamil. Agatyar came to Papanasam and established the Tamil culture from the Pothigai Malai.

Today the Tamil language as spoken in the Tirunelveli district is considered to be especially lucid. The Tirunelveli accent appeals to all Tamil speaking people. The version spoken here is considerably different and more pleasant than Madras Bashai, which is a corrupted form of Tamil.

Cuisine

Halwa: The city is noted for the sweet *halwa* (pronounced *alva*) which is made from wheat and sugar. Tirunelveli halwa is said to owe its peculiar taste to the water from the Thamirabarani river. The Halwa was made famous by a Marwari family which settled here more than 300 years ago. The original shop started by them is the Lakshmi Vilas. Slowly others borrowed the formula from them and now the halwa has become a synonym for this city. The other famous halwa stores are *Irutu Kadai halwa* (Dark Store halva) and Shanthi Sweets. Some claim that Iruttu Kadai Halwa is much tastier than *Lakshmi Vilas* Halwa. Now in 2007, a group started a shop in the name of *Irutu Kadai halwa* near the railway station and it is not the original. The original *Irutu Kadai halwa* is near the Nellayappar temple and it doesnt have a board or an electric lamp. There are many of the hot spots to buy halwa are around the Nellayappar temple and near the main railway station.

Halwa is brown and semi-solid in texture and contains lots of ghee/Vanaspati which gives it the oily look. It tastes the best when fresh and hot.

Local Dishes

Some of the unique and popular dishes in Tirunelveli are *Sodhi*, *Kootan Choru* and *Ulunthamparupu choru with yellu thovayal*. Sothi is a delicious gravy made of coconut milk and vegetables. This is served at marriage feasts, especially during the *Maruveedu* (return marriage) ceremony which takes place the day after a marriage. Kootan Choru is a hot spicy vegetable rice made with dhal, rice, vegetables and a mixture of coconut and red chillies. Ulunthamparupu choru is rice and ulunthamparupu (Urad Dhal) cooked together. Ulunthamparupu choru is taken with yellu (Sesame seeds) thovayal (chutney). Porotta of tirunelveli with the kuruma (salna) gives an added taste.

Filtered Coffee

Tirunelveli has numerous coffee houses which open in the wee hours of the morning, even before 4 am. A local favourite is that of the famous filter coffee from Pothi Hotel at Chandipillaiyar Kovil Mukku. Its exceptional quality and flavour addictively pulls elderly people to rise early and energize them, first thing in the morning.

Some Places of Interest

The two tier over Thiruvalluvar Bridge at Tirunelveli Junction was constructed to avoid the heavy traffic and railway line crossing. The total length of the bridge is 800 metres. This bridge is the first of its kind ever constructed in India. It was opened to traffic in 1972. It consists of 25 spans, of which 13 are bow string arch, each with a width of 30.3 metres, and 12 are single tier R.C.C. girder, each having a width of 11.72 metres.

Additional places of interest include:

- District Science Centre at Vannarpet.
- V. O. Chidhambaram Pillai Memorial Hall at the Exhibition Ground
- Krishnapuram Temple
- Papanasam, Manimuthar dam
- Agasthiyar falls, Papanasam
- Courtallam (the Spa of the South, 50 km from Nellai)
- Mancholai, Kakaachi, Kuthiravetti Hill Stations and Tea estates
- Sankarankovil Arulmigu Gomathi Amman Temple (50 km fom Nellai)
- Tenkasi Kasiviswanathar temple (50 km from Nellai)
- Tiruchendur subramaniyaswamy temple (50 km from Nellai

Local Problems

Although Tirunelveli is one of the major cities in Tamil Nadu, the dearth of industries and the climate has resulted in many people migrating to other parts of Tamil Nadu such as Chennai, Coimbatore, and Tirupur, both for higher education and for job opportunities. It has been speculated that failure of the government to create job opportunities could also be a factor in this migration, which results slowest development among all the cities in Tamil Nadu.

Many of the development proposals initiated and suddenly become standstill due to various reasons. Here is dearth of world class medical facilities. For major surgery one has to travel to nearby cities like Madurai and Chennai despite basic medical facilities and hospitals available.

Eventhough Madurai-Kanniyakumari through Tirunelveli, rail stretch is profitable one in Southern railways, it has not been double tracked, nor electrified which hampers the railway traffic heavily and people are forced to choose alternate mode of transport say buses and therefore many private buses take this opportunity to take a most of it. Moreover, the city does not have airport, which is the main instrument for IT parks and companies/other industrial developments.

Palayamkottai, Tirunelveli's Twin city

The twin city of Tirunelveli is Palayamkottai, on the eastern bank of the Thamirabarani river, while Tirunelveli is on the western bank.

Palayamkottai is known for its educational institutions and is referred to as "Oxford of South India." The town, surrounded by paddy fields, has a rich heritage in education dating back to the pre-independence era. Almost all the colleges and institutions of higher education located in the area are in Palayamkottai, some of them having been in existence for more than a century and a half. They include the Tirunelveli Medical College, Government Siddha College, Government Engineering College, Francis Xavier Engineering College, St. Xavier's College, St. John's College and Sarah Tucker College. This area is one which is well suited for IT sectors since it is in the city centre with all the facilities around.

The city is a main centre in South India for Christian missions and there are quite a few churches, the major church being Holy Trinity Cathedral, the cathedral church of a diocese of the Church of South India.

The city also has several Hindu temples: the Gopalaswamy temple, Shiva Temple, Ramar Temple, Uchini Makali temples and a number for the goddess Amman.

It has two sports grounds: Anna Stadium and the *VOC Ground*. The latter holds field hockey and kabbadi matches at both the district and state levels. Republic Day and Independence Day ceremonies are also held here.

There is a large market in Palayamkottai, along with the *Ulavar Santhai* where farmers sell their products directly.

Palayamkottai is also known for its Central Prison, which housed a lot of freedom fighters during the struggle for Indian Independence. It is still notable for its capacity and security. Tamil poet Subramanya Bharathy spent a part of his life here.

Palayamkottai Central Prison

The Palyamkottai Central Prison is another historically important land mark as some eminent personalities like kalaignar m.karunanithi and other political leaders had served their prison terms here.

Tirunelveli District

Tirunelveli District has an area of 6,838 km^2. It is bounded by Virudhunagar District to the north, Thoothukudi District to the east, the Indian Ocean to the south, Kanyakumari District to the southwest, and Kerala state to the west. The chief towns, in addition to Tirunelveli, are Courtallam (also called Kuttalam), Sankarankoil and Tenkasi. Tirunelveli district has substantial population of people who follow the Ayyavazhi belief system.

The famous Courtallam waterfalls are located in Tirunelveli District along such rivers as the Chittar River. It is said that a dip in any of the nine waterfalls rejuvenates the body and the mind. The water is supposed to have healing properties due to the herbs which grow in the area. The waterfalls are often dry and August is considered to be the best time to go. Thamira Sabhai is located in Courtallam. Special fruits like *Mongostaan* and *Ramtaan* are available only in Courtallam.

Many of India's freedom fighters have originated from this land. Veera Pandiya Kattabomman, V.O. Chidambaram Pillai and Bharathiar are from Thoothukudi District, which was a part of Tirunelveli District before 1990.

The great Tamil poet Subramanya Bharathy is from Ettayapuram in the erstwhile Tirunelveli District. He composed poems foreseeing India's freedom and wrote articles on a variety of subjects emphasizing the unity of India despite its variety in languages, religions, and cultures.

Mukkudal village, located in the Tirunelveli District, is famous for its beedi (tobacco) industry. Some of the famous textile showrooms of Tamil Nadu are also in Tirunelveli.

Udyana

The area is said to have supported some 500 Theravada Buddhist monasteries, at which travelling monks were provided lodgings and food for three days. It is said Buddha's footprint could be found there (refer petrosomatoglyph), a rock on which he dried his clothes and a place where he 'converted' a Naga.

Udyana is of vital importance in the Vajrayana schools of Buddhism, as most of the later tantras are identified as originating there.

Udyana is the modern day Swat Valley in Pakistan.

Fa Xian wrote: "There is a tradition that when Buddha came to North India, he came at once to this country, and that here he left a print of his foot, which is long or short according to the ideas of the beholder. It exists, and the same thing is true about it, at the present day." (This footprint can still be seen today, in the upper Swat valley, at Lat/Long: 35.1316, 72.459).

Swat (Pakistan)

Swat is a valley and a district in the North-West Frontier Province of Pakistan the capital is Saidu Sharif. With high mountains, green meadows, and clear lakes, it is a place of great natural beauty, and a popular destination for tourists. It was a princely state (see State of Swat) in the NWFP until it was dissolved in 1969.

This valley and the other areas along the banks of the river Swat, earliest known as *Shrivastu*, later *Suvastu* and currently the present name, is also the place of origin of the Shrivastava sub-clan of the Indo-Aryan Kayastha clan.

History

Swat has been inhabited for over two thousand years and was known in ancient times as Udyana. The first inhabitants were settled in well-planned towns. The independent monarchs of this region came under Achaemenid influence, before reverting back to local control in the 4th century BC. In 327 BC, Alexander the Great fought his way to Udegram and Barikot. In Greek accounts these towns have been identified as Ora and Bazira. By 305 BC, the region became a part of the Mauryan Empire.

Around the 2nd century BC, the area was occupied by Buddhists, the Indo-Greeks, and the Kushans who were attracted by the peace and serenity of the land. Swat is thought to be the probable birthplace of Vajrayana Buddhism. There are many archaeological sites in the district, and Buddhist relics are common, testimony to their skills as sculptors and architects.

Buddhist Heritage of Swat

Location of Swat District (highlighted in yellow) within the North West Frontier Province of Pakistan

The Swat museum has the footprints of the Buddha, which were found in the Swat valley and can now be seen in the Swat museum. When the Buddha died, His relics (or ashes) were distributed to seven kings, who built stupas over them for veneration..

The *Harmarajika stupa* (Taxila) and *Butkarha (Swat) stupa* at Jamal Garha were among the earliest stupas of Gandhara. These had been erected on the orders of king Ashoka and contained the real relics of the Buddha.

The Gandhara school is probably credited with the first representation of the Buddha in human form, the portrayal of Buddha in his human shape, rather than shown as a symbol.

As Buddhist art developed and spread outside India, the styles developed here were imitated. For example, in China the Gandhara style was imitated in images made of bronze, with a gradual change in the features of these images. Swat, the land of romance and beauty, is celebrated throughout the world as the holy land of Buddhist learning and piety. Swat acquired fame as a place of Buddhist pilgrimage. Buddhist tradition holds that the Buddha himself came to Swat during his last reincarnation as the Gautama Buddha and preached to the people here.

It is said that the Swat was filled with fourteen hundred imposing and beautiful stupas and monasteries, which housed as many as 6,000 gold images of the Buddhist pantheon for worship and education. There are now more than 400 Buddhist sites covering and area of 160 km in Swat valley only. Among the important Buddhist excavation in Swat an important one is Butkarha-I, containing the original relics of the Buddha. Source: Indo Pak Hist till 1951.

Advent of Islam

In the beginning of the 11th century AD, Mahmud of Ghazni advanced through Dir and invaded Swat, defeating Gira, the local ruler, near Udegram. Later, when the King of Kabul Mirza Ulagh Beg attempted to assassinate the dominant chiefs of the Yousafzais they took refuge under the umbrella of the Swati Kings of Swat and Bajour.

The whole area was being dominated by the Swati/Jahangiri Sultans of Swat for centuries. According to Major Raverty, Jahangiri Kings of Swat had ruled from Jalalabad to Jehlum. After more than two decades of guerilla war, they were dispossessed by the Yousafzais. The majority of the aboriginal inhabitants of Swat migrated to the Hazara region to the east, where Swatis predominate with their surname Swati, reflecting their link to the region.

State of Swat

Post 1970 Merger

Demographics: The main language of the area is Pashto. The people of Swat are mainly Pashtuns, Kohistanis and Gujars. Some have very distinctive features and claim to be descendants of the army of Alexander the Great.

The people of the Kalam region in northern Swat are known as Kohistanis and speak the Torwali and Kalami languages. There are also some Khowar speakers in the Kalam region.

This is because before Kalam came under the rule of Swat it was a region tributary to both Yasin and Chitral and after Yasin itself was assimilated into Chitral the Kalamis paid a tribute of mountain ponies to the Mehtar of Chitral every year.

Tourist Attractions

There is a ski resort in Swat at Malam Jabba as well. Malam Jabba is about 40km north east of Saidu Sharif. It is the most popular ski resort in Pakistan. The ski slope is also the longest in Pakistan at about 800m.

Administrative Set-up

The region has gone through considerable changes over the last few years. Since the dissolution of the princely state.

- Matta
- Swat

Local Politics

In August 2001, a new local government system was introduced by the military-led government of Pervez Musharraf, the new system consists of a District *Nazim* (or mayor) and a deputy *Naib Nazim*, the district in turn was subdivided into two *tehsils*. The first is *Swat tehsil* with 52 union councils and the other is *Matta Tehsil* with 13 union councils. Each tehsil has its own Nazim and Naib Nazim.

The District Nazim is *Jamal Nasir Khan* of the Pakistan Muslim League and his Naib Nazim is *Malik Sadiq Ahmed*. Swats tehsil's Nazim is *Fazal Rehman Nono* from the Pakistan People's Party, while its Naib Nazim is *Shah Dawran* from the Awami National Party. In Matta Tehsil the Nazim is *Abdul Jabbar Khan* and *Zakir Khan* both of the Awami National Party. Abdul jabbar khan has been killed by unknown gunman last night.

Provincial & National Politics

The region elects two Male M.N.A,s and one female M.N.A and seven male M.P.A,s as well as two female M.P.A,s. In the 2002 National and Provincial elections, the Muttahida-Majlise-Amal, an alliance of religious political parties won all the seats amidst a wave of anti Americanism that spread after the United States invasion of Afghanistan.

Mathura

Mathura pronunciation is a holy city in the Indian state of Uttar Pradesh. It was also spelt as Muttra during British Period. It is located approximately 50 km north of Agra, and 150 km south of Delhi. It is the administrative centre of Mathura District of Uttar Pradesh. During the ancient period, this was an economic hub, located at the junction of some relatively important caravan routes.

Mathura is reputed to be the birthplace of Krishna, Krishnajanmabhoomi. The Keshav Dev temple was built in ancient times on the site of Krishna's legendary birthplace (an underground prison). As per epic Mahabharata, Mathura was the capital of the Surasena Kingdom, ruled by Kansa the maternal uncle of Krishna. The city is mentioned in the Sherlock Holmes story 'The Sign of Four.'

History

In the 6th century BC Mathura became the capital of the Shursen republic. The city was later ruled by the Maurya empire (4th to 2nd centuries BC) and the Sunga dynasty (2nd century BC). It may have come under control of the Indo-Greeks some time between 180 BC and 100 BC. However, it would then have briefly reverted to Indian rule before being occupied by the Indo-Scythians during the 1st century BC. Archaeological evidence seems to indicate that, by 100 BC, there was a group of Jains living in Mathura (Bowker).

Megasthenes, writing in the early 3rd century BC, mentions Mathura as a great city under the name Methora.

Mathura served as one of the Kushan Empire's two capitals from the first to the third centuries. The Mathura Museum has the largest collection of redstone sculptures in Asia, depicting many famous Buddha figurines. In 634 Xuanzang had visited the Mathura town. He went east to Jalandhar in eastern Punjab, before climbing up to visit predominantly Theravada monasteries in the Kulu valley and turning southward again to Bairat and then Mathura, on the Yamuna river.

The city was sacked and many of its temples destroyed by Mahmud of Ghazni in 1018. The Keshav Dev temple was partially destroyed by the Mughal Emperor Aurangzeb, who built the city's Jami Masjid (Friday mosque) on the same site, reusing many of the temple's stones.

The main Krishna shrine is presently the Dwarkadeesh temple, built in 1815 by Seth Gokuldas Parikh, Treasurer of Gwalior.

Geography

Location: City of Lord Krishna, Mathura (27.28 N, 77.41 E) is district headquarters of Uttar Pradesh state of India. Mathura is located 145 km south to national capital 'New Delhi' and 50 km north to City of Taj Mahal, Agra. District Aligarh is in east and District Bharatpur of Rajasthan is in west.

Area: Geographical Area: 3329.4 km^2

Administration: District Mathura is divided in 3 tehsiles and 10 blocks for administrative purposes.

A: Tehsil: Chatta
1. Nandgaon
2. Chhata
3. Chaumuha

B: Tehsil: Mathura
4. Goverdhan
5. Mathura
6. Farah
7. Baldeo

C: Tehsil: Mant
8. Mant
9. Naujhil
10. Raya

Mathura is located at 27.5° N 77.68° E. It has an average elevation of 174 metres (570 feet).

Tourism

Tourism is still in a development stage in the city. There are quite a few places to visit in Mathura and its surroundings, most of them linked to the Hindu mythology. Major places are listed here:

Major Tourist Sites in Mathura

- Krishnajanmabhoomi
- Dwarikadheesh Temple
- Kans Kila
- Vishram Ghat (a bath and worship place on the banks of river Yamuna)

Educational Institutions

Home to the Uttar Pradesh Pandit Deen Dayal Upadhyaya Veterinary University (Uttar Pradesh Pandit Deen Dayal Upadhyaya Pashu Chikitsa Vigyan Vishwavidyalaya Evam Go Anusandhan Sansthan). First of its kind in the State and fourth in the Country to be made independent veterinary University, UP Pt. DDUVU was established by Government of Uttar Pradesh vide U. P. Act. No. 27 of 2001 on 25.10.2001 with the College of Veterinary Science & Animal Husbandry, the erstwhile UP. College of Veterinary Science & Animal Husbandry, Mathura as its main constituent College.

The University is located on the Mathura-Agra road and is about 5 km from Mathura Junction railway station and 4 km from new bus stand. The main campus of the University is spread over a vast land area of 782.32 acres in Mathura Cantt and about 1,400 acres (6 km^2) at Madhurikund, about 20 km from the main campus.

Places of Interest around Mathura

- Barsana
- Nandgaon
- Gokul
- Baldeo
- Vrindavan

- Goverdhan
- RadhaKund
- Mant
- Bharatpur, Rajasthan
- Agra
- Alwar, Rajasthan
- Deeg, Rajasthan
- Bird Sanctury, Kitham, Agra

Strategic Importance

Mathura is the home for Indian I Corps (Strike Formation) within the Indian Army's Central Command, hosting Strike I Corps headquarters in a large classified area in the outskirts of the city known as Mathura Cantonment (Central Command itself has its headquarters at Lucknow). It hosts Strike Infantry units, Air Defence units, Armoured Divisions, Engineer brigades, Aritillery Units and classified units of Strategic Nuclear Command. Corps I is primarily responsible for western borders of India. In 2007 during Exercise Ashwamedha, it had unleashed its armoured, artillery and infantry divisions in full flow to simulate operational ability of being prepared for high intensity, short duration and 'sudden' battles in an overall NBC (nuclear-chemical-biological) environment.

Industries

Today Mathura is situated on very important Road and Train routes in India. The famous Delhi-Agra highway (NH-2, National Highway-2) crosses Mathura, providing the city great connectivity. Also, the city houses a fairly large and important train station, named Mathura Junction. The city is home to the Delhi-Mumbai and Delhi-Chennai train routes.

Mathura is home to a large, technologically-advanced oil refinery owned by the Indian Oil Corporation. This refinery is one of the largest oil refineries of Asia. On the industrial aspect, Mathura is home to a flourishing Silver polishing industry, textile printing industry involving in Sari-printing and Fabric dyeing. In addition to this, water tap factories are also flourishing in the area.

A very famous twin-city to Mathura is Vrindavan. The small town hosts a lot of temples belonging to various sects of Hinduism preaching Lord Krishna in various forms/avatars. Some of the most famous temples are Banke Bihari Temple, Rang ji Temple, Iskcon Temple.

Ayodhya

Ayodhya pronunciation is an ancient city of India, the old capital of Awadh, in the Faizabad district of Uttar Pradesh. During the time of Gautama Buddha the city was called Ayojjha (Pali). Under the British Raj the city and the administrative area around it was called Oudh. It is on the right bank of the river Sarayu, 555 km east of New Delhi. The word ayodhya is Sanskrit for "not to be warred against". Some Puranas like the Brahmanda Purana (4/40/91) consider Ayodhya as one of the six holiest cities in Hinduism.

In the first few centuries of the Common Era it was called Saketa. Saketa, or (Pinyin: Shaqi) was conquered by the great Kushan / Yuezhi Emperor Kanishka c. 127 CE, who made it the administrative centre of his eastern territories. The name occurs again in Faxian as (Pinyin: Shazhi) in the early fifth century. It is not clear when the name changed, but by the time of the visit of the Chinese pilgrim monk, Xuanzang, c. 636 CE, it was known as Ayodhya.

Legacy and Importance

Ayodhya was one of the most ancient, largest and most magnificent of Indian cities. It is said to have covered an area of 250 km^2 (96 square miles), and was the capital of the Hindu kingdom of Kosala (Kaushal), the court of the great king Dasaratha, the 63rd monarch of the Solar line in descent from Vivaswan or the Sun God. The son of Vivaswan "Viavswat Manu" founded the city of Ayodhya.

The opening chapters of the Ramayana, a mythological religious epic of the Classical Hindu period, recount the magnificence of the city, the glories of the monarch and the virtues, wealth and loyalty of his people. Dasaratha was the father of Rama, the Seventh Avatar of the Vishnu. Many Hindus believe the birthplace of Rama to be in Ayodhya at the place called Ram Janmabhoomi, the site of the demolished Babri Mosque. According to the Ramayana, Ayodhya was ruled by the House of Ikshvaku, who was the son of Manu. Eventually, Rama ruled Ayodhya.

Ayodhya is also the birth place of five Tirthankars, including the first Tirthankar of Jainism, Shri Rishabh Dev. He is known as the father of Jain religion. The city is also important in the history and heritage of Buddhism in India, with several Buddhist temples, monuments and centers of learning having been established here during the age of the Mauryan Empire and the Gupta Dynasty. Ayodhya reached its glorious peak as known to history during the reign of the Guptas over India.

Bhagwan Swaminarayan, founder of the Swaminarayan Sect of Hinduism lived here during his childhood years. It was from Ayodhya that Bhagwan Swaminarayan started his seven year journey across India as Neelkanth.

Tulsidas is said to have begun the writing of his famous Ramayana poem Shri Ramacharitamanas in Ayodhya in 1574 CE. Several Tamil Alwar mention the city of Ayodhya. Ayodhya is also said to be the birthplace of Bhahubali, Brahmi, Sundari, King Dasaratha, Acharya Padaliptasurisvarji, King Harishchandra, Shri Rama, Achalbhrata, and the ninth Gandhara of Mahavir Swami.

The Atharva Veda called Ayodhya "a city built by gods and being as prosperous as paradise itself".

Ayodhya was the victim of pillage and sacking during the Ghaznavid raids and Ghorid invasions. Some Hindu temples were allegedly looted or destroyed. Some believe that the Babri Mosque was constructed on the remains of a temple, but this claim remains very controversial. With Muslim rulers established around the city under Mohammed of Ghor, it lost its strategic and economic importance to Lucknow and Kanpur.

Ayodhya today is a small, rustic city with ancient Hindu architecture predominating, and with some Mughal influence. Its population is mostly Hindu with a minority of Muslims, Jains and Buddhists. However, its history and heritage hold an unequivocal importance for over Hindus in India and across the world.

The Thai kingdom and city of Ayutthaya were named for Ayodhya, reflecting the common Southeast Asian practice of adopting place names from Hindu kingdoms.

According to an 11th century Korean chronicle the Samguk Yusa, the wife of King Suro of the ancient Korean kingdom of Geumgwan Gaya was a princess who travelled by boat from a faraway land called Ayuta to Korea in 48 CE. It is commonly thought that Ayodha is the foreign land referred to in the Korean chronicles, but some scholars believe that the foreign land may have been Ayutthaya of Thailand. The Koreans know the princess as Heo Hwang-ok, who was the first queen of Geumgwan Gaya and is considered an ancestor by several Korean lineages.

Geography

Ayodhya is located at 26.8° N 82.2° E. It has an average elevation of 93 metres (305 feet). Ayodhya is situated on the bank of the river Sarayu in Uttar Pradesh (northern India).

Demographics

As of 2001 India census, Ayodhya had a population of 49,593. Males constitute 59% of the population and females 41%. Ayodhya has an average literacy rate of 65%, higher than the national average of 59.5%; with 66% of the males and 34% of females literate. 12% of the population is under 6 years of age.

Ayodhya Debate

Ayodhya is also the centre of the Ayodhya Debate concerning the Ram Janmabhoomi temple and the Babri Mosque. The mosque was destroyed in 1992 by Kar Sevaks and rioters due to the belief that the Ram Janmabhoomi existed prior to the mosque's construction and that the temple was the birthplace of Rama. The title suit on the disputed site is currently pending in the Lucknow Bench of Allahabad High Court and its judgment is expected shortly.

Mob Attack

On 5 July 2005, five militants attacked the site of the makeshift Ramlalla temple, in Ayodhya. All five were shot down in the ensuing gunfight with the security forces guarding the area, and one civilian died in the bomb blast triggered by the terrorists to breach the cordon wall. The claim of police that the militants came from Pakistan could not be corroborated by independent evidence. The attack is still shrouded in mystery.

Koshambi

Koshambi (Pali) or Kausambi (Sanskrit) was one of the greatest cities in India in the Buddha's time (500 BC). It was the capital of the Vatsas (also: Vamsas), one of the Mahajanapadas (Great Kingdoms) of ancient India. Kausambi was a very prosperous city, where a large number of millionaire merchants resided. It was an important entreport of goods and passengers from north-west and south.

Koshambi is identified with the two villages of Kosam on the Jamuna river, about 35 miles south-west of Allahabad. The location of Koshambi is at the following coordinates: 25.338984° N 81.392899° E Coordinates: 25.338984° N 81.392899° E.

The Buddhist Commentarial scriptures give two reasons for the name Koshambi. The more favoured is that the city was so called because it was founded in or near the site of the hermitage once occupied by the sage Kusumba (v.l. Kusumbha). Another explanation is that large and stately margosa-trees (Kosammarukkha) grew in great numbers in and around the city.

Koshambi in Buddha's Time

In the time of the Buddha its king was Parantapa, and after him reigned his son Udena. Koshambi was evidently a city of great importance at the time of the Buddha for we find Ananda mentioning it as one of the places suitable for the Buddha's Parinibbana. It was also the most important halt for traffic coming to Kosala and Magadha from the south and the west.

The city was thirty leagues by river from Benares. (Thus we are told that the fish which swallowed Bakkula travelled thirty leagues through the Yamuna, from Koshambi to Benares). The usual route from Rajagaha to Koshambi was up the river (this was the route taken by Ananda when he went with five hundred others to inflict the higher punishment on Channa, Vin.ii.290), though there seems to have been a land route passing through Anupiya and Koshambi to Rajagaha).

In the Sutta Nipata (vv.1010-13) the whole route is given from Mahissati to Rajagaha, passing through Koshambi, the halting-places mentioned being: Ujjeni, Gonaddha, Vedisa, Vanasavhya, Koshambi, Saketa, Savatthi, Setavya, Kapilavatthu, Kusinara, Pava, Bhoganagara and Vaishali.

Near Koshambi, by the river, was Udena's park, the Udakavana, where Ananda and Pindola-Bharadvaja preached to the women of Udena's palace on two different occasions. The Buddha is mentioned as having once stayed in the Simsapavana in Koshambi. Maha Kaccana lived in a woodland near Koshambi after the holding of the First Buddhist Council.

Buddhist Historical Events in Koshambi

Buddhist Monasteries in Koshambi

Already in the Buddha's time there were four establishments of the Order in Koshambi-the Kukkutarama, the Ghositarama, the Pavarika-ambavana (these being given by three of the most eminent citizens of Koshambi, named respectively, Kukkuta, Ghosita and Pavarika), and the Badarikarama. The Buddha visited Koshambi on several occasions, stopping at one or other of these residences, and several discourses delivered during these visits are recorded in the books. (Thomas, op. cit., 115, n.2, doubts the authenticity of the stories connected with the Buddha's visits to Koshambi, holding that these stories are of later invention).

The Buddha spent his ninth rainy season at Koshambi, and it was on his way there on this occasion that he made a detour to Kammassadamma and was offered in marriage Magandiya, daughter of the brahmin Magandiya. The circumstances are narrated in connection with the Magandiya Sutta. Magandiya took the Buddha's refusal as an insult to herself, and, after her marriage to King Udena (of Koshambi), tried in various ways to take revenge on the Buddha, and also on Udena's wife Samavati, who had been the Buddha's follower.

The Schism at Koshambi

A great schism once arose among the monks in Koshambi. Some monks charged one of their colleagues with having committed an offence, but he refused to acknowledge the charge and, being himself learned in the Vinaya, argued his case and pleaded that the charge be dismissed. The rules were complicated; on the one hand, the monk had broken a rule and was treated as an offender, but on the other, he should not have been so treated if he could not see that he had done wrong.

The monk was eventually excommunicated, and this brought about a great dissension. When the matter was reported to the Buddha, he admonished the partisans of both sides and urged them to give up their differences, but they paid no heed, and even blows were exchanged. The people of Koshambi, becoming angry at the monks' behaviour, the quarrel grew apace. The Buddha once more counselled concord, relating to the monks the story of King Dighiti of Kosala, but his efforts at reconciliation were of no avail, one of the monks actually asking him to leave them to settle their differences without his interference.

In disgust the Buddha left Koshambi and, journeying through Balakalonakaragama and the Pacinavamsadaya, retired alone to keep retreat in the Parileyyaka forest. In the meantime the monks of both parties repented, partly owing to the pressure exerted by their lay followers in Koshambi, and, coming to the Buddha at Savatthi, they asked his pardon and settled their dispute

Other Events

Bakkula was the son of a banker in Koshambi. In the Buddha's time there lived near the ferry at Koshambi a powerful Naga-king, the reincarnation of a former ship's captain. The

Naga was converted by Sagata, who thereby won great fame. Ruja was born in a banker's family in Koshambi. Citta-pandita was also born there. A king, by name Kosambaka, once ruled there.

During the time of the Vajjian heresy, when the Vajjian monks of Vaishali wished to excommunicate Yasa Kakandakaputta, he went by air to Koshambi, and from there sent messengers to the orthodox monks in the different centres (Vin.ii.298; Mhv.iv.17).

It was at Koshambi that the Buddha promulgated a rule forbidding the use of intoxicants by monks (Vin.ii.307).

Koshambi is mentioned in the Samyutta Nikaya.

Kushinagar

Kushinagar or Kusinagar (26.45 N,83.24E)is a town and a nagar panchayat in Kushinagar district in the Indian state of Uttar Pradesh. It is an important Buddhist pilgrimage site, where Gautama Buddha died.

Demographics

As of 2001 India census, Kushinagar had a population of 17,982. Males constitute 52% of the population and females 48%. Kushinagar has an average literacy rate of 62%, higher than the national average of 59.5%: male literacy is 70%, and female literacy is 54%. In Kushinagar, 15% of the population is under 6 years of age.

Ancient History

In ancient times, it was known as Kushavati (Jatakas). Kushinagar was a celebrated centre of the Malla kingdom of ancient India. Later, it would be known as Kushinara, one of the most important four holy sites for Buddhists. At this location, near the Hiranyavati River, Gautama Buddha attained Parinirvana (or 'Final Nirvana') after falling ill from eating a meal of a species of mushroom which translates as "pig's delight".

Many of the ruined stupas and viharas here date back to 3rd century BCE-5th century CE when prosperity was at its peak. The Mauryan emperor Ashoka is known to have contributed to significant construction at this site.

Prior to its rediscovery in the 19th century, there was a silence of more than half a millennium at Kasia. Due to violent invasions, Kushinagar lost its vitality and eventually was neglected.

Visits by Buddha to Kushinagar

At the time of the Buddha, Kushinagar was the capital of the Mallas, and the scene of the Buddha's death. It was twenty-five yojanas from Rajagaha (DA.ii.609; acc. to Fa Hsien, p.40, it was twenty-four yojanas from Kapilavatthu) and lay on the high road from Alaka to Rajagaha, the road taken by Bavari's disciples (SN.v.1012). At that time it was a small city, "a branch-township with wattle-and-daub houses in the midst of the jungle," and Ananda was, at first, disappointed that the Buddha should have chosen it for his Parinibbana. But the Buddha, by preaching the Maha-Sudassana Sutta, pointed out to him that in ancient times it had been Kusavati, the royal city of Maha-Sudassana (D.ii.146).

It is said that the Buddha had three reasons for coming to Kusinara to die:

1. Because it was the proper venue for the preaching of the Maha-Sudassana Sutta;
2. Because Subhadda would visit him there and, after listening to his sermon, would develop meditation and become an arahant while the Buddha was still alive; and
3. Because the brahman Doha would be there, after the Buddha's death, to solve the problem of the distribution of his relics (UdA.402f; DA.ii.573f6).

Between Kusinara and Pava, three gavutas away (DA.ii.573)-from where the Buddha came to Kusinara on his last journey from Rajagaha, stopping at various places-lay the stream of Kakuttha on the banks of which was the Ambavana; beyond that was the Hirannavati river, and near the city, in a south-westerly direction, lay the Upavattana, the Sala-grove of the Mallas, which the Buddha made his last resting-place (UdA.238; DA.ii.572f).

After the Buddha's death his body was carried into the city by the northern gate and out of the city by the eastern gate; to the east of the city was Makutabandhana, the shrine of the Mallas, and there the body was cremated. For seven days those assembled at the ceremony held a festival in honour of the relics (D.ii.160f).

As the scene of his death, Kusinara became one of the four holy places declared by the Buddha to be fit places of pilgrimage for the pious, the other three being Kapilavatthu, Buddhagaya and Isipatana (D.ii.140).

Mention is made of other visits paid to Kusinara by the Buddha, prior to that when his death took place. Thus, once he went there from Apana and having spent some time at Kusinara, proceeded to Atuma. The Mallas of Kusinara were always great admirers of the Buddha, even though not all of them were his followers, and on the occasion of this visit they decided that any inhabitant of Kusinara who failed to go and meet the Buddha and escort him to the city, would be fined five hundred.

It was on this occasion that Roja the Mallan was converted and gave to the Buddha and the monks a supply of green vegetables and pastries (Vin.i.247f). During some of these visits the Buddha stayed in a wood called Baliharana, and there he preached two of the Kusinara Suttas (A.i.274f; v.79f) and the "Kinti" Sutta (M.ii.238f). A third Kusinara Sutta he preached while staying at Upavattana. (A.ii.79; for another discourse to some noisy monks at Upavattana, see Ud.iv.2).

According to a late tradition, one-eighth of the Buddha's relics were deposited in a cairn in Kusinara and honoured by the Mallas (D.ii.167; Bu.xxviii.3).

In Hiouen Thsang's day there still existed towers and Sarigharamas erected to mark the spots connected with the Buddha's last days and obsequies at Kusinara. According to his account (Beal. op. cit.li. lii. n) Kusinara was nineteen yojanas from Vaishali. A copper plate belonging to the thupa erected at the site of the Buddha's death has recently been discovered (CAGI.i.714).

Rediscovery

The remains of the Parinirvana Stupa and Parinirvana Temple, when rediscovered, were covered in a 40 foot high mound of bricks surrounded by a dense thorny forest. After E. Buchanan, an officer of the East India Company, arrived in Kasia in the course of his survey-work, H. H. Wilson, in 1854, made the suggestion that ancient Kushinagar and Kasia were the same. Work resumed around 1861-1862 when General Alexander Cunningham, an archaeological surveyor, would prove the site to be that of Gautama Buddha's passing. A British officer named Mr. A.C.L. Carlleyle followed suit. Excavations began in the late 1800s and many important remnants of the main site such as the Matha Kuar and Ramabhar stupa were unveiled.

Today

Today, Kushinagar is a much-frequented pilgrimage site for Indian and foreign tourists, and temples have been constructed by Indian, Chinese, Sri Lankan, Thai, Burmese, South Korean, Tibetan and Japanese Buddhists, alongside the ruins of monasteries and stupas. Kushinagar is one of the main four Buddhist pilgrimage sites related to the life of Gautama Buddha. The other three are Lumbini, Bodh Gaya, and Sarnath.

The two places most frequently visited in Kushinagar are the Mahaparinirvana Stupa, which is built on the place of Buddha's Mahaparinirvana (Great Nirvana or passing away), and the place of his cremation, which is 1.6 km away. Close to the Mahaparinirvana Stupa is located a 1500 year old Buddha-image of the Buddha as he attained Parinirvana. The Mahaparinirvana Stupa is surrounded by ruins of ancient monasteries.

Sarnath

Sarnath (also Mrigadava, Migadaya, Rishipattana, Isipatana) is the deer park where Gautama Buddha first taught the Dharma, and where the Buddhist Sangha came into existence through the enlightenment of Kondanna. Sarnath is located 13 kilometres north-east of Varanasi, in Uttar Pradesh, India.

Isipatana is mentioned by the Buddha as one of the four places of pilgrimage which his devout followers should visit.

Origin of Names

Mrigadava means "deer-park". Isipatana is the name used in the Pali Canon, and means the place where holy men (Pali: isi, Sanskrit: rishi) fell to earth.

The legend says that when the Buddha-to-be was born, some devas came down to announce it to 500 rishis. The rishis all rose into the air and disappeared and their relics fell to the ground.

Another explanation for the name is that Isipatana was so called because sages, on their way through the air (from the Himalayas), alight here or start from here on their aerial flight (isayo ettha nipatanti uppatanti cati-Isipatanam). Pacceka Buddhas, having spent seven days in contemplation in the Gandhamadana, bathe in the Anotatta Lake and come to the habitations of men through the air, in search of alms.

They descend to earth at Isipatana. Sometimes the Pacceka Buddhas come to Isipatana from Nandamulaka-pabbhara.

Hiouen Thsang quotes the Nigrodhamiga Jataka (J.i.145ff) to account for the origin of the Migadaya. According to him the Deer Park was the forest gifted by the king of Benares of the Jataka, where the deer might wander unmolested.

The Migadaya was so-called because deer were allowed to roam about there unmolested.

Sarnath, from Saranganath, means "Lord of the Deer" and relates to another old Buddhist story in which the Bodhisattva is a deer and offers his life to a king instead of the doe the latter is planning to kill.

The king is so moved that he creates the park as a sanctuary for deer. The park is still there today.

History

Gautama Buddha at Isipatana

The Buddha went from Bodhgaya to Sarnath about 5 weeks after his enlightenment. Before Gautama (the Buddha-to-be) attained enlightenment, he gave up his austere penances and his friends, the Pancavaggiya monks, left him and went to Isipatana.

After attaining Enlightenment the Buddha, leaving Uruvela, travelled to the Isipatana to join and teach them. He went to them because, using his spirital powers, he had seen that his five former companions would be able to understand Dharma quickly. While travelling to Sarnath, Gautama Buddha had to cross the Ganges. Having no money with which to pay the ferryman, he crossed the Ganges through the air. When King Bimbisara heard of this, he abolished the toll for ascetics. When Gautama Buddha found his five former companions, he taught them, they understood and as a result they also became enlightened.

At that time the Sangha, the community of the enlightened ones, was founded. The sermon Buddha gave to the five monks was his first sermon, called the Dhammacakkappavattana Sutta. It was given on the full-moon day of Asalha. Buddha subsequently also spent his first rainy season at Sarnath at the Mulagandhakuti. The Sangha had grown to 60 in number (after Yasa and his fiends had become monks), and Buddha sent them out in all directions to travel alone and teach the Dharma. All 60 monks were Arahants.

Several other incidents connected with the Buddha, besides the preaching of the first sermon, are mentioned as having taken place in Isipatana. Here it was that one day at dawn Yasa came to the Buddha and became an Arahant.

It was at Isipatana, too, that the rule was passed prohibiting the use of sandals made of talipot leaves. On another occasion when the Buddha was staying at Isipatana, having gone there from Rajagaha, he instituted rules forbidding the use of certain kinds of flesh, including human flesh. Twice, while the Buddha was at Isipatana, Mara visited him but had to go away discomfited.

Besides the Dhammacakkappavattana Sutta mentioned above, several other suttas were preached by the Buddha while staying at Isipatana, among them

- the Anattalakkhana Sutta,
- the Saccavibhanga Sutta,
- the Panca Sutta (S.iii.66f),
- the Rathakara or Pacetana Sutta (A.i.110f),
- the two Pasa Suttas (S.i.105f),
- the Samaya Sutta (A.iii.320ff),
- the Katuviya Sutta (A.i.279f.),
- a discourse on the Metteyyapanha of the Parayana (A.iii.399f), and
- the Dhammadinna Sutta (S.v.406f), preached to the distinguished layman Dhammadinna, who came to see the Buddha.

Some of the most eminent members of the Sangha seem to have resided at Isipatana from time to time; among recorded conversations at Isipatana are several between Sariputta and Mahakotthita, and one between Mahakotthita and Citta-Hatthisariputta. Mention is made, too, of a discourse in which several monks staying at Isipatana tried to help Channa in his difficulties.

According to the Udapana Jataka (J.ii.354ff) there was a very ancient well near Isipatana which, in the Buddha's time, was used by the monks living there.

Isipatana after the Buddha

According to the Mahavamsa, there was a large community of monks at Isipatana in the second century B.C. For, we are told that at the foundation ceremony of the Maha Thupa in Anuradhapura, twelve thousand monks were present from Isipatana led by the Elder Dhammasena.

Hiouen Thsang found, at Isipatana, fifteen hundred monks studying the Hinayana. In the enclosure of the Sangharama was a vihara about two hundred feet high, strongly built, its roof surmounted by a golden figure of the mango. In the centre of the vihara was a life-size statue of the Buddha turning the wheel of the Law. To the south-west were the remains of a stone stupa built by King Ashoka.

The Divy. (389-94) mentions Ashoka as intimating to Upagupta his desire to visit the places connected with the Buddha's activities, and to erect thupas there. Thus he visited Lumbini, Bodhimula, Isipatana, Migadaya and Kusinagara; this is confirmed by Ashoka's lithic records, *e.g.* Rock Edict, viii.

In front of it was a stone pillar to mark the spot where the Buddha preached his first sermon. Near by was another stupa on the site where the Pancavaggiyas spent their time in meditation before the Buddha's arrival, and another where five hundred Pacceka Buddhas entered Nibbana. Close to it was another building where the future Buddha Metteyya received assurance of his becoming a Buddha.

Buddhism flourished in Sarnath in part because of kings and wealthy merchants based in Varanasi. By the third century Sarnath had become an important centre for the arts, which reached its zenith during the Gupta period (4th to 6th centuries CE). In the 7th century by the time Xuan Zang visited from China, he found 30 monasteries and 3000 monks living at Sarnath.

Sarnath became a major centre of the Sammatiya school of Buddhism, one of the early Buddhist schools. However, the presence of images of Heruka and Tara indicate that Vajrayana Buddhism was (at a later time) also practised here. Also images of Brahminist gods as Shiva and Brahma were found at the site, and there is still a Jain temple located very close to the Dhamekh Stupa.

At the end of the 12th century Sarnath was sacked by Turkish Muslims, and the site was subsequently plundered for building materials.

Discovery of Isipatana

Isipatana is identified with the modern Sarnath, six miles

from Benares. Alexander Cunningham found the Migadaya represented by a fine wood, covering an area of about half a mile, extending from the great tomb of Dhamekha on the north to the Chaukundi mound on the south.

Legendary Characteristics of Isipatana

According to the Buddhist Commentarial Scriptures, all the Buddhas preach their first sermon at the Migadaya in Isipatana. It is one of the four avijahitatthanani (unchanging spots), the others being the bodhi-pallanka, the spot at the gate of Sankassa, where the Buddha first touched the earth on his return from Tavatimsa, and the site of the bed in the Gandhakuti in Jetavana

In past ages Isipatana sometimes retained its own name, as it did in the time of Phussa Buddha (Bu.xix.18), Dhammadassi (BuA.182) and Kassapa (BuA.218). Kassapa was born there (ibid., 217). But more often Isipatana was known by different names (for these names see under those of the different Buddhas). Thus in Vipassi's time it was known as Khema-uyyana. It is the custom for all Buddhas to go through the air to Isipatana to preach their first sermon. Gotama Buddha, however, walked all the way, eighteen leagues, because he knew that by so doing he would meet Upaka, the Ajivaka, to whom he could be of service.

Current Features of Isipatana

Most of the ancient buildings and structures at Sarnath were damaged or destroyed by the Turks. However, amongst the ruins can be distinguished:

- The Dhamek Stupa; it is an impressive 128 feet high and 93 feet in diameter.
- The Dharmarajika Stupa is one of the few pre-Ashokan stupas remaining, although only the foundations remain. The rest of the Dharmarajika Stupa was removed to Varanasi to be used as building materials in the 18h century. At that time, also relics were found in the Dharmarajika Stupa. These relics were subsequently thrown in the Ganges river.

- The Chaukhandi Stupa commemorates the spot where the Buddha met his first disciples, dating back to the fifth century or earlier and later enhanced by the addition of an octagonal tower of Islamic origin. In recent years it is undergoing restoration.
- The ruins of the Mulagandhakuti vihara mark the place where the Buddha spent his first rainy season.
- The modern Mulagandhakuti Vihara is a monastery buiilt in the 1930s by the Sri Lankan Mahabodhi Society, with beautiful wall paintings. Behind it is a the Deer Park (where deer are still to be seen).
- The Ashoka Pillar erected here, originally surmounted by the "Lion Capital of Ashoka" (presently on display at the Sarnath Museum), was broken during Turk invasions but the base still stands at the original location.
- The Sarnath Archeological Museum houses the famous Ashokan lion capital, which miraculously survived its 45 foot drop to the ground (from the top of the Ashokan Pillar), and became the National Emblem of India and national symbol on the Indian flag. The museum also houses a famous and refined Buddha-image of the Buddha in Dharmachakra-posture.
- There is also a Bodhi tree planted by Anagarika Dharmapala which was grown from a cutting of the Bodhi tree at Bodh Gaya.

For Buddhists, Sarnath (or Isipatana) is one of four pilgrimage sites designated by Gautama Buddha, the other three being Kushinagar, Bodh Gaya, and Lumbini.

Varanasi

Varanasi also known as Benares, Banaras, or Benaras is a famous Hindu holy city situated on the banks of the river Ganges (Ganga) in the Indian state of Uttar Pradesh. It is one of the oldest continually inhabited cities in the world, dating back thousands of years and contemporaneous with the Sumer civilisation. The city is called Kasi, "the luminous" in the Rigveda. It is often also referred to as "city of temples and learning."

The culture of Varanasi is deeply associated with the river Ganges and the river's religious importance. The city has been a cultural and religious centre in northern India for thousands of years. Varanasi has its own style of classical Hindustani music, and has produced prominent philosophers, poets, writers and musicians in Indian history, including Kabir, Ravi Das, Munshi Premchand, Jaishankar Prasad, Acharya Ram Chandra Shukla, Pandit Ravi Shankar, Hariprasad Chaurasia and Ustad Bismillah Khan. Varanasi is the home of Banaras Hindu University. Tulsidas wrote his Ramcharitmanas here, and Gautam Buddha gave his first sermon at Sarnath near Kashi. The language spoken in Varanasi is Kashika Bhojpuri related to Hindi.

Geography

Varanasi is closely associated with the Ganges and has many temples along its banks

The city of Varanasi is located in the middle Ganga valley of North India, in the Eastern part of the state of Uttar Pradesh, along the left crescent-shaped bank of the Ganga river. The Varanasi City is the district headquarters of the Varanasi district. The "Varanasi Urban Agglomeration"-an agglomeration of seven urban sub-units-covers an area of 112.26 km^2 (approximately 43 mi^2). The urban agglomeration is stretched between 82° 56'E-83° 03'E and 25° 14'N-25° 23.5'N. Being located in broad plain of North India, (also called as Gangetic plains), the land can be very much called as plain. Due to yearly low level floods in river, the soil is repeatedly replenished and hence is very productive for agriculture for most of the city.

On a local level though, Varanasi is located on a higher ground between rivers Ganga and Varuna, the mean elevation being 80.71 m. The main land is relatively stony, which with the absence of small distributaries and canals, provides a continuous and relatively dry land, which was perfect for settling down in the ancient times.

It is often difficult to suggest the original geography of Varanasi, due to conflicts between descriptions provided in old texts and city's current status. It is often said that Varanasi is situated between the two confluences: one of Ganga and Varuna and other of Ganga and river Assi. The statement gets its weight from the fact that the distance between these two confluences is around 2.5 miles, and a round trip to between these two places is considered holy by Hindus, and is called Pancha-kroshi Yatra (the five mile journey). At the end of this journey, Sakshi Vinayak Temple is located where devotees go on to complete the circle.

On the contrary, though Varuna and Ganga do exist as rivers, Assi also exists but only as a nullah. Also, there is no evidence that Assi was ever a big river.

Climate

Varanasi has a humid subtropical climate with high variation between summer and winter temperatures. Summers are long, from early April till October, with the monsoon season in between. Cold waves from the Himalayan region dip temperatures across the city in the winter from December to February. The average temperature is 32°C-46 °C (90°F-115 °F) in the summer; 5 °C-15 °C (41 °F-59 °F) in the winter. The average annual rainfall is 1110 mm (44 in).. Fog is common in winter while hot dry winds called loo blow in summer. The city is relatively free from the air pollution. Recently due to water pollution, making of dams, and increase in temperature due to climate change etc., the water level of the river has gone down significantly and small portions of land can be seen in the middle of the river.

People and Culture

Regions near the banks of river Ganga are extremely crowded and house several Hindu temples, narrow winding lanes and road-side shops. The main residential areas of Varanasi (especially for the middle and upper classes) are situated in regions far from the ghats; they are more spacious and less polluted. Such a place in an Indian city is called a housing colony. Varanasi has nearly 100 ghats, most of which are bathing ghats, while some others are for cremation. According to Hindu belief, dying at Kasi ensures release from the eternal cycle of birth and rebirth. Many of these ghats were built when the Marathas controlled the city and the Scindias, the Peshwas, Holkars and Bhonsles stand out as patrons of present day Varanasi. Even today many of the ghats are privately owned. Shivala or Kali ghat is still owned by the former Maharaja of Kasi.

Various legends are associated with the ghats and it is believed that Dasaswamedh Ghat is where Lord Brahma sacrificed 10 horses in a yajna. Manikarnika Ghat is the place where Lord Vishnu dug a pit with his Chakra and while performing various penances filled it with perspiration. As Lord Shiva watched him, his earring (Manik) fell into the pit, hence the name. According to another legend, in order to keep Lord Shiva moving around with his devotees, Goddess Parvati asked him to find her earrings, which she hid, lost on the bank of Ganga and make Lord Shiva stay at the place and search forever.

It is said that when the body is cremated at Mani Karnika Ghat Lord Shiva asks every soul whether they have seen the earring (Mani Karnika). Other interesting ghats are Man Mandir Ghat built in 1770 CE by Jai Singh of Jaipur, the intrepid astronomer who built his observatories here, Mansarover Ghat built by Man Singh of Amber. Bachraj is used by Jain devotees for it has three river bank Jain temples. Tulsi Ghat is where Tulsidas wrote Ramcharitmanas. Lalita Ghat was built by late King of Nepal.

Holy City

Varanasi is a holy city in Hinduism, one of the most sacred pilgrimage places for Hindus of all denomination. The Hindu God Shiva supposedly once lived there making many Hindus want to go there on a pilgrimage. More than 1,000,000 pilgrims visit the city each year. Here is the holy shrine of Lord Kashi Vishwanath, (an aspect of Lord Shiva) and one of the twelve revered Jyotirlingas of the Lord Shiva. Hindus believe that bathing in the river Ganga will remit sins and that dying in the holy city of Kashi (Varanasi) circumvents rebirth. This holy city is worshipped as one of the Shakti Peethas where Divine

Mother Sati's earring fell and so devotees believe that on that spot stands the present Vishalakshi Temple and hindus of the shakti sect come to the city because the river it self is said to be shakti (goddess) its self It is here that Adi Shankara wrote his commentaries on Hinduism, leading to the great Hindu revival.

It is not just the Hindus venerate Varanasi today, for the city has links with Buddhism and Jainism as well. In the residential neighbourhood of the city lies Sarnath, the site of the deer park where Gautama Buddha is said to have given his first sermon about the basic principles of Buddhism. It is one of the four pilgrimage sites designated by Gautama Buddha, the other three being Kushinagar, Bodh Gaya, and Lumbini. The Dhamek Stupa is one of the few pre-Ashokan stupas remaining, although only the foundations remain. Also remaining is the Chaukhandi Stupa commemorating the spot where the Buddha met his first deciples, dating back to the fifth century or earlier and later enhanced by the addition of an octagonal tower.

Varanasi is also a pilgrimage place for Jains. It is believed to be the birthplace of Parshvanatha, the twenty-third Tirthankar. Vaishnavism and Shaivism have coexisted in Varanasi harmoniously. The city has also been influenced by Islamic culture.

This explains the continuous tension between communities in the city and the fact that really ancient monuments are few. However, Varanasi has kept its sacred position as the Holy City of Hinduism.

Temples

Varanasi is a city of temples. Almost every road crossing has a nearby temple. Such small temples form the basis of daily local prayers and other rituals. But there are many large temples too, erected at different times through out the history of Varanasi.

Kashi Vishwanath Temple, also called Golden Temple, which in its present shape was built in 1780 by Maharani Ahilyabai Holkar of Indore, is located on the outskirts of the

Ganga. This temple makes Varanasi a place of great religious importance to the Hindus, as Vishweshwara or Vishwanatha, the aforementioned Jyotirlinga of the Lord Shiva is enshrined here. It is said that a single view of Vishwanatha Jyotirlinga is considered to merit more than that of other jyotirlingas. A Naubatkhana was built up in front of the Temple by the collector Mohammed Ibrahim Khan at the instance of Governor General Warren Hastings in 1785. In 1839, Punjab Kesari, the Sikh Maharaja Ranjit Singh, the ruler of Punjab donated gold to cover the two domes of the temple. On January 28, 1983 the Temple was taken over by the government of Uttar Pradesh and its management was transferred to a trust with Late Dr. Vibhuti Narayan Singh, then Kashi Naresh, as president and an executive committee with Divisional Commissioner as chairman.

The temple was once destroyed by Aurangzeb who built a mosque on it. It was later resurrected at a location near the mosque, and is many times a cause of local strain among Hindus and Muslims.

Durga Temple, also called Monkey temple, was built at some point of time in 18th century by a Bengali Maharani. The temple got its name as 'Monkey temple' because of the presence of large number of monkeys in the temple. According to legends, the present statue of Goddess Durga was not made by man but appeared on its own in the temple. Thousands of Hindu devotees visit the Durga temple during Navratri and other auspicious occasions. Non-Hindus can enter the courtyard of the Durga temple but not the inner sanctum.

The architecture is of Nagara Style, which is typical of North India. The temple is accompanied by a rectangular tank of water called Durga Kund. The temple has multi-tiered spires and is stained red with ochre, signifying the red colour of Durga. The Kund was earlier connected to the river itself thus refreshing the water. This tunnel was later closed, leading to locked water which is replenished only by rain or drainage from the Temple. Every year on the occasion of Nag panchami, the act of depicting Lord Vishnu reclining on the coiled-up Shesha is repeated in the Kund.

Sankat Mochan Temple is dedicated to Lord Hanuman and is very popular with the local citizens. It is a place for many yearly religious as well as cultural festivals. On 7 March 2006, one of the three explosions carried out by Islamic militants hit the temple, while the aarti, in which numerous worshippers and wedding attendees participated, was in progress.

The new Vishwanath Temple, called Birla Mandir, mainly funded by Raja Birla of the Birla family of industrialists, was built as a replica of the old Kashi Vishwanath Temple. Planned by Pandit Madan Mohan Malaviya, the temple is part of the Banaras Hindu University, and stands for national revival.

The temple is open to people of all castes and religions. Kadar Temple is also dedicated to Lord Shiva this is very popular because it is called svyambu Ling of Shiva it is near Harischandra Ghat it has two part one Shiva and second is Parvati some pandit says one is visnu (Hari) second part is Shive (Har).

Art

A holy city, Varanasi does not take a backseat when it comes to fine arts and literature. Great Indian writers have lived in this city from Kabir, Ravi Das, and Tulsidas to Bharatendu Harishchandra, Jayshankar Prasad, Acharya Ram Chandra Shukla, Munshi Prem Chand, Jagannath Prasad Ratnakar, Devaki Nandan Khatri, Hazari Prasad Dwivedi, Tegh Ali, Kshetresa Chandra Chattopadhyaya, Vagish Shastri, Baldev Upadhyaya, Vidya Niwas Mishra, Kashi Nath Singh, Namvar Singh, Rudra Kashikeya, Nirgun among many other notables.

Art lovers and historians like Rai Krishnadas, his son Prof. Anand Krishna, musicians like Pt. Omkarnath Thakur, P t. Ravi Shankar, Ustad Bismillah Khan, Siddheshwari Devi, Dr. Lalmani Misra and his son Dr. Gopal Shankar Misra, Dr. N. Rajam, Dr.Rajbhan Singh, Pt. Anokhelal, Pt. Samta Prasad, Kanthe Maharaj, Pt. M. V. Kalvint, Sitara Devi, Gopi Krishna, Pt. Kishan Maharaj, Rajan and Sajan, Mahadev Mishra, Girija Devi and numerous others have kept the city alive to the spiritual aspect of fine arts apart from their ability to entertain. Numerous festivals are celebrated that preserve traditional styles of classical and folk culture. All night, open music concerts like ones organised at Sankat Mochan Temple, Hori, Kajri and Chaiti Mela, Budwa Mangal, are annual features that draw connoisseurs from all over.

Economy

Varanasi has several small cottage industries, including Silk sari making, the production of textiles such as hand-woven carpets, and handicrafts. The Banarasi Pan (betel leaves) and Banarasi Khoa (a milk product, somewhat similar to cheese) are popular, and the related small-scale industries employ many people.

Indian Railways runs a major diesel locomotive factory in Varanasi, Diesel Locomotive Works (DLW). According to Macaulay, Varanasi was the "city which, in wealth, population, dignity and sanctity was among the foremost in Asia". He described the commercial importance saying "from the looms of Benaras went forth the most delicate silks that adorned the halls of St. James and of Vesailles."

Demographics

The population of Varanasi urban agglomeration in 2001 was 1,371,749; the sex ratio was 879 females every 1000 males. However, the area under Varanasi Municipal Corporation has a population of 1,100,748 with the sex ratio being 883 females for every 1000 males.

The literacy rate in the urban agglomeration is 61.5% while that in the municipal corporation area is 61%. Approximately 138,000 people in the municipal area live in slums. The crime rate in the city in 2004 was 128.5 per 100,000 which is higher than Uttar Pradesh rate of 73.2 but lower than the national rate of 168.8.

Transport

Auto Rickshaw and Rickshaw are the most widely available public transport within Varanasi. In outer regions of the city, mini-buses are common. Small boats and small steamers are used to cross the river Ganga.

Varanasi is well connected by air, rail and buses with all the important places of India. Its distance from Delhi is 776 km. The Babatpur airport is about 25 km from the city centre and it is well connected to Delhi, Mumbai, Bangalore, Kolkata, and Nepal. All the major domestic Indian carriers like Jet Airways, Kingfisher Airlines, Indian, Spicejet, and Alliance Air operate from here.

One of the major factors for sustainment of Varanasi for such a long time as an inhabited city, is its effective transport between different cities. From ancient times the city was connected to cities like Taxila, Gazipur, Patliputra, Vaishali, Ayodhya, Gorakhpur, Agra etc.

The city was connected through a single road from Taxila going through Patliputra during the Mauryan empire. This road was later renovated and extended by Sher Shah Suri during the 16th century and later came to be known as the famous Grand Trunk Road.

Civic Administration and Utility Services

Varanasi is governed by a number of bodies, the prime being the Varanasi Nagar Nigam (Municipal Corporation) and Varanasi Development Authority, which is responsible for the master planning of the city. Water supply and sewage system is maintained by Jal Nigam, a subsidiary of Nagar Nigam. Power supply is by the Uttar Pradesh Power Corporation Limited. The city produces about 350 million litres per day of sewer and 425 tonnes per day of solid waste.

The solid wastes are disposed in one landfill site. A huge amount of sewer flows into the river Ganga daily. Nagar Nigam also runs a bus service in the city and suburban areas. The city is within the Varanasi range of Varanasi zone of Uttar Pradesh Police. A Special Superintendent of Police is the highest ranking police officer in the city. The city constitutes one parliamentary constituency. Indian National Congress won the constituency in Indian general election, 2004.

Varanasi was one the five cities where Ganga Action Plan was launched.

Education

University Education

Varanasi is the site of three public universities. Banaras Hindu University, which includes Institute of Technology and Institute of Medical Sciences, is among the top 3 largest residential universities in the world having more than 128 independent teaching departments. Mahatma Gandhi Kashi Vidyapeeth University and Sampurnanand Sanskrit University are the other two universities.

Banaras Hindu University (1916) was founded by Pandit Madan Mohan Malaviya with the cooperation of Dr. Annie Besant. Its 1350 acre (5.5 km^2) campus was built on land donated by the then Maharaja of Kashi.

Governor General Lord Cornwallis establish the Sanskrit College (1791), which was the first college in Varanasi. The first principal of Sanskrit College was Sanskrit Professor J. Myor, ICS followed by Dr. J.R. Ballentien, RTH Griffith, Dr. G. Thevo, Dr. Aurthor Venice, Dr. Ganganath Jha, and Gopinath Kaviraj among others. After independence this college turned to in Sampurnanand Sanskrit University.

Central Institute for Higher Tibetan Studies at Sarnath is a deemed university with a preference for the traditional Tibetan method of teaching within a framework of modern universities. Uday Pratap College, another rdeemed university, is the centre of sports and science study for the suburban students of modern Benares. Varanasi is also noted for many private and public institutes that provide Hindu religious teaching. Since ancient times people have been coming to Varanasi to learn philosophy, Sanskrit, astrology, social science and religious teachings. In Indian tradition, Varanasi is often called "Sarva Vidya Ki Rajdhani" (capital of knowledge). The city also has the Jamiah Salafiah, a Salafi Islamic institution.

Basic and Special Education

Varanasi's schools are either run by the state government or by private (many of which are religious) organizations. Schools mainly use English or Hindi as the medium of instruction. The schools are affiliated with the Indian Certificate of Secondary Education (ICSE), the Central Board for Secondary Education (CBSE), or the UP. Board of High School & Intermediate Education.

Under the 10+2+3 plan, after completing their secondary education, students typically enroll in a 2 year junior college (also known as a pre-university) or in schools with a higher secondary facility. Students usually choose from one of three streams-liberal arts, commerce, or science, though vocational streams are also available. Upon completing the required coursework, students may enroll in general or professional degree programmes.

Tourism

Probably due to its unique culture, Varanasi is a major tourist destination for foreign tourists in India. A number of 3, 4 and 5 star hotels are present in the city. All sort of cuisines are available mostly as street food due to rich and hospitable culture of Varanasi.

Varanasi is a noted centre for silk weaving and brassware. Fine silks and brocaded fabrics, exquisite saris, brassware, jewellery, woodcraft, carpets, wall hangings, lamp shades and masks of Hindu and Buddhist deities are some of Varanasi's shopping attractions. The main shopping areas include the Chowk, Godaulia, Vishwanath Lane, Lahurabir and Thatheri Bazaar.

Varanasi in Popular Culture

- A major section of Hindu's believe that Varanasi (KASHI) is the 'Centre of Universe', hence they call it as Universal Capital Banaras.
- In Kurt Weill's "Benares Song" from the opera Rise and Fall of the City of Mahagonny.
- In Dan Simmons' Hyperion Cantos the barge, transporting the pilgrims to the Sea of Grass, was called Benares.
- Ian McDonald's novel River of Gods is partly set in Varanasi.

- In a song by Krishna Das entitled "Kashi Vishwanath Gange" on the CD Breath of the heart.
- In a song by Waterjuice entitled "Varanasi Space Station" on the CD World Fusion.
- Bibhutibhushan Bandopadhyay's seminal novel 'Aparajito' was partly set in Benaras. It was further immortalized by Satyajit Ray in his 'Apu Trilogy'. A part of the film was shot in Varanasi (Benaras)

Vaishali

Vaishali District is a district in Bihar state, India. It is named after the Vaishali (ancient city). The history of Vaishali district is thus very ancient, and finds mention in the Indian classic Mahabharata, as well as in Buddhist and Jain tradition.

Ancient Vaishali

Vaishali derives its name from King Vishal of the Mahabharata age. Even before the advent of Buddhism and Jainism, Vaishali was the capital of the vibrant republican Licchavi state since before the birth of Mahavira (c. 599 BC), which suggests that it was perhaps the first republic in the world, similar to those later found in ancient Greece. In that period, Vaishali was an ancient metropolis and the capital city of the republic of the Vaishali state, which covered most of the Himalayan Gangetic region of present-day Bihar state, India. Very little is known about the early history of Vaishali. The Vishnu Purana records 34 kings of Vaishali, the first being Nabhaga, who is believed to have abdicated his throne over a matter of human rights and believed to have declared: "I am now a free tiller of the soil, king over my acre." The last among the 34 was Sumati, who is considered a contemporary of Dasaratha, father of the Hindu god, Lord Rama.

Numerous references to Vaishali are found in texts pertaining to both Jainism and Buddhism, which have preserved much information on Vaishali and the other Maha Janapadas. Based on the information found in these texts, Vaishali was established as a republic by the 6th century BC, prior to the birth of Gautama Buddha in 563, making it the world's first republic. In the republic of Vaishali, Lord Mahavira was born. Gautama Buddha delivered his last sermon at Vaishali and announced his Parinirvana there. Vaishali is also renowned as the land of Ambapali (also spelled as Amrapali), the great Indian courtesan, who appears in many folktales, as well as in Buddhist literature. Ambapali became a disciple of Buddha.

A kilometre away is Abhishek Pushkarini, the coronation tank. The sacred waters of the tank anointed the elected representatives of Vaishali. Next to it stands the Japanese temple and the Vshwa Shanti Stupa (World Peace Pagoda) built by the Nipponzan Myohoji sect of Japan. A small part of the Buddha's relics found in Vaishali have been enshrined in the foundation and in the chhatra of the Stupa. Near the coronation tank is Stupa 1 or the Relic Stupa. Here the Lichchavis reverentially encased on of the eight portions of the Master's relics, which they received after the Mahaparinirvana.

After his last discourse the Awakened One set out for Kushinagar, but the Lichchavis kept following him. Buddha gave them his alms bowl but they still refused to return. The Master created an illusion of a river in spate which compelled them to go back. This site can be identified with Deora in modern Kesariya village, where Ashoka later built a stupa. Ananda, the favourite disciple of the Buddha, attained Nirvana in the midst of the Ganga outside Vaishali.

Patna

Patna is the capital of the Indian state of Bihar, and one of the oldest continuously inhabited places in the world.

The modern city of Patna lies on the southern bank of the Ganges, as it flows past with the combined waters of the rivers Ghagra, Son and Gandak. At the point where the city is located, the sacred Ganges looks more sea than river: mighty, wide and never-ending.

A bustling city of 1,800,000 people, the city is approximately 25 km long and 9 km to 10 km wide.

The Buddhist and Jain pilgrim centres of Vaishali, Rajgir or Rajgriha, Nalanda, Bodhgaya, and Pawapuri are all nearby.

Patna is a sacred city for Sikhs also.

The tenth and last "human" guru, Guru Gobind Singh, was born here. It is the ideal gateway for all the places on this circuit. The monuments in and around the city take one down the history to its glorious past.

Apart from being the administrative centre of the state and its historic importance, the city is also a major educational centre and medical centre. It's the epicentre for all the students from Bihar preparing for various competitive examinations. Various educational instituitions are coming up here.

The walled old area, called Patna City by the locals, is also a major trading centre.

Origin of Name

The appellation Patna is etymologically derived from Patan, the name of the Hindu goddess Patan devi. Another theory says the name comes from Pattan, or a port in Sanskrit since the city, located near the confluence of four rivers, has been a thriving river port. Another theory suggests that the name Patna may be a short form of Patliputra, one of the most popular ancient names of this city.

The city has been known by various names during its more than two millennia long existence-Pataligram, Patliputra, Kusumpur, Pushpapura, Azimabad, and the present day Patna. It got its name of Patna during the reign of Sher Shah Suri, a Bihari ruler who has the distinction of making the only interruption to the long rule of Mughals. His tomb is at Sasaram, a place near to Patna.

History of Patna

Legend ascribes the origin of Patna to a mythological king Putraka who created Patna by magic for his queen Patali, literally Trumpet flower, which gives it its ancient name Pataligrama. It is said that in honour of the first born to the queen, the city was named Patliputra. Gram is the Sanskrit for village and Putra means son.

From a scientific history perspective, it would be appropriate to surmise that the history of Patna started around the year

490 BC when Ajatashatru, the king of Magadh, wanted to shift his capital from the hilly Rajagriha to a more strategically located place to combat the Licchavis of Vaishali. He chose the site on the bank of Ganges and fortified the area. From that time, the city has had a continuous history, a record claimed by few cities in the world. Gautam Buddha passed through this place in the last year of his life, and he had prophesized a great future for this place, but at the same time, he predicted its ruin from flood, fire, and feud.

With the rise of the Mauryan empire, the place became the seat of power and nerve centre of the sub-continent. From Patliputra, the famed emperor Chandragupta Maurya (a contemporary of Alexander) ruled a vast empire, stretching from the Bay of Bengal to Afghanistan.

Early Mauryan Patliputra was mostly built with wooden structures. Emperor Ashoka, the grandson of Chandragupta Maurya, transformed the wooden capital into a stone construction around 273 BC. Chinese scholar Fa Hein, who visited India sometime around A.D. 399-414, has given a vivid description of the stone structures in his travelogue.

Megasthenes, Greek historian and ambassador to the court of Chandragupta gives the first written account of Patliputra. Much later, a number of Chinese travellers came to India in pursuit of knowledge and recorded their observation about Patliputra in their travelogues.

Megasthenes (350 BC-290 BC), in his book Indica has mentioned that the city of Palibothra (Patliputra, modern day Patna) was situated on the confluence of the rivers Ganges and Arennovoas (Sonabhadra-Hiranyawah) and was 9 miles long and 1.75 miles wide.

In the years that followed, the city saw many dynasties ruling the Indian subcontinent from here. It saw the rules of the Gupta empire and the Pala kings. However, it never reached the glory that it had under the Mauryas.

With the disintegration of the Gupta empire, Patna passed through uncertain times. Bakhtiar Khilji captured Bihar in the 12th century AD and destroyed many ancient seats of learning,

Patna lost its prestige as the political and cultural centre of India.

The Mughal period was a period of unremarkable provincial administration from Delhi. The most remarkable period during these times was under Sher Shah Suri who revived Patna in the middle of the 16th century. He visualised a fort and a town on the banks of Ganga. Sher Shah's fort in Patna does not survive, but the mosque built in Afghan architectural style survives.

Mughal emperor Akbar came to Patna in 1574 to crush the Afghan Chief Daud Khan. Akbar's navratna and state's official historian and author of Ain-i-Akbari Abul Fazl refers to Patna as a flourishing centre for paper, stone and glass industries. He also refers to the high quality of numerous strains of rice grown in Patna famous as Patna rice in Europe.

Mughal Emperor Aurangzeb acceded to the request of his favourite grandson Prince Muhammad Azim to rename Patna as Azimabad, in 1704 while Azim was in Patna as the subedar. However, very little changed during this period other than the name.

With the decline of Mughal empire, Patna moved into the hands of the Nawabs of Bengal, who levied a heavy tax on the populace but allowed it to flourish as a commercial centre.

During 17th century, Patna became a centre of international trade. The British started with a factory in Patna in 1620 for trading in calico and silk. Soon it became a trading centre for saltpetre, urging other Europeans-French, Danes, Dutch and Portuguese-to compete in the lucrative business. Peter Mundy, writing in 1632, calls this place, "the greatest mart of the eastern region".

After the decisive Battle of Buxar (1765), Patna fell in the hands of the East India Company and continued as a trading centre.

In 1912, Patna became of the capital of Orissa Province and Bihar when Bengal Presidency was partitioned. It soon emerged as an important and strategic centre. A number of imposing structures were constructed by the British. Credit for designing the massive and majestic buildings of colonial Patna goes to the architect, I. F. Munnings. Most of these buildings reflect either Indo-Saracenic influence (like Patna Museum and the state Assembly), or overt Renaissance influence like the Raj Bhawan and the High Court. Some buildings, like the General Post Office (GPO) and the Old Secretariat bear pseudo-Renaissance influence. Some say, the experience gained in building the new capital area of Patna proved very useful in building the imperial capital of New Delhi.

Patna is important seat of business in the eastern part of India, major trading centre of cotton, tusser, readymade garments. Now it is emerging as a big centre of higher education as got has started Chankya Law University, BIT Mesra Extension Centre etc. There are several prestigious educational institutions in Patna like Patna College, Patna Women's College, Patna Science College, Bihar National College, Anugrah Narayan College, Bihar College of Engineering, now National Institute of Technology, Patna, Patna Medical College (formerly, Prince of Wales Medical College), Nalanda Medical College, Patna Dental College, Bihar Veterinary College and the Lalit Narayan Mishra Institute. A new IIT is coming up at Bihta, near Patna. Japan is helping Bihar in it. Also the prestigious IGIMS is starting medical education in the near future. A few private medical & engineering colleges are also coming up in the near future.

Orissa was created as a separate province in 1935. Patna continued as the capital of Bihar province under the British Raj.

Patna played a major role in the Indian independence struggle. Most notable are the Champaran movement against the Indigo plantation and the 1942 Quit India Movement. Patna's contribution in the freedom struggle has been immense with outstanding national leaders like Swami Sahajanand Saraswati, Basawon Singh (Sinha), Bihar Bibhuti Anugrah Narayan Sinha, Loknayak Jayaprakash Narayan, Bihar Kesari Sri Krishna Sinha, Sheel Bhadra Yajee, Sarangdhar Sinha (Singh), Yogendra Shukla, and many others who worked for India's freedom relentlessly.

Patna continued to be the capital of the state of Bihar after independence in 1947, though Bihar itself was partitioned again in 2000 when Jharkhand was carved out as a separate state of the Indian union.

Geography

Patna is located on the south bank of the Ganges River, called Ganga locally. Patna has a very long riverline, and it is surrounded on three sides by rivers-the Ganga, Sone, and Poonpun (also spelt Punpun). Just to the north of Patna across the river Ganga flows the river Gandak making it a unique place having four largish rivers in its vicinity. It is the largest riverine city in the world a historical city on the banks of Ganges was nomenclated by princess Sarika, daughter of king Patliputra.

The bridge over the river Ganga, named after Mohandas Gandhi, is 5850m long is said to be the longest single river bridge in the world.

- Altitude: 53 meters
- Temperature: Summer 43 °C to 21 °C, Winter 20 °C to 5 °C
- Rainfall (average): 1,200 mm

Climate

In Patna, as in most of Bihar, the summer temperatures rise very high as the hot tropical sun beats down with all its intensity coupled with a heat wave which is more severe than Delhi. The city, being near four large rivers, experiences a rather high humidity throughout the year.

The summer begins in April and peaks in June/July with the temperature soaring up to 43° C till the moisture laiden monsoon wind bring some much-needed relief to the parched fields. The rains last through August & September and continue into early October. The northern Indian winters bring bitter cold nights and sunny days to Patna from November to February till the arrival of the spring that brings the weather to a full cycle.

The local almanac divides the year into six seasons of roughly two months each. Apart from the usual four seasons: Summer, Monsoon, Winter and Spring, you may add mild winter between Monsoon and Winter and Mild summer just before the onslaught of the severe north Indian summer.

Demographics

The population of Patna is over 1,885,470, The population density is 1132 persons per square kilometre. There are 839 females to every 1,000 males. Overall Literacy rate is 62.9%, and female Literacy rate is 50.8%. Source-District Elementary Education Report Card 2004 of National Institute of Educational Planning and Administration, New Delhi

Many languages are spoken in Patna. Hindi is the official language you can see official board and all official adds and works in Hindi and in Urdu too. Thanks to the British influence since early days, English is also spoken extensively.

The native dialect is Magahi named after Magadha the ancient name of Bihar. Other dialects from other regions of Bihar spoken widely in Patna are Angika, Bhojpuri, and Maithili. Other languages spoken in Patna include Bengali, and Oriya.

People and Culture

Though geographically located in the Magadh region of Bihar, there are ample people who are natives from the Bhojpur, Mithila, Vajj and Ang regions. These are the five regions of Bihar, which differ from each other slightly. Intermarriages and cultural intemixing between the people from these five regions have always been there. Hence it may be difficult for an outsider to even discern the differences between them.

Family Orientation

People are religious and family oriented, and their lives are deeply rooted in tradition. The interests of the family take precedence over that of an individual. Families are generally large, though the government is actively encouraging family planning to curb rapid population growth. Extended families often live together in one home because of economic necessity.

Although the culture is same but the language varies among all these regions. Also the dilect of the people is quite different.

Marriage

Most marriages are still arranged by parents; the degree to which the children are consulted depends on the family. Marriage is sacred and is considered to endure beyond death. Weddings are times of great celebration, expense, and feasting. Ceremonies are often elaborate. In many ceremonies, the bride and groom exchange garlands and promises before they circle around a fire seven times to solemnize the marriage. Bright clothing, jewellery, and flowers are part of almost every type of ceremony. The bride's parents may still give a dowry, such as money or land, to the groom, even though the practice is illegal. This practice is often called Tilak. Mostly marriages (arranged ones) are caste based.

But things are changing rapidly. People are getting progressive and have started understanding that modernization is the order of the day. People are marrying people from different cultures and castes.

Cuisine

Staple food of majority of the population is "bhat, dal, roti, tarkari and achar", prepared basically from rice, lentils, wheat flour, vegetables, and pickle grade raw, unripe fruits. Traditionally, mustard oil has been the popular cooking medium for Patnaites. Plain boiled milk as well as curd is widely used by all section of the Patnaites. "Khichdi", the broth of rice and lentils, seasoned with spices, and served with several accompanying items like curd, chutney, pickles, papads, ghee (clarified butter) and chokha (boiled mashed potatoes, seasoned with finely cut onions, green chilies) constitutes the lunch for most Patnaites on Saturdays.

Patna is also known for the sweet delicacies of central Bihar including Khaja, Motichoor ka Ladoo, Kala Jamun, Kesaria Peda, Parwal ki Mithai, Khubi ka Lai and Chena Murki. These owe their origin to towns in the vicinity of Patna: Khaja from Silao, Ladoo from Maner, Kala Jamun from Vikram,

Khubi ka Lai from Barh, Kesaria Peda from Gaya and Chena Murki from Koelwar, Poori from Behea. Descendants of the original family members of the cooks, called halwais in the local language, have migrated to urban Patna and authentic sweet delicacies are now available in the city itself. Unlike the Bengali sweets which are soaked in syrup of sugar and are therefore wet, sweets of Patna and Bihar are mostly dry. The mangoes of Digha, Patna are very delicious & famous.

There are several other traditional snacks and savouries:

- Pua', prepared from a mixture of refined wheat flour(maida), milk, ghee (clarified butter), sugar, dry fruits and honey
- Pittha, steam cooked, made by powdered rice with sttufed ground gram(chana)OR khoya etc.
- Tilkut, referred to as 'Palala' in Buddhist literature, is made of pounded 'tila' or sesame seeds (Sesamum indicum) and jaggery or sugar
- Chiwra, beaten rice, served with a coat of creamy curd and sugar or jaggery
- Makhana (a kind of water fruit) is prepared from lotus seeds and is taken puffed or as kheer, prepared with milk and sugar
- Sattu, powdered baked gram, is a high energy giving food. It is taken mixed with water or with milk. Sometimes, sattu mixed with spices are used to prepare stuffed 'chapattis', locally called as 'makuni roti'.
- Litti Chokha, A baked round shape, made by wheat flour with stuffed sattu (litti), the combination of smashed boiled potatoes, bringals & tomatoes (chokha).
- Makuni, a stuffed paratha with sattu (ingredients:sattu, onion, chilli, pickles, mustard oil, salt)
- Paan, a dessert made out of betel nuts, spices, tobacco, and certain other ingredients, wrapped in a betel leaf and had after a meal.

A variety of non-vegetarian items are also prepared by a section of the population. Fish curries are widely used by a cross section of non-vegetarian population of all social groups. Mughal cuisine are well known and widely relished in Patna. Of late, Continental dishes are also catching up fancy. Various types of rolls which are also available in New York owe their origin to Patna.

Some Muslim families moved from here to Karachi in Pakistan during partition, and then to the U.S., taking with them their culture and cuisine. They sell various vegetarian and non vegetarian rolls and are rather popular by the generic name Roll Bihari in and around Lexington Avenue (South) in New York.

Economy

From the very ancient time patna has rich socio economic background. Patna has long been a major agricultural centre of trade, its most active exports being grain, sugarcane, sesame, and medium-grained Patna rice. It is also an important business centre of eastern India.

The hinterland of Patna is endowed with excellent agro-climatic resources and the gains of the green revolution have enabled the older eastern part of Patna (locally called as Patna City) to develop as a leading grain market of the state of Bihar, and one of the biggest in eastern India. Patna, being the state capital, with a growing middle income group households, has also emerged as a big and rapidly expanding consumer market, both for Fast Moving Consumer Goods (FMCG), as also for other consumer durable items. A large and growing population, and expanding boundaries of the city, is also spurring growth of service sector. The old and established educational institutions of the city have always been contributing to the national pool of excellent human resources.

Places of Interest

In Patna

Some of the places of interest in the city are:

- Agam Kuan, literally the unfathomable well which is said to date back to the Ashokan period.

- Hanuman Mandir The favourite Deity of the Patnaite. It is situated right in front of the Patna Junction, the central railway station of the City. Long winding queues can be seen at the temple on Saturdays and Tuesdays, the traditional worshipping days of the deity.
- Kumhrar, the site of the ruins of the Ashokan Patliputra.
- Takht Shri Harmandir Saheb, constructed by Punjab ruler Maharaja Ranjit Singh, consecrates the birthplace of Guru Gobind Singh Jee.
- State Secretariat Building and its Clock Tower, including the Martyrs Memorial commemorating the seven school and college students who were brutally killed by the armed forces under the command of the British Raj in front of the Patna Secretariat during the Quit India movement of 1942.
- Phulwari Shareef is a place of great Religious & Historical importance for Muslims.
- Imarat-e-Shariya or the "Shariyat" of Patna looks after whole of Bihar, Jharkhand, Orrisa, West Bengal and all North-Eastern states.
- High Court Building and a famous Dargah beside it.
- Patna Planetorium one of the largest in the country.
- Moin-ul-Haque Stadium boasts of its Cricket Ground which is 2nd largest in India, next only to "The Eden Gardens".
- Golghar (a beehive shaped granary)-One of the oldest British buildings in Patna.
- Patna Museum called the Jadu Ghar: The well-known museum has a fine collection of stone and bronze sculptures and terracota figures of Hindu and Buddhist artists. Didarganj Yakshi is the most prized collection of this museum.
- Khuda Baksh Oriental Library: It has a collection of rare ancient manuscripts.
- Lalit Narayan Mishra Institute of Economic Development and Social Change, Bailey Road.. One of the prominent educational centre for Management

studies and Computer Sciences in Eastern India. The Institute offers courses like MBA, PGHRM, MCA et al. It is one of the most important and reputed education centre in Bihar with modern amenities, well built infrastructure, clubs and excellent Placement opportunity for Students.

- A. N. Sinha Institute Of Social Sciences: A prominent social research institute with has vast literary collection and rare historical documentation.
- SINHA Library which owns the reputation of being one of the largest in the region.
- Begu Hajjam's mosque, built in 1489 by the Bengal ruler Alauddin Hussani Shah.
- Pathar ki Masjid built by Pervez, the elder brother of Shah Jehan and the first Mughal prince who made Bihar his residence.
- Qila House (Jalan House) houses an interesting museum famous for its jade collection, Chinese paintings and other far eastern work of art, Collected by Diwan Bahadur Radhakrishan Jalan.
- Sadaqat Ashram on the banks of the river Ganga (The land was donated by Mulana Mazharul Haque to the then congress party) which later became the retreat of Dr. Rajendra Prasad.
- Zoological and Botanical garden called Sanjay Gandhi Jaivik Udyan.
- Padri Ki Haveli, deemed to be the oldest church in Bihar dating back to 1772.
- Bankipore Club on the banks of the river Ganges. The dance hall of this club is said to be one of the original buildings built by the Dutch in the 17th century.
- Congress Maidan A historic ground that symbolises the Indian independence movement in Bihar.It was used to hold meetings by great illumanaries like Rajendra Prasad,Nehru,Anugrah Narayan Sinha, Sri Babu, Jayaprakash Narayan and others.

- Darbhanga House, also called Nav Lakha building. This was built by Maharaja Sir Kameshwar Singh of Darbhanga. This beautiful building on the banks of Ganges now houses the post graduate departments of Patna University. It houses the Kali Mandir, which has been a place of worship of the goddess, the Maharaja himself was a great devotee and the students of the Patna University rarely take an exam without offering a prayer.
- Patna College administrative block building was initially part of a Dutch Opium factory established on the banks of the Ganga as a part of the flourishing Opium Trade from the northern China and Nepal region.
- Patna Science College boasts of its numerous great Alumnis and very good research facilities, as said by Sir C V Raman when he first visited the varsity "...it has its mark at the international platform."
- National Institute of Technology, Patna—6th oldest engg. college of the country. (B.C..) was upgraded into NIT on 28th JAN 2004.
- Gandhi Maidan called the Patna Lawns during the British Raj.
- Anugrah Seva Sadan It was established by Loknayak Jayprakash Narayan to serve the underprivilaged masses and to serve as a care home for the poor.It bears the pious name of reverend leader Bihar Bibhuti Dr. Anugrah Narayan Sinha.
- Very old Church Known as Christ Church which also has a school with same name near Gandhi Maidan.
- Kargil Chowraha near gandhi maidan built in the memory of our brave soldier who get shaheed in kargil war "SALUTE TO THEM"
- Saheed smarak, situated near Bihar Vidhan Sabha. is a memory of seven extra ordinary students who attempted to hoist the Indian flag on the top of Bihar Vidhan Sabha in 1942 during English rule. The six were shot dead by the forces under the command of the-

then colonial government of India, while the last and the seventh one was able to hoist the flag.

- Nagholkothi Located in Old city of Patna. Built by Nawabs of Patna is an example of unique architecture of midlive time with beautiful garden of Mughal style.

Around Patna

Education

Most of the government-run schools in Patna are affiliated to Bihar School Examination Board, whereas most of the private schools are affiliated to ICSE and CBSE boards. The major ones being Notre Dame Academy, St. Joseph's Convent High School, Loyola High School, St. Xavier's High School, Patna, Don Bosco Academy, St. Michael's Higher Secondary School, and St. Karen's School. There are a plenty of government schools too but they lack many facilities.

Unlike the rest of India, many colleges also provide an option for the plus 2 level of education (Class 11 and 12) raising the standard of education due to access to superior teachers of colleges. As a result, a high percent of the students are able to qualify in All India competitive examinations like IIT JEE, All India Medical Entrance Exam and CAT.

Bihar need much development in the field of primary & higher education.

Bodh Gaya

Bodh Gaya or Bodhgaya (24° 41' 60N, 84° 58' 60E) is a city in Gaya district in the Indian state of Bihar. It is famous for being the place of Buddha's attainment of Enlightenment.

Historically, it was known as the Bodhimanda (ground round the Bodhi-tree), and there was a large monastic settlement there. The main monastery of Bodhgaya used to be called the Bodhimanda-vihara (Pali). Now it is called the Mahabodhi Temple.

For Buddhists, Bodh Gaya is the most important of the main four pilgrimage sites related to the life of Gautama Buddha, the other three being Kushinagar, Lumbini, and Sarnath. In

2002, Mahabodhi Temple, located in Bodh Gaya, became a UNESCO World Heritage Site.

History

According to Buddhist traditions, circa 500 BC Prince Gautama Siddhartha, wandering as a monk, reached the sylvan banks of Falgu River, near the city of Gaya. There he sat in meditation under a bodhi tree (Ficus religiosa). After three days and three nights of meditation, Siddharta attained enlightenment and insight, and the answers that he had sought. He then spent seven weeks at seven different spots in the vicinity meditating and considering his experience. After seven weeks, he travelled to Sarnath, where he began teaching Buddhism.

Disciples of Gautama Siddhartha began to visit the place where he had gained enlightenment during the full moon in the month of Vaisakh (April-May), as per the Hindu calendar. Over time, the place became known as Bodh Gaya, the day of enlightenment as Buddha Purnima, and the tree as the Bodhi Tree.

The history of Bodh Gaya is documented by many inscriptions and pilgrimage accounts. Foremost among these are the accounts of the Chinese pilgrims Faxian in the 5th century and Xuanzang in the 7th century. The area was at the heart of a Buddhist civilization for centuries, until it was conquered by Turkish armies in the 13th century.

Mahabodhi Temple

The complex, located about 96 kilometers from Patna, at 24°41'43?N, 84°59'38?E, contains the Mahabodhi Temple with the diamond throne (called the Vajrasana) and the holy Bodhi tree. This tree was originally a sapling of the Sri Maha Bodhi tree in Sri Lanka, itself grown from a sapling of the original Bodhi tree.

It is believed that 250 years after the Enlightenment of the Buddha, Emperor Ashoka visited Bodh Gaya. He is considered to be the founder of the original Mahabodhi temple. It consisted of an elongated spire crowned by a miniature stupa and a chhatravali on a platform. A double flight of steps led up to the platform and the upper sanctum.

The mouldings on the spire contained Buddha images in niches. Some historians believe that the temple was constructed or renovated in the 1st century during the Kushan period. With the decline of Buddhism in India, the temple was abandoned and forgotten, buried under layers of soil and sand.

The temple was later restored by Sir Alexander Cunningham as part of his work for the British Archaeological Society in the late 19th century. In 1883, Cunningham along with J. D. Beglar and Dr. Rajendralal Miitra painstakingly excavated the site. Extensive renovation work was carried out to restore Bodh Gaya to its former glory.

Other Buddhist Temples

Kittisirimegha of Sri Lanka, contemporary of Samudragupta, erected with the permission of Samudragupta, a Sangharama near the Mahabodhi-vihara, chiefly for the use of the Singhalese monks who went to worship the Bodhi tree. The circumstances in connection with the Sangharama are given by Hiouen Thsang (Beal, op. cit., 133ff) who gives a description of it as seen by himself. It was probably here that Buddhaghosa met the Elder Revata who persuaded him to come to Ceylon.

Presently, several Buddhist temples and monasteries have been built by the people of Bhutan, China, Japan, Myanmar, Nepal, Sikkim, Sri Lanka, Thailand, Tibet and Vietnam in a wide area around the temple. These buildings reflect the architectural style, exterior and interior decoration of their respective countries. The statue of Buddha in the Chinese Temple is 200 years old and was brought from China. Japan's Nippon Temple is shaped like a pagoda.

The Myanmar (Burmese) Temple is also pagoda shaped and is reminiscent of Pagan. The Thai Temple has a typical sloping, curved roof covered with golden tiles. Inside, the temple holds a massive and spectacular bronze statue of Buddha. Next to the Thai temple there is a recent 25 meter statue of Buddha located within a garden which has existed there for over 100 years. For Tibetan buddhism there are two temples.

Demographics

As of 2001 India census, Bodh Gaya had a population of 30,883. Males constitute 54% of the population and females 46%. Bodh Gaya has an average literacy rate of 51%, lower than the national average of 59.5%; with male literacy of 63% and female literacy of 38%. 18% of the population is under 6 years of age.

Nalanda

Nalanda is the name of an ancient university in India.

The name is a Sanskrit word that means giver of knowledge, (possibly from nalam, lotus, a symbol of knowledge and da, to give). The Chinese pilgrim-monk Xuanzang gives several explanations of the name Nalanda. One is that it was named after the Naga who lived in a tank in the middle of the mango grove. Another-and accepted by him-is that the Bodhisatta once had his capital here and gave "alms without intermission," hence the name.

It is located about 55 miles south east of Patna, and was a Buddhist centre of learning from 427 CE to 1197 CE partly under the Pala Empire. It has been called "one of the first great universities in recorded history." Nalanda is located at 25.135766° N 85.444923° ECoordinates: 25.135766° N 85.444923° E. Nalanda was identified by Alexander Cunningham with the village of Baragaon.

Nalanda in the Time of the Buddha (500 BC)

The Buddha is mentioned as having several times stayed at Nalanda. When he visited Nalanda he would usually reside in Pavarika's mango grove, and while there he had discussions with Upali-Gahapati and Dighatapassi, with Kevatta, and also several conversations with Asibandhakaputta.

The Buddha visited Nalanda during his last tour through Magadha, and it was there that Sariputta uttered his "lion's roar," affirming his faith in the Buddha, shortly before his death. The road from Rajagaha to Nalanda passed through Ambalatthika, and from Nalanda it went on to Pataligama. Between Rajagaha and Nalanda was situated the Bahuputta cetiya.

According to the Kevatta Sutta, in the Buddha's time Nalanda was already an influential and prosperous town, thickly populated, though it was not till later that it became the centre of learning for which it afterwards became famous. There is a record in the Samyutta Nikaya, of the town having been the victim of a severe famine during the Buddha's time. Sariputta, the right hand disciple of the Buddha, was born and died in Nalanda.

Nalanda was the residence of Sonnadinna. Mahavira is several times mentioned as staying at Nalanda, which was evidently a centre of activity of the Jains. Mahavira is believed to have attained Moksha at Pavapuri, which is located in Nalanda (also according to one sect of Jainism he was born in the nearby village called Kundalpur).

King Ashoka (250 BC) is said to have built a temple there. According to Tibetan sources, Nagarjuna taught there.

Arising and Establishment of Nalanda University

Historical studies indicate that the University of Nalanda was established 450 CE under the patronage of the Gupta emperors, notably Kumaragupta.

Description of Nalanda University

Nalanda was one of the world's first residential universities, *i.e.*, it had dormitories for students. In its heyday it accommodated over 10,000 students and 2,000 teachers. The university was considered an architectural masterpiece, and was marked by a lofty wall and one gate. Nalanda had eight separate compounds and ten temples, along with many other meditation halls and classrooms. On the grounds were lakes and parks. The library was located in a nine storied building where meticulous copies of texts were produced. The subjects taught at Nalanda University covered every field of learning, and it attracted pupils and scholars from Korea, Japan, China,

Tibet, Indonesia, Persia and Turkey. The Tang Dynasty Chinese pilgrim Xuanzang left detailed accounts of the university in the 7th century.

Influence on Buddhism

A vast amount of what is considered to be Tibetan Buddhism (Vajrayana) actually stems from the late (9th-12th century) Nalanda teachers and traditions. Other forms of Buddhism, like the Mahayana followed in Vietnam, China, Korea and Japan, found their genesis within the walls of the ancient university.

Also Theravada Buddhism was taught at Nalanda University. But the teachings of Theravada were not developed further in Nalanda, as Nalanda was not a strong centre of Theravada.

Decline and End

Due to the disappearance of Buddhism from India during the 12th century, the university was in decline. In 1193, the Nalanda University suffered a final blow after the complex was sacked by Muslim armies under Bakhtiyar Khilji; this event is seen as a milestone in the decline of Buddhism in India. It is said that Khilji asked if there was a copy of the Koran at Nalanda before he sacked it.

When the Tibetan translator Chag Lotsawa visited them in 1235, he found them damaged and looted, but still functioning with a small number of monks. Ahir blames the destruction of the temples, monasteries, centers of learning at Nalanda and northern India for the demise of ancient Indian scientific thought in mathematics, astronomy, alchemy, and anatomy. Ling and Scott, however, point out that centres of learning were already declining, before the presence of Muslims.

Fortified Sena monasteries along the main route of the invasion were destroyed, and being off the main route both Nalanda and Bodh Gaya survived. Many institutions off the main route such as the Jagaddala Monastery in northern Bengal were untouched and flourishing.

Ruins

A number of ruined structures survive. Nearby is the Surya Mandir, a Hindu temple. The known and excavated ruins extend over an area of about 150,000 square metres, although if Xuanzang's account of Nalanda's extent is correlated with present excavations, almost 90% of it remains unexcavated.

Nalanda is no longer inhabited. Today the nearest habitation is a village called Bargaon.

In 1951, a modern centre for Pali (Theravadin) Buddhist studies was founded nearby by Bhikshu Jagdish Kashyap, the Nava Nalanda Mahavihara. Presently, this institute is pursuing an ambitious programme of satellite imaging of the entire region.

The Nalanda Museum contains a number of manuscripts, and shows many examples of the items that have been excavated.

Delhi

Delhi sometimes referred to as Dilli, is the second-largest metropolis in India after Mumbai with a population of 13 million. Located in northern India on the banks of the River Yamuna, Delhi has the political status of a federally-administered union territory known as the National Capital Territory of Delhi (NCT). A constitutional amendment in 1991 gave Delhi a special status among the Union Territories; Delhi has its own legislative assembly with limited powers. The National Capital Territory of Delhi comprises nine districts, 27 tehsils, three statutory towns *viz.* Municipal Corporation of Delhi (MCD), New Delhi Municipal Committee (NDMC) and Delhi Cantonment Board (DCB), 59 census towns and 165 villages.

Delhi is one of the oldest continually inhabited cities in the world. Having been the capital of several empires in ancient India, Delhi was a major city in the old trade routes from northwest India to the Gangetic Plains. Many ancient monuments, archaeological sites and remains of national importance have been erected in its history. The Mughals built a section of the city (now known as Old City or Old Delhi) that served as the capital of Mughal Empire for a long period. During the British Raj, New Delhi was built as an administrative quarter of the city. New Delhi was declared the capital of India after India gained independence from British rule in 1947.

As the seat of the Government of India, New Delhi houses important offices of the federal government, including the Parliament of India. Delhi has grown up to be a cosmopolitan city owing to the immigration of people from across the country. Like many other large cities of the world, Delhi suffers from urbanisation problems such as pollution, traffic congestion and scarcity of resources. The rapid development and urbanisation of New Delhi and surrounding areas coupled with the high average income of the populace has largely eclipsed socio-cultural traits that used to represent Delhi until a few years after independence.

Etymology

The etymology of "Delhi" is uncertain. The most common view is that it is an eponym of Dhillu, a king who ruled the area in ancient times. Raja Dhillu (King Dhillu) founded ancient Delhi in 800 BC. Some historians believe that the name is derived from Dilli, a corruption of dehleez or dehali-Hindustani for 'threshold'-and symbolic of city as a gateway to the Indo-Gangetic Plain. Another theory suggests that the city's original name was Dhillika. The Hindi/Prakrit word dhili ("loose") was also used for the area, and gradually transformed into the local name "Dilli". The coins in circulation in the region under the Tomara Rajputs were called dehliwal.

Delhi has had over 10 different names.

History

Human habitation was probably present in and around Delhi during the second millennium BC and before, as evidenced by archeological relics. The city is believed to be the site of Indraprastha, legendary capital of the Pandavas in the Indian epic Mahabharata. Settlements grew from the time of the Mauryan Empire (c. 300 BC). Remains of seven major cities have been discovered in Delhi. The Tomara dynasty founded the city of Lal Kot in 736 AD. The Chauhan Gurjars of Ajmer conquered Lal Kot in 1180 AD and renamed it Qila Rai Pithora. The Chauhan king Prithviraj III was defeated in 1192 by the Afghan Muhammad Ghori. In 1206, Qutb-ud-din Aybak, the first ruler of the Slave Dynasty established the Delhi Sultanate. Qutb-ud-din started the construction the Qutub Minar and Quwwat-al-Islam (might of Islam), the earliest extant mosque in India.

After the fall of the Slave dynasty, a succession of Turkic and Central Asian dynasties, the Khilji dynasty, the Tughluq dynasty, the Sayyid dynasty and the Lodhi dynasty held power in the late medieval period, and built a sequence of forts and townships that are part of the seven cities of Delhi. Delhi was a major centre of sufism (a mystic tradition of Islam) during the Sultanate period. In 1526, Zahiruddin Babur defeated the last Lodhi sultan in the First Battle of Panipat and founded the Mughal Empire that ruled from Delhi, Agra and Lahore.

The Mughal Empire ruled northern India for more than three centuries, with a five-year hiatus during Sher Shah Suri's reign in the mid-16th century. Mughal emperor Akbar shifted the capital from Delhi to Agra. Shah Jahan built the seventh city of Delhi that bears his name (Shahjahanabad), and is more commonly known as the Old City or Old Delhi. The old city served as the capital of the Mughal Empire since 1638. In 1761, Delhi was raided by Ahmed Shah Abdali after the Third battle of Panipat.

Delhi came under direct British control after the Indian Rebellion of 1857. Shortly after the Rebellion, Calcutta was declared the capital of British India and Delhi was made a district province of the Punjab. In 1911, Delhi was again declared as the capital of British India. Parts of the old city were pulled down to create New Delhi; a monumental new quarter of the city designed by the British architect Edwin Lutyens to house the government buildings. New Delhi, also known as Lutyens' Delhi, was officially declared as the seat of the Government of India and the capital of the republic after independence on 15 August 1947. During the partition of India thousands of Hindu and Sikh refugees from West Punjab and Sindh migrated to

Delhi. Migration to Delhi from the rest of India continues, contributing more to the rise of Delhi's population than the birth rate, which is declining.

In 1984, the assassination of Indira Gandhi (Prime Minister of India) led to violent backlash against the Sikh community, resulting in over two thousand seven hundred deaths. The Constitution (Sixty-ninth Amendment) Act, 1991 declared the Union Territory of Delhi to be formally known as National Capital Territory of Delhi. The Act gave Delhi its own legislative assembly, though with limited powers.

Geography

The Great Gangetic Plains cover most of Delhi, as can be seen in this NASA image.

The National Capital Territory of Delhi is spread over an area of 1,483 km^2 (573 sq. mi), of which 783 km^2 (302 sq. mi) is designated rural, and 700 km^2 (270 sq. mi) urban. Delhi has a maximum length of 51.9 km (32 mi) and the maximum width of 48.48 km (30 mi). There are three local bodies (statutory towns) namely, Municipal Corporation of Delhi (area is 1,397.3 km^2 (540 sq. mi)), New Delhi Municipal Committee (42.7 km^2 (16 sq. mi)) and Delhi Cantonment Board (43 km^2 (17 sq. mi)).

Delhi is located at 28°61'N, 77°23'E, and lies in northern India. It borders the Indian state of Uttar Pradesh on the south and Haryana on the west. Delhi lies almost entirely in the Gangetic plains. Two prominent features of the geography of Delhi are the Yamuna flood plain and the Delhi ridge. The low-lying Yamuna flood plains provide fertile alluvial soil suitable for agriculture.

However, these plains are prone to recurrent floods. Reaching up to a height of 318 m (1043 ft), the ridge forms the most dominating feature in this region. It originates from the Aravalli Range in the south and encircles the west, northeast and northwest parts of the city. Yamuna, a sacred river in Hinduism, is the only major river flowing through Delhi. Most of the city, including New Delhi, lies west of the river. East of the river is the urban area of Shahdara. Delhi falls under seismic zone-IV, making it vulnerable to major earthquakes.

Delhi has a semi-arid climate with high variation between summer and winter temperatures. Summers are long, from early April to October, with the monsoon season in between. During the summer season, the city faces extreme power and water shortages.

The summer heat waves kill dozens each year. Winter starts in November and peaks in January and is notorious for its heavy fog, which often disrupts road, air and rail traffic. Extreme temperatures range from-0.6 °C (30.9 °F) to 47 °C (116.6 °F). The annual mean temperature is 25 °C (77 °F); monthly mean temperatures range from 14 °C to 33 °C (58 °F to 92 °F). The average annual rainfall is approximately 714 mm (28.1 inches), most of which is during the monsoons in July and August. The average date of the advent of monsoon winds in Delhi is 29 June.

Civic Administration

The Delhi metropolitan area lies within the National Capital Territory of Delhi (NCT). The NCT has three local municipal corporations: Municipal Corporation of Delhi (MCD), New Delhi Municipal Council (NDMC) and Delhi Cantonment Board. MCD is one of the largest municipal corporations in the world providing civic amenities to an estimated 13.78 million people. The capital of India, New Delhi, falls under the administration of NDMC. The chairperson of the NDMC is appointed by the Government of India in consultation with the Chief Minister of Delhi.

Delhi has four major satellite cities which lie outside the National Capital Territory of Delhi. These are Gurgaon and Faridabad (in Haryana), and NOIDA and Ghaziabad (in Uttar Pradesh). Delhi is divided into nine districts. Each district (division) is headed by a Deputy Commissioner and has three subdivisions. A Subdivision Magistrate heads each subdivision. All Deputy Commissioners report to the Divisional Commissioner. The District Administration of Delhi is the enforcing department for all kinds of State and Central Government policies and exercises supervisory powers over numerous other functionaries of the Government.

The Delhi High Court has jurisdiction over Delhi. Delhi also has lower courts; the Small Causes Court for civil cases, and the Sessions Court for criminal cases. The Delhi Police, headed by the Police Commissioner, is one of the largest metropolitan police forces in the world. Delhi is administratively divided into nine police-zones, which are further subdivided into 95 local police stations.

Government and Politics

As a special Union Territory, the National Capital Territory of Delhi has its own Legislative Assembly, Lieutenant Governor, Council of Ministers and Chief Minister. The legislative assembly seats are filled by direct election from territorial constituencies in the NCT. However, the Union Government of India and the Government of National Capital Territory of Delhi jointly administer New Delhi. The legislative assembly was re-established in 1993 for the first time since 1956, with direct federal rule in the span.

In addition, the Municipal Corporation of Delhi (MCD) handles civic administration for the city as part of the Panchayati Raj act. New Delhi, an urban area in Delhi, is the seat of both the State Government of Delhi and the Government of India. The Parliament of India, the Rashtrapati Bhavan (Presidential Palace) and the Supreme Court of India are located in New Delhi. There are 70 assembly constituencies and seven Lok Sabha (Indian parliament's lower house) constituencies in Delhi.

Delhi was a traditional stronghold of the Indian National Congress, also known as the Congress Party. In the 1990s the Bharatiya Janata Party (BJP) under the leadership of Madan Lal Khurana came into power. However in 1998, Congress regained power. Sheila Dixit of Congress is the incumbent Chief Minister. The Congress retained power in the Legislative Assembly in the 2003 election as well by a large margin. However, in 2007, the BJP scored a crushing victory over the ruling Congress in the MCD election, signalling a near certain return to power in the elections of Dec, 2008. Both parties have advocated full-fledged statehood for Delhi, but the process to establish this has been slow.

Utility Services

The water supply in Delhi is managed by the Delhi Jal Board (DJB). As of 2006, it supplied 650 MGD (million gallons per day) of water, while the water demand for 2005-06 was estimated to be 963 MGD. The rest of the demand is met by private and public tube wells and hand pumps. At 240 MGD, the Bhakra storage is the largest water source for DJB, followed by river Yamuna and Ganges. With falling groundwater level and rising population density, Delhi faces severely acute water shortage. Delhi daily produces 8000 tonnes of solid wastes which is dumped at three landfill sites by MCD. The daily domestic waste water production is 470 MGD and industrial waste water is 70 MGD. A large portion of the sewerage flows untreated into the river Yamuna.

The city's per capita electricity consumption is about 1,265 kWh but actual demand is much more. In 1997, Delhi Vidyut Board (DVB) replaced Delhi Electric Supply Undertaking which was managed by the MCD. The DVB itself cannot generate adequate power to meet the city's demand and borrows power from India's Northern Region Grid. As a result, Delhi faces a power shortage resulting in frequent blackouts and brownouts, especially during the summer season when energy demand is at its peak.

Several industrial units in Delhi rely on their own electrical generators to meet their electric demand and for back up during Delhi's frequent and disruptive power cuts. A few years ago, the power sector in Delhi was handed over to private companies. The distribution of electricity is carried out by companies run by TATA'S & Reliance Energy Ltd. in Delhi. Delhi has 43 fire stations (under Delhi Fire Service) that attend about 15,000 fire and rescue calls per year.

State-owned Mahanagar Telephone Nigam Limited (MTNL) and private enterprises like Hutch, Airtel, Idea cellular, Reliance Infocomm and Tata Indicom provide telephone and cell phone service to the city. Cellular coverage is extensive, and both GSM and CDMA (from Reliance and Tata Indicom) services are available. Affordable broadband internet penetration is increasing in the city.

Economy

With an estimated net State Domestic Product (SDP) of 83,085 crores (830.85 billion) Indian rupee (INR) (for the year 2004-05), Delhi is an important commercial centre in South Asia. Delhi has a per capita income of 53,976 INR which is around 2.5 times of the national average. The tertiary sector contributes 70.95% of Delhi's gross SDP followed by secondary and primary sectors with 25.2% and 3.85% contribution respectively. Delhi's workforce constitutes 32.82% of the population showing an increase of 52.52% between 1991 and 2001. Delhi's unemployment rate decreased from 12.57% in 1999-2000 to 4.63% in 2003. In December 2004, 636,000 people were registered with various employment exchange programmes in Delhi.

In 2001, the total workforce in all government (union and state) and quasi government sector was 620,000. In comparison, organised private sector employed 219,000. Delhi's service sector has expanded due in part to the large skilled English-speaking workforce that has attracted many multinational companies. Key service industries include information technology, telecommunications, hotels, banking, media and tourism. Delhi's manufacturing industry has also grown considerably as many consumer goods industries have established manufacturing units and headquarters in and around Delhi. Delhi's large consumer market, coupled with the easy availability of skilled labour, has attracted foreign investment in Delhi. In 2001, the manufacturing sector employed 1,440,000 workers while the number of industrial units was 129,000. Construction, power, telecommunications, health and community services, and real estate form integral parts of Delhi's economy. Delhi's retail industry is one of the fastest growing industries in India. However, as in the rest of India, the fast growth of retail is expected to affect the traditional unorganised retail trading system.

Transport

Public transport in Delhi is provided by buses, auto rickshaws, a rapid transit system, taxis and suburban railways.

Buses are the most popular means of transport catering to about 60% of the total demand. The state-owned Delhi Transport Corporation (DTC) is a major bus service provider for the city. Private vehicles account for 30% of the total demand for transport. At 1922.32 km of road length per 100 km^2, Delhi has one of the highest road densities in India. Delhi is well connected to other parts of India by five National Highways: NH 1, 2, 8, 10 and 24. Roads in Delhi are maintained by MCD (Municipal Corporation of Delhi), NDMC, Delhi Cantonment Board, Public Works Department (PWD) and Delhi Development Authority.

Delhi's high population growth rate, coupled with high economic growth rate has resulted in an ever increasing demand for transport creating excessive pressure on the city's existent transport infrastructure. The city faces acute transport management problems leading to air pollution, congestion and resultant loss of productivity. In order to meet the transport demand in Delhi, the State and Union government started the construction of a mass rapid transit system, including the Delhi Metro. As of 2007, the metro operates three lines with a total length of 65 km (40 miles) and 59 stations while several other lines are under construction. In 1998, the Supreme Court of India ordered all public transport vehicles to use compressed natural gas (CNG) as fuel instead of diesel and other hydrocarbons. The DTC now operates the world's largest fleet of environment-friendly CNG buses. Though pollution from road transport has decreased in recent years, it is still at a high level.

Railways served only 1% of the local traffic until 2003. However Delhi is a major junction in the rail map of India and is the headquarters of the Northern Railway. The four main railway stations are Old Delhi, Nizamuddin Railway Station, Sarai Rohilla and New Delhi Railway Station.

Indira Gandhi International Airport (IGI) is situated in the southwestern corner of Delhi and serves for domestic and international connections. In 2005-06, the airport recorded a traffic of more than 8.5 million passengers, making it one of the busiest airports in South Asia. Safdarjung Airport is the other airfield in Delhi used for general aviation purpose.

Demographics

Many ethnic groups and cultures are represented in Delhi, making it a cosmopolitan city. A seat of political power and a centre of commerce, the city attracts workers-both blue collar and white collar-from all parts of India, further enhancing its diverse character. A diplomatic hub, represented by embassies of 160 countries, Delhi has a large expatriate population as well.

According to the 2001 Census of India, the population of Delhi that year was 13,782,976. The corresponding population density was 9,294 persons per km^2, with a sex ratio of 821 women per 1000 men, and a literacy rate of 81.82%. The literacy rate on increase day by day with more number of people studying higher and professional education. Mr. Imran Khan who is a resident of Delhi has done Master of Human Resource Management and Master of Library and Information Science. He is presently working as a Library Professional at Jamia Hamdard, New Delhi. He has been entrusted with the responsibilities of University Library Membership and Library Networking. He is presently pursuing his M.Phil. degree in Library and Information Science. By 2003, the National Capital Territory of Delhi had a population of 14.1 million people, making it the second largest metropolitan area in India after Mumbai.

This included 295,000 people living in New Delhi and another 125,000 in Delhi Cantonment. By 2004, the estimated population had increased to 15,279,000. That year, the birth rate, death rate and infant mortality rate (per 1000 population) were 20.03, 5.59 and 13.08, respectively. According a 1999-2000 estimate, the total number of people living below the poverty line in Delhi was 1,149,000 (which was 8.23% of the total population). In 2001, the population of Delhi increased by 285,000 as a result of migration and by an additional 215,000 as a result of natural population growth. The resulting high migration rate, made Delhi is one of the fastest growing cities in the world. By 2015, Delhi is expected to be the third largest agglomeration in the world after Tokyo and Mumbai.

Hinduism is the religion of 82% of Delhi's population. There are also large communities of Muslims (11.7%), Sikhs (4.0%), Jains (1.1%) and Christians (0.9%) in the city. Other minorities include Buddhists and Jews. Hindi is the principal spoken and written language of the city. Other languages commonly spoken in the city are English, Punjabi and Urdu. Of these, English is an associate official language, and Punjabi and Urdu second official languages. Linguistic groups from all over India are well represented in the city; among them are Maithili, Tamil, Kannada, Telugu, Bengali and Marathi. Punjabis, Jats and Gujjars are examples of the various ethnic communities in the city.

In 2005, Delhi accounted for the highest percentage (16.2%) of the crimes reported in the 35 cities in India with populations of one million or more. The city also has the highest rate of crime against women (27.6 compared to national average rate of 14.1 per 100,000) and against children (6.5 compared to national average of 1.4 per 100,000) in the country.

Culture

Delhi's culture has been influenced by its lengthy history and historic association as the capital of India. This is exemplified by the many monuments of significance found in the city; the Archaeological Survey of India recognises 175 monuments in Delhi as national heritage sites. The Old City is the site where the Mughals and the Turkic rulers constructed several architectural marvels like the Jama Masjid (India's largest mosque) and Red Fort. Three World Heritage Sites-the Red Fort, Qutab Minar and Humayun's Tomb-are located in Delhi. Other monuments include the India Gate, the Jantar Mantar (an 18th century astronomical observatory) and the Purana Qila (a 16th century fortress).

The Lotus Temple, Laxminarayan Temple and Akshardham are examples of modern architecture. Raj Ghat and associated memorials houses memorials of Mahatma Gandhi and other notable personalities. New Delhi houses several government buildings and official residences reminiscent of the British colonial architecture. Important structures include the

Rashtrapati Bhavan, the Secretariat, Rajpath, the Parliament of India and Vijay Chowk. Safdarjung's Tomb is an example of the Mughal gardens style.

Delhi's association and geographic proximity to the capital, New Delhi, has amplified the importance of national events and holidays. National events such as Republic Day, Independence Day and Gandhi Jayanti (Gandhi's birthday) are celebrated with great enthusiasm in Delhi. On India's Independence Day (15 August) the Prime Minister of India addresses the nation from the Red Fort. Most Delhiites celebrate the day by flying kites, which are considered a symbol of freedom. The Republic Day Parade is a large cultural and military parade showcasing India's cultural diversity and military might.

Religious festivals include Diwali (the festival of light), Guru Nanak's Birthday, Durga Puja, Holi, Lohri, Maha Shivaratri, Eid ul-Fitr, Eid ul-Adha and Buddha Jayanti. The Qutub Festival is a cultural event during which performances of musicians and dancers from all over India are showcased at night, with the Qutub Minar as the chosen backdrop of the event. Other events such as Kite Flying Festival, International Mango Festival and Vasant Panchami (the Spring Festival) are held every year in Delhi.

Punjabi cuisine and Mughlai delicacies like kababs and biryanis are popular in several parts of Delhi. Due to Delhi's large cosmopolitan population, cuisines from every part of India, including Rajasthani, Maharashtrian, Bengali, Hyderabadi cuisines, and South Indian food items like idli, sambar and dosa are widely available. Local delicacies include Chaat and Dahi-Papri. There are several food outlets in Delhi serving international cuisine including Italian and Chinese.

Historically, Delhi has always remained an important trading centre in northern India. Old Delhi still contains legacies of its rich Mughal past that can be found among the old city's tangle of snaking lanes and teeming bazaars. The dingy markets of the Old City has an eclectic product range from oil-swamped mango, lime and eggplant pickles, candy-coloured herbal potions to silver jewelry, bridal attire, uncut material and linen, spices, sweets. Some of old regal havelis (palacial residences) are still there in the Old City. Chandni Chowk, a three century old shopping area, is one of the most popular shopping areas in Delhi for jewellery and Zari saris. Notable among Delhi's arts and crafts are the Zardozi (an embroidery done with gold thread) and Meenakari (the art of enameling). Dilli Haat, Hauz Khas, Pragati Maidan offer a variety of Indian handicrafts and handlooms. However, the city is said to have lost its own identity and socio-cultural legacies as it went to absorb multitude of humanity from across the country and has morphed into an amorphous pool of cultural styles.

Education

Schools and higher educational institutions in Delhi are administered either by the Directorate of Education, the NCT government, or private organizations. In 2004-05, there were 2,515 primary, 635 middle, 504 secondary and 1,208 senior secondary schools in Delhi. That year, the higher education institutions in the city included 165 colleges, among them five medical colleges and eight engineering colleges, six universities-Delhi University, Jawaharlal Nehru University, Guru Gobind Singh Indraprastha University, Jamia Millia Islamia and Indira Gandhi National Open University, Jamia Hamdard,-and nine deemed universities.

Private schools in Delhi-which employ either English or Hindi as the language of instruction-are affiliated to one of two administering bodies: the Indian Certificate of Secondary Education (ICSE) and the Central Board for Secondary Education (CBSE). In 2004-05, approximately 15.29 lakh (1.529 million) students were enrolled in primary schools, 8.22 lakh (0.822 million) in middle schools and 6.69 lakh (0.669 million) in secondary schools across Delhi. Female students represented 49% of the total enrollment. The same year, the Delhi government spent between 1.58% and 1.95% of its gross state domestic product on education.

After completing the ten-year secondary phase of their education under the 10+2+3 plan, students typically spend the next two years either in junior colleges or in schools with senior secondary facilities, during which their studies become more focused.

They select a stream of study-liberal arts, commerce, science, or, less commonly, vocational. Upon completion, those who choose to continue, either study for a 3-year undergraduate degree at a college, or a professional degree in law, engineering, or medicine. Notable higher education or research institutes in Delhi include All India Institute of Medical Sciences, Indian Institute of Technology Delhi, Indian Institute of Foreign Trade, Delhi School of Economics, Shri Ram College of Commerce, Lady Shri Ram College for Women, Netaji Subhas Institute of Technology, and Delhi College of Engineering.

Media

As the capital of India, New Delhi is the focus of political reportage, including regular television broadcasts of Indian parliament sessions. Many country-wide media agencies, among them the state-owned Press Trust of India and Doordarshan, are based in the city.

Television programming in the city includes two free terrestrial television channels offered by Doordarshan, and several Hindi, English and regional-languages cable channels offered by Multi system operators. Satellite television, in contrast, is yet to gain large-scale subscribership in the city.

Print journalism remains a popular news medium in Delhi. During the year 2004-05, 1029 newspapers-in thirteen languages-were published from the city. Of these, 492 were Hindi language newspapers, and included Navbharat Times, Dainik Hindustan, Punjab Kesri, Dainik Jagran, Dainik Bhaskar and fastest growing weekly The Stageman International. Among the English language newspapers, The Hindustan Times, with over a million copies in circulation, was the single largest daily.

Other major English newspapers include Indian Express, Business standard, Times of India, The Hindu, The Pioneer and Asian Age. Recently in the year 2006 two English daily tabloids were launched in Delhi. While one is a joint production of Times of India and Hindustan Times named "Metro Now", the other is Mumbai's most famous and widely recognised tabloid "MiD DAY". With the launch of the tabloids, he culture of reading tabloids in Delhi is fast catching up. Radio is a less popular mass medium in Delhi, although FM radio has been gaining ground since the inauguration of several new FM channels in 2006. A number of state-owned and private radio stations broadcast from Delhi, including All India Radio (AIR), one of the world's largest radio service providers, which offers six radio channels in ten languages. Other city-based radio stations include Radio Mirchi (98.3 FM), Red FM (93.5 FM) and Radio City (91.1 FM).

Sports

As in the rest of India, cricket is a popular sport in Delhi. There are several cricket grounds (or maidans) located across the city, including the Feroz Shah Kotla stadium, one of the oldest cricket grounds in India to be granted status as venue for international cricket matches. The Delhi cricket team represents the city in the Ranji Trophy, a domestic first-class cricket championship played between different cities and states of India. Other sports such as field hockey, Football (soccer), tennis, golf, badminton, swimming, kart racing, weightlifting and table tennis are also popular in the city.

Sports facilities in Delhi include the Jawharlal Nehru Stadium and the Indira Gandhi Indoor Stadium. In the past, Delhi has hosted several domestic and international sporting events, such as the First and the Ninth Asian Games. The coming years will see the city host the 2010 Commonwealth Games, projected to be the largest multi-sport event ever held in the city. Delhi lost bidding for the 2014 Asian Games,(81) but is bidding for 2020 Olympic Games.

Anantnag

Anantnag is a city and a municipality in Anantnag district in the state of Jammu & Kashmir, India.

Anantnag is the 3rd largest city of Jammu and Kashmir in population and largest city according to area. It is also regarded as commercial and financial capital of the valley of

Kashmir. It is the largest business and trading centre of the valley.

Demographics

As of 2001 India census, Anantnag had a population of 183,437. Males constitute 55% of the population and females 45%. Anantnag city has an average literacy rate of 79%, higher than the national average of 59.5%; with 84% of the males and 79% of females literate. 10% of the population is under 6 years of age.

History

The city finds its place in the Bhagavadgita that says "I am Ananta Naga" It is also well mentioned in ancient Naga and Pichash cronicals of ancient aboriginals of the valley. Anantnag is an ancient city which came into existence as a market town around 5000 B.C. making it of the oldest urban human settlements in the whole world. It was also known by the name of Kashyapteshwara in ancient times linking it to the mythology of Rishi Kashyapa. It has one spring called Inder Spring Hydro sphere. It has two Sulphur springs and countless fresh water springs. There are about 7 temples in Anantnag (Anantnag Bhawan Complex): two Shiva Temples, one Radha Krishna Mandir, one Durga Temple, one Ganesh Temple, Sita Ram Temple, Hanuman Temple, four Dharmshallas and one school building.

Outside the complex in the town are three temples-Ancient temples-Devibal, Shiva Temple at Nai Basti, and third at Hara Mohalla. All three temples outside the complex were burnt and damaged by Muslim fundamentalists during riots against Kashmiri Hindus in February 1986, and rebuilt with assistance of the then Governor of Jammu and Kashmir Mr. Jag Mohan. Now both the Shivala temples outside complex are reported to have been again damaged and partially burnt by Kashmiri Militants.

The district as well as its headquarters city are called by same name. Regarding this second name no mention is to be found in the old chronicles of Kashmir. It is however, said that the name of Islamabad was assigned to the city by one Islam Khan who was the Governor of Kashmir during the Mughal rule in 1663 A.D., but the change in its nomenclature proved temporary and during the reign of Maharaja Gulab Singh the town as well as district again resumed their old name, Anantnag, but the name Islamabad is still popular among the common masses, though officially the name Anantnag is used.

According to ancient mythological stories, the name was derived from Anant, the serpent of Vishnu and the emblem of eternity. Anant also means numerous in the Sanskrit language and Naga means spring in the Kashmiri language. Thus Anantnag is believed to mean numerous springs, because there are many springs, including Nag Bal, Salak Nag and Malik Nag in the town. Nag Bal issues from the foot-hill of table land. Its waters are received into tanks, whose sides are built with stones and which are over shadowed by Chinar trees. Houses of worship of the adherents of three religions Hindus, Muslims, and Sikhs are built adjacent to each other near the tanks, which depicts a rare example of communal harmony between those particular faiths in the area.

Another example of religious tolerance is the Mosque of Baba Dawood Khaki, which contains a small Hindu temple in its courtyard. Among the mosques of the town of Anantnag, one is built indirectly near the mausoleum of famous Kashmiri saint Rishi Malo to whose prayers the defeat of Akbar's first attempt to invade Jammu and Kashmir was attributed. The place is venerated by Kashmiris of all faiths.

Anantnag is a city of various handicrafts. Shawl weaving, Gabbah and Namdah manufacturing are the main trades. Near Anantnag three streams namely Arapath, Brengi and Sandran confluence together, thus giving birth to river Veth (Jhelum). Another stream Lidar also joins the flow with them at a little distance downstream further ahead. From this place the river becomes navigable.

In olden times river Jhelum was the main source of transportation between Anantnag and other towns downstream. The distances of different towns and cities from Anantnag are

Achhabal-6 miles, Kokarnag-14 miles, Verinag-17 miles, Pahalgam-24 miles and Srinagar-33 miles.

Geography

Anantnag is situated at 33.44 latitude and 75.12 longitude, at an elevation of 5400 feet above sea level, at a distance of 33 miles from the main state-headquarters Srinagar. Anantnag is located at 33.73° N 75.15° E. It has an average elevation of 1601 metres (5252 feet). The city is constituted by three main boroughs or towns Viz Anantnag, Khanabal, Martand and half a dozen small townships. Most of the population of city resides in the Anantnag borough.

The old city of Anantnag comprises Nagbal, Maliknag, Kadipora, Cheeni Chowk, Doni Pawa, Sarnal Bala, Janglatmandi, Old Port Khanabal, Downtown martand, & Dangarpora areas. The new city consists civil lines areas like New Colony, Iqbalabad, Fasilabad, Moomin-Abad, Harnag, Sultan Bah-i-Rum Shah and Mid town areas like Ashshjipora, Naibasti, Batpora and Mir Bazaar. Anantnag has quite a population inhabiting several satellite areas like Wanpoh, Dialgam, Fatehpora, Nowgam, Seer, Anchidora, Fateh Garh University town and NH 1 A north and east.

Anantnag has for long enjoyed the status of the second largest city of Jammu and Kashmir, India, but in last few years has become largest city with respect to the area. The name of Anantnag District according to a well known archaeologist, Sir A. Stein from the great spring Ananta Naga issuing at the centre of the city. This is also corroborated by almost all local historians including Kalhana according to whom the city has taken the name of this great spring of Cesha or Ananta Naga land of countless springs. The spring is mentioned in the Neelmat Purana as a sacred place for the Hindus and Koshur Encyclopedia testifies it.

Anantnag, like the rest of the Kashmir Valley, has witnessed many vicissitudes and experienced many upheavals from time to time. Hugel found here some monuments of the Mughal period in ruins when he visited Jammu and Kashmir in 1835. No significant ancient building or archaeological site is found in the district today except the Martand temple as most of the ancient architectural monuments in area were destroyed during rule of Sikander Hyat Khan. What must have once been magnificent architectural show pieces like the Martand complex of temples situated at a distance of nine kilometers from the district headquarters or the palaces of Laltaditya and Awantivarman at Awantipora lying midway between Srinagar and Anantnag are now in grand ruins.

The majestic Martand temple is one of the important archaeological sites of the country. Its impressive architecture reveals the glorious past of the area. Martand temple is the clear expression of Kashmir's pristine glory. The Mughal Emperors especially Jehangir developed many beauty spots of the district, but of their noble and magnificent edifices only fainted traces survive. All the same, even in their present ruinous conditions, these monuments do not fail to feast the eye or excite the imagination of admirers at large.

Holy Places

Kashmir is the land of saints, Sufis, and Munis and the Anantnag district being part of the Kashmir Valley is no exception. Anantnag is bestowed with religious wealth in the form of numerous shrines and places of worship enjoying reverence and allegiance of people professing different faiths. There are numerous sepulchers of saints which have enchanting environs, while visiting these shrines, one feels in close proximity of the Almighty. Some of the shrines have historical importance in addition to religious significance attached to them.

These shrines belong to both Hindus and Muslims and are visited by thousands of devotees. Some of the shrines are the world famous shrine of Baba Hyder Gazi (ra), Amarnath Ji, Devibal, Gautam Nag, Verinag, Nila Nag, Vitasta, Mattan, Bawan, Uma Devi of Uma Nagri, Nagdandi, Domtabal Asthapan, Khana Barnain Triporsundari Asthapan Devsar, Goswami Gund Ashram, Guddar Asthapan, Lok Bhawan, Swami Mirza Kak Asthapan Hangulgund, Durga, Shiva Bhagwati at Akingam, Kulwagishiri Asthapan Kulgam, Liddar Syandhai Asthapan, Trisandhia Asthapan, Gauri Temple at

Pahalgam, Shillagram Temple. Other famous shrines of Reshis like Reshi Maloo (Anantnag), the last of the giants of the Rishi order in Jammu and Kashmir about whose resting place the Alamda-i-Kashmir (Flag Bearer of Kashmir), Sheikh Noor-ud-Din Rishi had foretold his diciples. The devotees of the district and other places visit these shrines particularly on days when the festivals connected with the shrines are celebrated here.

Sports

Adventure sports are popular among tourists. Pahalgam has potential for canoeing and water skiing. Water trekking is local name for three to four day trip along the river Jhelum in a shikara with camping gear. Aru (58 km) and Pahalgam (45km) are popular destinations for hikers, trekkers and fishermen.

Sports like football and cricket are popular among schoolchildren as well as adults.

Performing Arts

Performing arts of the city include:

- Bhand Pather, a form of traditional folk theatre art form of play and dance, is performed by a group of about ten to fifteen artists. They depict in a satirical style social evils. Performance is accompanied by light music.
- Chakri is a major and popular form of Kashmiri folk music.
- Another form of Kashmiri genre of music called Sufiana music is also practised in the city. It was introduced in the valley in the 15th century from Iran. Over centuries, it has assimilated a number of Indian Ragas, and has established itself as a classical music of the region. The instruments used in the music include santoor, sitar, Kashmiri saz, tabla, and wasool.
- Hafiz Nagma, a form of dance, is performed to the accompaniment of Sufiana music. The dancer is a female while males play different instruments used in Sufiana music.

Anantnag at a Glance

Hospitals

- Distt. Hospital Janglat mandi
- Maternity Hospital Nagbal
- Childrens hospital Nag bal
- St. Bishop Hospital Kadipora
- Rahmet-e-Alam Hospital Sarnal Bala
- Sub District Hospital Martand
- Central Military Hospital Dakbunglow Khanabal

Universities

- University of Kashmir South campus Fateh garh
- Sheri Kashmir Agricultural university Wanpoh

Colleges

- Govt Degree College Boys Khanabal
- Govt Woman's Degree College K.P Road
- Hanfia college of science and commerce
- Rahmet-e-Alam B.ed College Chee
- ITI Asajipora
- NIET KP Road

Main Schools

- Islamia Hanfia College Lal Chowk
- Boys Hr Sec School Batengoo
- IMI Institute Takibal
- IMI Institute Girls Moominabad
- Girls Hr Sec School Lal Chowk
- Al Sarwat Convent Hr sec School Krangsoo
- St. Lukes High school Nai Basti
- Bloosom Public School Nai Basti Near LIC.
- Govt. Hr School Wanapoh
- Govt. Hr School dialgam
- Govt Higher secondary School Uttersoo Anantnag.

- Govt Primary School Kreeri kuthar Anantnag (From 1950 With out Building)
- Govt Higher Secondary School Chittergul Anantnag
- Govt Higher Secondary School Shangus Anantnag

Tehsil

- ANANTNAG
- SHANGUS
- PAHALGAM

Bhojakata

Bhojakata was the capital of Rukmi a Bhoja-Yadava king of Vidarbha Kingdom. Rukmi wanted his sister Rukmini to be married by the Chedi king Shishupala. But she was in love with Vasudeva Krishna. Krishna abducted Rukmini against the will of Rukmi. Then king Rukmi left the capital of Vidarbha, viz Kundinapuri and chased Krishna. He pledged that he will not return to his capital without Rukmini. But he was defeated by Krishna's army. Rukmi kept his promise by constructing another capital for Vidarbha, to the west of Kundinapuri called Bhojakata. Since then he started ruling from this new capital. He never returned to Kundinapuri.

Ancient Indian (Bharata) cities and Places (Title and location names are in English.)

Bhojakata is situated to the western boundary of Vidharbha region of Maharashtra state of India.

Gokarna

Gokarna or Gokarn is a village in the Uttara Kannada district of the Karnataka state, India. It is a Hindu pilgrimage centre as well as a tourist destination in India. Gokarna is a beach town with tourists enjoying the sun, the surf and the sea gulls.

Etymology

Gokarna means Cows' Ear. It is believed that Lord Shiva emerged from the ear of a cow (Prithvi, the Mother Earth) here.

It is also located at the ear-shaped confluence of two rivers Gangavali and Aghanashini.

Legends

Legends in the Sahyadri Khand of the Puranas indicate that the State of Kerala was reclaimed from the sea by the Warrior-Sage Parashuram who came from the North (of the Vindhya ranges) after his wanderings in which he killed the kshatriyas 21 times and threw his axe, the weapon by which he annihilated the kshatriyas, in the sea to prevent the erosion of the land stretching from Gokarna to the Southernmost tip of India.

Gokarna is also mentioned in the Shrimad Bhagawat Purana as being the home of the two brothers Gokarna and Dhundhakari and the Bhagawat also gives details of the difference in their temperament and nature and their exploits.

Ravana, a demonic king from Lanka, did penance for the grace of Lord Shiva at Mount Kailash. Lord Shiva agrees to give Atmalingam with condition that the atmalingam should be physically carried and not placed anywhere on the ground, and it establishes wherever it is placed on earth. On his way, Ravana stops for bath and gives the atmalingam to Lord Ganesha dressed like a Vatu (brahmin boy), who promptly puts it down. Ravan tries to extricate it resulting in throwing the coverings of the Linga to Dhareshwar, Gunavanteshwar, Murudeshwar and Shejjeshwar temples. Refer full story in article on Murudeshwar.

History

The earliest history of the city is not known. It was a centre for India's traditional and ancient Ganja Culture. A sect of brahmins called Gaud Saraswat Brahmins fled from the Gomantak to escape forcible conversions by the Portuguese and British and settled in and around Gokarna in 15th century. It was part of Sodhe and Vijayanagar kingdoms. Later when Konkan region including Goa was occupied by Portuguese, it became part of their rule. Few temples were destroyed by the Portuguese in 1714 and then rebuilt later in the 18th century and also under the supervision of Guru H.H. Shrimat Anandashram Swamiji in 1928.

Geography

Gokarna is about 453 km from Bangalore, 240 km north of Mangalore and about 59 km from Karwar. It is between the Gangavali and Agnashini rivers and situated along the Karwar coast by the Arabian Sea. It is near to college towns Suratkal and Manipal.

Economy

Government

It is a town in Uttar Kannada district of Karnataka.

Transport

Gokarna can be reached by buses and maxicabs from Kumta(36 km), Ankola(25km) and Karwar(59km) on national highway 17. Karnataka state road transport corporation also runs long journey buses from many cities like Goa and Mangalore. It can be reached by train run by Konkan railway on Mumbai to Mangalore route. The railway station is 6km away from the town.

Demographics

Culture

Gokarna is town of contrasts as it is a temple town and also a holiday destination by the sea. Gokarna is full of coconut and palm trees, blue seas and clean sands. It is an attractive town with two main streets with shops and traditional tile roofed brick houses. Gokarna is a hippy paradise with drums, guitars and hammocks. The beaches near Gokarna have shacks (huts) for rent.

Religious Attractions

Gokarna is also an important centre of Sanskrit learning and houses Bhandikeri Math and Toggu Math. It is a place where sanksrit knowledge is passed from generations in Brahmis families. Many Hindus also perform last rites of a person here. It is town of temples like Mahabaleshwar Temple, Maha Ganapathi, Tamra-Gauri, Venkataramana, Uma-Maheshwari, Varadraj, Bhadrakali etc.

The Mahabaleshvara Temple is one of the major temples in Gokarna. It is situated at the western end of the main street. The main deity here is two-armed, standing, and at least 1500 years old. The idol of Lord Ganesha also is ancient. In the sanctuary is a stone linga, encased in brass, placed on a coiled stone serpent. The floor of the hall in front has an intricate engraving of a giant tortoise. Kotiteertha tank lake is surrounded by temples. During festivals, giant wooden cart is drawn by humans along the main street.

Shivaratri festival is celebrated here with great enthusiasm. Each year a team builds up two great temple chariots which is used during the Shiva Ratri festival. The two great temple chariots lead a procession through the town's narrow streets, while priests and pilgrims chant hymns in praise of Shiva. More than a hundred people are needed to pull the chariots with thick ropes while priests conduct religious ceremonies inside. During the four day Shiva Ratri festival the small town of Gokarna is visited by up to 20,000 pilgrims.

Beaches

The drive up the winding path that leads to Gokarna is a scenic one, with the rocky mountains and Western Ghats on one side and the Arabian Sea on the other.

Gokarna is also famous for its beautiful beaches and landscapes. The four beaches in Gokarna are the Gokarna beach, Kudle, Om, Half moon and Paradise (also known as Full moon). The Gokarna beach forms the coast of the town while the other four beaches lies towards the south of Gokarna. Kudle and Om are around 6 km from Gokarna town along a muddy hill; they are accessible by rickshaw or foot. Half moon and Paradise are beyond Om beach and are accessible only by foot or boat. Om beach is named because it's shaped like the auspicious ? (Om) symbol. Om beach is the only naturally Om shaped beach. Two other beaches Paradise and Half Moon are smaller and remote beaches.

Hastinapur

Hastinapur (Hastinapura in Sanskrit) is a town and a nagar panchayat in Meerut district in the Indian state of Uttar Pradesh.

History

Hastinapura was the capital of the kingdom of the Kauravas, belonging to the Kuru dynasty of kings. The throne of this city was the prize over which the Kurukshetra War of the epic Mahabharata was fought. All incidents in the epic Mahabharata have taken place in this city of Hastinapura. The first reference to Hastinapur in Hindu mythology comes as the capital of Emperor Bharata.

Present-day Location

In the present day Hastinapura is a small town in the Doab region of Uttar Pradesh, called Hastinapur, 37 km from Meerut and 110 km from Delhi. Geographical Details: Situated at 29 degree 09'31.50 degree North & 77 degree 59'19.46" East. Hastinapur is 120 KM North-East of Delhi on Delhi-Meerut-Bijnore Highway. You need to take a turn to Bijnore highway from Meerut from where Hastinapur is approx 39 KM away. Road is good & clean (average speed is 50 KM/hour) & green with trees and agricultural farms both sides. Hastinapur is a small town. Population is approx. 20,000. Regular buses are available from 7 AM to 9 PM from Meerut which is the nearest Railway station (42km). Nearest Airport: New Delhi. (120 km)

Brief History

Historical Details: Hastinapura = Hastin (elephant) + pura (city) = city named after the elephants. History of this place begins from the period of Mahabharata. It is also described as Gajpur, Hastinapur, Nagpur, Asandivat, Brahmasthal, Shanti Nagar and Kunjarpur etc. in Shashtras. Grandson of Samrat Ashok, king Samprati has built many temples here during his empire. The ancient temple & the stoops are not present today since this city has come across through many ups & downs. Hastinapur city was located on the earlier course of the of holy river Ganga.

Excavation at Hastinapur was carried out in early 1950s, by B.B. Lal, of the Archaeological Survey of India. Although the main aim of this excavation, mentioned by Lal himself, "was to find out the stratigraphic position of the Painted Grey Ware with reference to other known ceramic industries of the early historical period"1, Lal could not resist attempting a correlation between Mahabharata, the text, and the material remains that he uncovered at Hastinapur. This exercise led him to historicize some of the traditions mentioned in the text, as well as link the appearance of the Painted Grey Ware with the arrival of the "Aryans" in upper Ganga basin areas.

Bharata's Lineage:-Rulers of Hastinapura as per epic Mahabharata:

- Bharadwaj-Appointed as king by Bharat
- Hasti-Established Hastinapur
- Ajmeedh-Son of Hasti
- Kuru
- Jahnu-Son of Kuru
- Shantanu-12th in generation of Jahnu
- Chitrangada
- Vichitravirya-Younger brother of Chitrangada
- Pandu-Son of Ambalika (younger wife of Vichitravirya)
- Dhritarashtra-Son of Ambika (elder wife of Vichitravirya)
- Yudhishthira-Son of Kunti
- Parikshit-Son of Abhimanyu (Son of Arjun) and Uttara
- Janamejaya-Son of Parikshit
- Chemak-last king from Chandra Vansh

Geography

Hastinapur is located at 29.17° N 78.02° E. It has an average elevation of 202 metres (662 feet).

Demographics

As of 2001 India census, Hastinapur had a population of 21,248. Males constitute 53% of the population and females

47%. Hastinapur has an average literacy rate of 58%, lower than the national average of 59.5%: male literacy is 67%, and female literacy is 47%. In Hastinapur, 15% of the population is under 6 years of age.

Places to Visit

Jain Temples

Acharya (teacher) of Kharatargatchh Shri Jinchandrasuriji has described 4 stoops (pillars) at the time of his visit in VS 1627. Muni Shri Soubhagya Vijayji has visited this place in 18th century of VS and described about three stoops (pillars). The Shwetambar temple is renovated recently & the re-establishment (pratishtha) took place on Margshirsh Shukla 10 of VS 2021. Re-establishment (pratishtha) of Digambar temple took place in VS 1863. Digambar Jain Bada Mandir and Old Pandeshwer Temple was renovated by Gurjar king Nain Singh. Old Pandeshwer Temple: Its an old temple of Lord Shiva, situated in the ruins of old Hastinapur.

Hastinapur National Park

(Best Time:October to February) Dense forest of Hastinapur lies astride the canal. It is rich in faunal wealth because of the various types of ecological niches existing in the reserve. The main groups occur are mammals, birds, reptiles (snakes and lizards), amphibians (frogs & toads) butterflies and fishes, and chiefly the invertebrate groups are, the Scorpions, Centipedes, Odonata (dragon & damselflies), Hymenoptera (wasps, bees, etc.) Isoptera (termites) and Lepidoptera which comprises more than 60 species. Our National Bird Peacock is found here in abundance. Other inhabitants include the sloth bear, jackal, wild pig and the lesser cats-fishing cat, leopard cat, jungle cat, monkeys and civet.

Gangetic dolphins have been spotted in certain stretches along the river, especially between Haridwar and Bijnor.

Hastinapur has also an abundance of birds. Water reserve near river Ganga is one of the major wintering areas for large numbers of aquatic birds from Afghanistan, Turkmenistan,

China and Siberia. Over 230 species of birds are known to have made the National Park their home. Some 364 species of birds, including the rare Siberian Crane, have been recorded in the park. The sanctuary hosts a small wintering population of the rare Siberian Cranes.

Last year most of the birds here as an alternate avenue to Bharatpur's Keoladeo National Park. Other species include the ruddy shelducks, gulls, northern shovelers, northern pintails, coots, garganey, tufted ducks and common pochard. There are spectacular painted storks, black and white necked storks, sarus cranes and varied night birds of prey, ranging from the great Indian horned owl to the jungle owlet, Colorful woodpeckers, barbets, kingfishers, minivets, bee eaters and bulbuls flit through the forest canopy.

Where to Stay?

The Forest Rest House, Hastinapur; PWD Inspection House, Hastinapur. There are many dharamsalas in the town. You can avail aircondition flats with nominal charges.

The antiquity of the present location of Hastinapur is testified by the existence of ancient Shiva-lingas worshipped by the venerable Best of Munis, Sage Ved Vyas, by the Pandavas, by Draupadi, and Guru Dronacharya. Presence of the township of Parikshitgarh, close by at a distance of 10 miles, further solidifies the definite geographical location of Hastinapur. The town of Parikshitgarh is named after the grandson of Arjuna, who became king of Hastinapur when the five brothers renounced the world and went into the Himalayas.

Both the towns are similarly located on small hillocks which were the original fortresses at these locations. A massive inundation about 3000 yrs ago during a great flood in the Ganges totally drowned the cities and left them choked with silt up to roof level. 1 B.B. Lal, ' Excavation at Hastinapur and other explorations in the Upper Ganga and Sutlej Basins 1950-52', Ancient India, No. 10&11, 1954 & 1955, ASI, New Delhi.

When Yudhisthira, the eldest of the five Pandava brothers is given the kingdom of Khandavaprastha, a region northwest to the city of Hastinapura, a land cursed with barren and arid soils, diseased and dangerous forests and famine. However Lord Krishna summons Indra, the king of the Devas to help Yudhisthira, who in turn summons the Deva architect Vishwakarman.

Performing sacred ceremonies to bless the land, Vishwakarman builds a glorious new city, which becomes the capital. Millions of people flock to this new city, and soon prosperity and health spread across Khandavaprastha, thanks to the perfectly pious rule of Yudhisthira and his brothers. After the Kurukshetra War, Yudhisthira, now king of Hastinapura retains control of his city.

Indraprastha was said to be 5,000 years old. Legend suggests that Indraprastha once stood where Purana Qila is today. A village called Indrapat existed in Delhi until the beginning of the 20th century; the village was levelled and the British city of New Delhi was made upon it. The excavations of the ancient mound of Indraprastha, capital of the Pandavas, located within Purana Qila revealed evidence of continuous habitation of the site for almost 2,500 years.

Since much of the historical record of ancient India is blurred, it is not known what happened after the Mahabharata epic. Indraprastha remained a major city for many centuries, from the time of the Mauryan Empire to the Gupta Empire in India, but became less significant with the rise of cities like Patliputra, southeast of the river plains, which was the source of India's two most powerful empires. Indraprastha was probably sacked by Hun invaders after the fall of the Gupta empire.

Hindu monarch Raja Dhilu is said to have founded the ancient city of Delhi close to Indraprastha.

Mithila

Mithila was a kingdom in ancient India. It existed in the eastern Gangetic plains in areas which is today spread over more than half of Bihar state of India, and parts of adjoining Nepal. Mithila was the capital of Videha Kingdom as per epic Ramayana. This city is identified as modern day Janakpur in

Dhanusa district of Nepal. The country of Videha is sometimes referred as Mithila though it was the capital city, much the same way as Kosala Kingdom is referred as Ayodhya though Ayodhya was the capital of Kosala kingdom.

According to D.D. Koshambi, Satpath Brahmana tells that Mathava Videgha, led by his priest Gotama Rahugana, was the first king who crossed Sadanira (supposed to be Gandaka) and founded a kingdom, where the people named videhas lived at the time of composition of Satpath Brahmana. Gotama Rahugana was a vedic rishi who composed many hymns of the first mandala of Rgveda. Most notable Rgvedic hymns of Gotama Rahugana are those which praise Sva-rajya, which was indisputably the State of Videgha which later became Videha due to phonetic change. Mathava Videgha, therefore, must belong to the Rigvedic period and must have preceded the period of Satpath Brahmana by a considerable gap. Rigveda also mentions hymns by Kasiraja Pratardana in tenth mandala. Hence, Mithila and Kashi formed part of the region in which Rigvedic peoples lived. Descendandants of Gotama Rahugana were called Gautama. One such sage lived near Ahilya-sthana during the age of Ramayana.

The legend of Mithila extends over many centuries. Both Gautama Buddha and Vardamana Mahavira are said to have lived in Mithila. It also formed the centre of Indian history during the first millennium, and has contributed to various literary and scriptural works.

Maithili is the language spoken in Mithila. Linguists consider Maithili to be an Eastern Indic language, and thus a different language from Hindi, which is Central Indic. Maithili has previously been considered a dialect of both Hindi and Bengali. In fact Maithili is now a part of the Eighth Schedule of Indian official languages.

The most important reference to Mithila is in the Hindu epic, Ramayana where Lord Rama's wife Sita is said to have been the princess of the land, born to King Janaka, who ruled Mithila from Janakpur. Other famous kings of Mithila during ancient period are King Bhanumath, Satghumanya, Suchi,

Urjnama, Satdhwya, Kriti, Anjan, Arisnami, Srutayu, Supasyu, Suryasu, Srinjay, Sourmabi, Anena, Bhimrath, Satyarath, Upangu, Upgupt, Swagat, Snanand, Subrachya, Supraswa, Subhasn, Suchurut, Susurath, Jay, Vijay, Critu, Suny, Vith Habya, Dwati, Bahulaswa, Kriti Tirtiya.1

Mithila is also the name of a style of Hindu art created in the Mithila area. It started as ritual geometric and symbolic decorations of households done by women, especially before a marriage, on the walls and floors of a house, and not known to many outside the region. After paper was brought to the area, women began to sell their artwork and expand their subjects to popular and local Hindu deities as well as to the depiction of everyday events. Ganga Devi is perhaps the most famous Mithila artist; she illustrated traditional ritual Mithila decorations, depictions of popular deities, scenes from the Ramayana, and events in her own life.

Geography and Climate

The whole Mithila region is situated in the northern plain of Ganges. Main places in this region are Darbhanga, Madhubani and Janakpur, Janakpur is now in Nepal's region. The climate in this region is mainly dry and cool. In summers the temperature wanders around the 35 to 45 degree Celsius range and in winter it is 5 to 15 degrees Celsius. This area is very near to the mean sea level hence the winter becomes uncomfortable. The months of February to March and then October to November are the best ones to roam around.

The soil is suited for agriculture, which is the region's main economic stake. Rainfall is sufficient for agriculture.

This area is flooded every year causing terrific problem in the life of peoples and loss of billions of rupees. Dams on various rivers are felt by some people to be urgent necessary for the people. But others fear that large dams in an earthquake-prone zones will be more disastrous than annual floods.

Economy

Agriculture is the main economic stake of the region. Main crops are paddy, wheat, pulses, moong, urad, arhar, jute (with a recent decline in its production), and maize. These days, with agriculture not able to compete with other parts of the country, it's becoming one of the most backward regions. Flood destroys enormous amounts of crop every year.

Vrindavan

Vrindavan pronunciation (help·info) (alternate spellings Vrindaban or Brindavan), or Vraj in Mathura district, Uttar Pradesh, India is a town on the site of an ancient forest which is believed to have been the region where the famous cowherd boy, Krishna, from Hindu scriptures spent his childhood days. It is about 15km away from Mathura city (said to be Krishna's birthplace), near the Agra-Delhi highway.

The town includes many hundreds of temples dedicated to the worship of Radha and Krishna and is considered sacred by a number of religious traditions such as Gaudiya Vaishnavism, Vaishnavism, and Hinduism in general.

In recent decades the name of Vrindavan has often been used within India, to represent an idyllic place or garden. Even in urban areas the town is busy with wildlife, including peacocks, cows, monkeys and a variety of bird species. Some of the ancient forest still remains, including a number of protected tulsi woods, which are of special significance to the local inhabitants, many of whom use leaves from the tulsi plant each day in their worship (puja).

Religious Heritage

According to tradition, Krishna was raised in the cowherding village of Gokul by his foster parents Nanda Maharaj and Yasoda. The Bhagavata Purana describes Krishna's early childhood pastimes in Vrindavan forest wherein he, his brother Balarama, and his cowherd friends stole butter, engaged in childhood pranks and fought with demons.

Along with these activities, Krishna is also described as meeting and dancing with the local girls of Vrindavan village including Radharani who were known as gopis. These pastimes were the source of inspiration for the famous poem, Gita Govinda.

Temples

The most popular temples include:

- The Madan Mohan Temple located near the Kali Ghat which was built by Kapur Ram Das of Multan. This is the oldest existent temple in Vrindavan today. The temple is closely associated with the saint Chaitanya Mahaprabhu. The original image of Lord Madan Gopal was shifted from the shrine to Karauli in Rajasthan for safe keeping during Aurangzeb's rule. Today, a replica of the image is worshiped at the temple.
- The Banke-Bihari Temple, built in 1862 is the most popular shrine at Vrindavan. The image of Banke-Bihari was discovered in Nidhi Vana by Swami Haridas, the great Krishna devotee, belonging to the Nimbarka sampradaya.
- The famous Radha Vallabh Temple set up by the Radha-Vallabh sampradaya, has the crown of Radharani placed next to the Shri Krishna image in the sanctum.
- The Jaipur Temple which was built by Sawai Madho Singh II, the Maharaja of Jaipur in 1917, is a richly embellished and opulent temple. The fine hand-carved sandstone is of unparalleled workmanship. The temple is dedicated to Shri Radha Madhava.
- Sri Radha Raman Mandir constructed at the request of Gopala Bhatta Goswami around 1542 is one most exquisitely crafted and revered temples of Vrindavan, especially by the Goswamis. It still houses the original saligram deity of Krishna, alongside Radharani.
- The Shahji Temple, another popular temple at Vrindavan, was designed and built in 1876 by a wealthy jeweller, Shah Kundan Lal of Lucknow. The deities (images) at the temple are popularly known as the Chhote Radha Raman. Noted for its magnificent architecture and beautiful marble sculpture, the temple has twelve spiral columns each 15 feet high. The `Basanti Kamra'-the darbar hall is famed for its Belgian glass chandeliers and fine paintings.

- The Rangaji Temple, built in 1851 is dedicated to Lord Ranganatha or Rangaji depicted as Lord Vishnu in his sheshashayi pose, resting on the coils of the sacred Sesha Naga. The temple built in the Dravidian style (as a replica of Srivilliputhur) has a tall gopuram (gateway), of six storeys and a gold-plated Dhwaja stambha, 50 feet high. A water tank and a picturesque garden lie within the temple enclosure. The annual festival of Jal Vihar of the presiding deity is performed with great pomp and splendour at the tank. The temple is also famous for its `Brahmotsdav' celebration in March-April, more popularly known as the `Rath ka Mela'. The ten day long celebrations are marked by the pulling of the rath (the chariot car) by the devotees from the temple to the adjoining gardens. The prayers within the temple are performed, following in the style of Andal, one of the twelve Vaishnava Saints of South India.
- The Govind Deo (Govindaji) Temple was once a magnificent seven storeyed structure built in the form of a Greek cross. It is said that the Emperor Akbar donated some of the red sandstone that had been brought for the Red Fort at Agra, for the construction of this temple. Built at the astronomical cost of one crore rupees in 1590 by his general Raja Man Singh, the temple combines western, Hindu and Muslim architectural elements in its structure. It was destroyed by Mughal ruler Aurangzeb.
- The Sri Krishna-Balrama Temple built by the International Society for Krishna Consciousness (ISKCON) in a location known as 'Raman-Reti', is one of the most beautiful temples in Vrindavan today. The principal deities of this temple are Krishna & Balaram, with Radha-Shyamasundar and Gaura-Nitai alongside. Adjoining the temple is the samadhi of A. C. Bhaktivedanta Swami Prabhupada, the founder of ISKCON, built in pure white marble.
- The Radha Damodar Mandir Located at Seva Kunj, the

Mandir was established in 1542 by Srila Jiva Goswami. The deities Sri Sri Radha Damodar are here. The bhajan kutir of A. C. Bhaktivedanta Swami Prabhupada is also situated at the Mandir.

Other Sacred Sites

Other places of interest include Seva Kunj, Kesi Ghat, Sriji Temple, Jugal Kishore Temple, Lal Babu Temple, Raj Ghat, Kusuma Sarovar, Meera-Bai Temple, Imli Tal, Kaliya Ghat, Raman Reti, Varaha Ghat and Chira Ghat, and across the river, a short boat-ride away is the samadhi shrine of Devraha Baba, a revered saint of the last century.

The Seva Kunj is where Lord Krishna once performed the Raaslila with Radha-Rani and the gopis and Nidhi Van where the divine couple rested. The samadhi of Swami Haridas, the guru of Tansen, is situated here. Every year, in his honour, Swami Haridas Sammelan is organized, in which all renowed musicians of India take part.

Another famous temple of Sri Vrindavan is Sri Kathia Baba Ka Sthan" at Gurukul Road, the mahanta of which is entitled as "brajobidehi mahanta" and the acharya of Swabhuram Dwara of Nimbarka sect, Sri Swami Rash Behari Das Kathia Babaji Maharaj.

Geography

Vrindavan is located at 27.58° N 77.7° E. It has an average elevation of 170 metres (557 feet).

Demographics

As of 2001 India census, Vrindavan had a population of 56,618. Males constitute 56% of the population and females 44%. Vrindavan has an average literacy rate of 65%, higher than the national average of 59.5%: male literacy is 73%, and female literacy is 55%. In Vrindavan, 13% of the population is under 6 years of age.

Vrindavan is also known as the City of Widows. According to some Hindu traditions, upper-caste widows may not remarry, so many of those abandoned by their families on the death of their husband make their way here. In exchange for singing bhajan hymns for 7-8 hours in bhajanashrams, the women are given a cup of rice and a pittance of money (around Rs.10), which they try to supplement by begging on the streets or in some instances, even through prostitution.

There are an estimated 15,000 to 20,000 widows living on the streets, many of whom have spent over 30 years there. An organization called Guild of Service was formed to assist these deprived women and children. In 2000 the organization opened Amar Bari (My Home), a refuge for 120 Vrindavan widows, and a second shelter for 500 widows is expected to open.

Allahabad

Allahabad is the English name of a city in the north Indian state of Uttar Pradesh.

The name is derived from the one given to the city by the Mughal Emperor Akbar in 1583. The name in Indian languages or in India generally is Ilahabad; ilah being Arabic for "(a) god" (in this context from Din-i-Ilahi, the religion founded by Akbar), and "-abad" is Persian for "place of".

The ancient name of the city is Prayaga (Sanskrit for "place of sacrifice", Prayag in modern Hindi) and is believed to be the spot where Brahma offered his first sacrifice after creating the world. It is one of four sites of the Kumbh Mela, the others being Haridwar, Ujjain and Nasik.

It has a position of importance in the Hindu religion and mythology since it is situated at the confluence of the holy rivers Ganga and Yamuna, and Hindu belief says that the invisible Saraswati River joins here also.

Because solar events in Allahabad occur 5 hours and 27.4 minutes ahead of Greenwich, the city is very close to the reference point for IST or Indian Standard Time which is + 5 hours and 30 minutes ahead of Greenwich. Allahabad is-2.6 minutes behind IST and Varanasi is +2 minutes ahead of IST. Actual IST longitude is between these two cities.

Amarkantak

Amarkantak is a town and a nagar panchayat in Anuppur District in the state of Madhya Pradesh, India. Amarkantak region is a unique natural heritage area and is the meeting point of the Vindhyas and the Satpuras, with the Maikal Hills being the fulcrum. This is the place from where the Narmada River, the Sone River and Johila River emerge.

Location

Amarkantak is situated in Anuppur District of Madhya Pradesh in India. Amarkantak is located at 22.67° N 81.75° E. It has an average elevation of 1048 metres (3438 feet). Roads running through Rewa, Shahdol, Bilaspur, Jabalpur, Katni and Pendra connect it. The nearest railway station is Pendra Road (48 km) in Chhatisgarh. The nearest Airport is Dumna Jabalpur (240 km).

Demographics

As of 2001 India census, Amarkantak had a population of 7074. Males constitute 54% of the population and females 46%. Amarkantak has an average literacy rate of 68%, higher than the national average of 59.5%; with 62% of the males and 38% of females literate. 13% of the population is under 6 years of age.

Geography

It is not only the Narmada which arises from Amarkantak, because the Son River, initially referred to as Jwalawanti of Johila, the Mahanadi and the Amadoh, which is a major early tributary of the Godavari, all rise from within the Amarkantak plateau. The beauty of the plateau can well be gauged from the fact that it lies 1000 metres a.m.s.l. in the midst of a moist sal and mixed forest. A little distance from Gaumukh, the source of the Narmada, is Kapildhara, where the Narmada leaves Anuppur District and enters Dindori District by cascading more than 20 metres down a sheer basalt rock. Four kilometers from Amarkantak is Kabir Chabutara, the exact junction point of Dindori, Bilaspur and Anuppur districts. As the source of the Narmada, which is more than 150 million years older than the Ganga and is considered by many Hindus to be the most sacred for all the rivers of India, Amarkantak itself is sacred to the Hindus and is deemed to be a door-way to 'nirwana'. In these hills dwell some of the most primitive of the Madhya Pradesh tribals, the Hill Korwas and Pandavas. Even today the Pandavas run away if they see any strangers approaching their village.

Geologically the Amarkantak Hills have underlying basalt (Deccan Traps). The overburden consists of bauxite and laterite, making the soil ferruginous and clayey, with an acidic or neutral reaction. There is schist and gneiss, which is why sal is to be found here despite underlying trap. Climatically Amarkantak is temperate.

July, August and September are the real monsoon months, but there is also some winter rain. February is about the only month which is dry.

The Flora and Fauna

The temperate climate and the equitable distribution of rain make Amarkantak an ideal plateau for dense vegetation cover. From 1970 to 1976 H.O. Saxena, the Forest Botanist, State Forest Research Institute conducted intensive studies on the flora of Amarkantak, which is classified by Champion as Central Indian sub-tropical hill forests. He identified 635 species, including 612 angiosperms, 2 gymnosperms and 21 pteridophytes. 7 of these species were new for Central India and 14 for Madhya Pradesh.

Whilst the forest is sal dominated, there are associate species such as Mallotus Philipensis, Buchanania lanzan, Ougeinia oojeinesis, Terminalia chebula, Bauhinia spp, Grewia spp, Gardenia latifolia, Anogeissus latifolia, together with climbers and shrubs such as Bauhinia vahilii, Dioscorea, Smilax, Celastrus painiculata and such ground flora as Desmodium, Moghania, Sida, Crotalaria, Leucas, Pogostemon benglaensis, Strobilantihes, Setaria, Oplismenus etc. As one moves down into the valleys sal gradually is replaced by mixed forests, which include Bauhinia retusa, Grewia spp. Bursera serrata (which is normally to be found in the north-east and whose presence in Amarkantak shows the catholicity of vegetation here), Rhamnus wightii, Schleichera oleosa, Schefflera venulosa, Butea monosperma, Lagerstoemia parviflora, Boswellia serrata, Garuga pinnata, Ficus spp, Lannea coromandelica, etc., with a wide variety of grasses and other ground flora. Interestingly enough there are plants of the north-west and central Himalayas to be found in Amarkantak, including Thalictrum foliolosum, Ceranium Ocellatum, Androsace umbellata, Mazur delavavi, Lindernia Hookeri var. Kumannensis, etc. Because of the high percentage of grasses in Amarkantak the ratio of Dicotyledons to monocotyledons here is 68.3 to 26.5 whereas the world average is 81.3 to 18.7.

Pinus caribaea, known as Tropical pine, was planted in Amarkntak in 1968 on advice of Forest Research Institute, Dehradun on the recommendations of National Agricultural Commission of India looking to the future demand of quality pulp wood. This work was undertaken under the World Bank Technical Assistance Project by clearing natural Sal forests. The naturalists and environmentalists in India raised a controversy over it and ultimately the project of Tropical pine Plantation was abolished.

In isolated eco-system, such as remote valleys and islands, there is an extremely wide variety of floristic genera, but with the proportion of species to genera being very small. This is because each genus is unique to itself and does not proliferate and subdivide into many species. The general rule of the botanical world, however, is that there is a very high proportion of species to genera.

The eco-system of Amarkantak is truly unique, closely resembling that of isolated valleys or islands, because whereas the proportion of species genera is 13:1 in the world, in India it is 7:1 and in Amarkantak it is 15:1. This makes every genus in Amarkantak of great botanical importance because if a particular plant becomes extinct the genus itself will die because it does not live through any of its variant species. There are very few such spots in India and this makes Amarkantak a natural heritage area of national and even international importance.

Amarkantak has some extremely valuable medicinal plants, which are now gravely endangered. Two of these call for special mention, Hedychium coronarium, or Gulbakavali and Curcuma caesiaRoxburghii, or Kali Haldi. Gulbakavali belong to the family zinziberaceae. Gulbakavali grows on marshy land, with pure water and under dense shade on deep soil. Its natural habitat is Mai-ki-bagia, Sonmuda, Kabir Chabutara, Dudhdhara and some private gardens in Amarkantak. Kali haldi belong to the same family as ginger, turmeric and amba haldi.

It tastes very much like ginger and is used extensively as an anti-inflammatory drug for dealing with sprains and bruised. The rhizome gives off new shoots in the rains, with the leaves being about 30cms. long and 15to 16cms. broad. The leaves are a deep, dark green in colour. Kali haldi prefers marshy land and is to be found in Kabir Chabutara, Chadha and the foot hills of Amarkantak.

The rhizome contains essential oils and resins, sugar, starch, albuminoids, gums and organic acids and substantial coarse figure. With the other Curcuma Varieties including C. aromatica and C. augustifolia, kali haldi is an endangered species, especially because it is highly localised around Amarkantak, and it requires total protection.

Religious Importance of Amarkantak

Amarkantak situated on the western edge of ancient Kingdom of Kalinga is a place of worship for all the three worlds. Gods and Gandharvas (Celestial beings), Asuras (demons), Saints and Sages have all achieved great spiritual powers here. It is believed that who ever dies at Amarkantak is assured of a place in heaven. A lady who makes offerings of fruits and flowers will gain the respect of her husband, and no doubt she will also achieve a place in heaven.

When Lord Shiva destroyed Tripura (The three cities) by fire, the ashes of one fell upon mount Kailash, the ashes of another fell upon Amarkantak, and the ashes of the third were saved by Lord Shiva and kept in heaven. The ashes that fell upon Amarkantak turned into crores of Shivalingas. Only one is visible at Jwaleshwar in Amarkantak.

Amarkantak is a Sanskrit word the literal meaning of which is immortal (amar) obstruction (kantak). The place was abode of Gods but was disturbed by the hindrances of Rudraganas and hence called Amarkantak. The poet Kalidas has mentioned it as Amrakoot. Myth is that the dense forests of this region were full of mango (amra) trees. So Kalidas named it as Amrakoot, which later became Amarkantak.

History of Amarkantak

Amarkantak and rivers originating from it do not find mention in Vedic literature, but these have been mentioned in Puranas, Ramayana, Mahabharata, Vashishtha samhita and "Shatapatha Brahmana". After Mahabharata the history of a period of about 3000 years is in dark. Professor Arjun Chaube Kashyap concludes that the Puranic name of Amarkantak was Riksh parvat.

About 6000 years back the Suryavanshi samrat Mandhata founded a town in the valley Riksh parvat and named it Mandhata. The queen of samrat Purukutsa, who was son of Mandhata, gave the title of Narmada to the river. Due to occupation of this area by Mandhata the descendents of Yayati moved from this area to west of Madhya Pradesh and settled on the banks of Narmada River.

According to tradition, this Vindhyachal area was included in the Kingdom of Ayodhya, Kapila Muni, Bhrigu Rishi and Markandeya Rishi had ashrams here. It is also said that Pandavas stayed here and gained spiritual benefits during their exile.

After about 3000 years of Mahabharata the Adi Shankarachrya was born in 788 AD and consecrated on the banks of Narmada River. He founded Pataleshwar Mahadev in Amarkantak at the origin of Narmada from the bamboo clumps. This place is known as Surajkund today. There is no bamboo clumps here now.

In the more recent history, this area was given in dowry to the Kalachuri King by the Chedi King (10th to 11th century AD). The Kalchuri Maharaja Karnadeva (1042-1072 AD) had constructed temples at Surajkund. In 1808 Amarkantak was ruled by the King of Nagpur and later came under foreign rule.In the latestnews, amarkantak selected as the place for india's first tribal university.UPA government decided to form a tribal university.

Places of Tourist Importance

Amarkantak being a unique natural heritage is very rich in biodiversity. It has got a number of places of scenic beauty. Apart from this it is source of origin of three important rivers. It is a great pilgrim centre for Hindus. It is thus a great-unexplored tourism destination.

Narmadakund and Temples

At the place of origin of Narmada River there is an open pool known as Narmadakund. Around this kund there are number of temples such as Narmada and Shiva temple, Kartikey temple, Shri Ram Janki temple, Annapurna temple, Guru Gorakhnath temple, Sri Shuryanarayan temple, Vangeshwar Mahadev temple, Durga temple, Shiv Pariwar, Siddheswar Mahadev temple, Sri Radha Krishna temple, Eleven Rudra temple etc.

Ancient Temples of Kalachuri Period

The ancient temples of Kalachuri period are situated in the south of Narmadakund just behind it. These were built by Kalachuri Maharaja Karnadeva (1042-1072 AD). The Machhendranath and Pataleshwar temples are excellent examples of architecture. There is also Keshav Narayan temple built by the Bhonsle ruler of Nagpur in the 18th century.

Sonemuda

Sonemuda is the place of origin of Sone River. It is situated at a distance of 1.5 km from Narmadakund at the very edge of Maikal Mountain. The Sone River cascades from the mountain in a waterfall hundreds of feet long. As we stand on the viewing platform facing east, we see a panorama of forested hills and valleys. According to Megasthanes and other Aryan writers the river Sone gets its name from gold as the gold dust is found in the water of Sone.

Mai ki Bagiya (Goddess garden)

A grove of trees in dense forests situated at a distance of one km from Narmadakund is named "Mai ki Bagiya" in honour of the goddess Narmada. In this natural garden Mango, Banana and other fruit trees along with Gulbakavli, roses and other flower plants are there.

Kapildhara (Kapil waterfall)

Six km northwest of Narmadakund is situated the famous waterfall called Kapildhara with a fall of about hundred feet. According to scriptures, Kapil Muni lived here. There is a scene of natural beauty with mountains and dense forest down hills. According to 'Vindhya Vaibhav' Kapil Muni performed severe austerities here and received divine light. He also wrote 'sankhya philosophy' (an advanced treatise on mathematics) at this place. The Kapileshwar temple is also situated nearby. The surrounding mountains are full of caves where saints have been performing their spiritual practices.

Kabir Chabutra (the platform of saint Kabir)

It is an old belief that the great saint Kabir performed austerities here and achieved spiritual powers. It is therefore a holy place for the Kabir panth sect. The local people, the Panikas, consider Kabir Chabutara as one of the holiest places of the Kabirpanthis because Sant Kabir spent many years here in meditation.At this very place Kabir and Nanak met and discussed spiritual matters and introduced the way of better living for human being. It is also the meeting point of three districts, Anuppur and Dindori districts of Madhya Pradesh and Bilaspur district of Chhatisgarh. There is also a Kabir waterfall here.

Shri Jwaleshwar Mahadev (the temple of Shiva)

The Jwaleshwar temple and the source of origin of the third river Juhila River is situated at a distance of 8 km from Amarkantak on Shahdol road. According to 'Vindhya Vaibhav' Lord Shiva himself established a Shivling here and also scattered crores of other Shivlings over Maikal Mountain. According to puranic traditions a rectangular area containing crores of

Shivlings is known as 'Maha Rudra Meru' and is the abode of lord Shiva himself. There are only two 'Maha Rudra Meru' places Varanasi and Amarkantak. Lord Shiva and Parvati live here because of this special spiritual quality.

Chitrakuta

Chitrakuta (also spelt Chitrakoot) is a town and a nagar panchayat in Satna district in the state of Madhya Pradesh, India. It is a town of religious, cultural, historical and archaeological importance, situated in the Bundelkhand region, bordering Chitrakoot district in Uttar Pradesh, India. Chitrakoot Dham (Karwi) is a nearby town. It is known for a number of temples and sites mentioned in Hindu mythology.

Many people gather here on each Amavasya. Somwati Amavasyas, Deepawali, Sharad-Poornima, Makar Sankranti and Ramanavami are special occasions for such gatherings and celebrations. It attracts crowds throughout the year including above occasions and for Free Eye Hospital Camps. Noted 'Ayurvedic' and 'Yoga' centres like 'Arogyadham' are located in Chitrakuta.

Geography

Chitrakuta means the 'Hill of many wonders'. Chitrakuta falls in the northern Vindhya range of mountains spread over the states of Uttar Pradesh and Madhya Pradesh. The Chitrakuta region is included in the District Chitrakuta of Uttar Pradesh and the District Satna of Madhya Pradesh. Chitrakuta district in Uttar Pradesh was created on 4 September 1998.

Chitrakoot Parvat Mala includes Kamad Giri, Hanumaan Dhara, Janki Kund, Lakshman pahari, and Devangana famous Religious mountains.

History

Chitrakuta's spiritual legacy stretches back to legendary ages: It was in these deep forests that Rama, Sita and his brother Lakshmana spent eleven and half years of their fourteen years of exile; the great sage Atri, Sati Anusuya, Dattatreya,

Maharshi Markandeya, Sarbhanga, Sutikshna and various other sages, seers, devotees and thinkers meditated; and here the principal trinity of the Hindu pantheon, Brahma, Vishnu and Mahesh, took their incarnations.

It is said that all the gods and goddesses came to Chitrakuta when Rama performed the Shraddha ceremony of his father to partake of the shuddhi (*i.e.* a feast given to all the relatives and friends on the thirteenth day of the a death in the family). The first known mention of the place is in the Valmiki Ramayana, which is believed to be the first ever Mahakavya composed by the first ever poet.

As Valmiki is said to be contemporaneous with (or even earlier than) Rama and is believed to have composed the Ramayana before the birth of Rama, the antiquity of its fame can well be gauged. Valmiki speaks of Chitrakuta as an eminently holy place inhabited by the great sages, abounding in monkeys, bears and various other kinds of fauna and flora. Both the sages Bharadwaja and Valmiki speak of Chitrakuta in glowing terms and advise Rama to make it his abode during the period of his exile. Lord Rama himself admits this bewitching impact of this place.

In the 'Ramopakhyana' and descriptions of teerthas at various places in the Mahabharata, Chitrakuta finds a favoured place. In 'Adhyatma Ramayana' and 'Brihat Ramayana' testify to the throbbing spiritually and natural beauty of Chitrakuta. The Rev. Father Kamil Bulke even mentions a 'Chitrakoot-Mahatmya'; found among the collections of Mackenzie. Various Sanskrit and Hindi poets also have paid similar tributes to Chitrakuta. Mahakavi Kalidas has described this place beautifully in his epic 'Raghuvansha'. He was so much impressed with its charms that he made Chitrakuta (which he calls Ramgiri because of its time-honoured associations with lord Rama) the place of exile of his yaksha in Meghdoot.

Tulsidas, the saint-poet of Hindi has spoken very reverently of this place in all his major works-Ramcharit Manas, Kavitawali, Dohawali and Vinay Patrika. The last-mentioned work contains many verses which show a deep personal bond between Tulsidas and Chitrakuta. He spent quite some part of his life here worshipping Rama and craving his darshan. It was here that he had what he must have considered the crowning moment of his achievements—*i.e.* the darshan of his beloved deity Lord Ram at the intercession of Hanumanji. His eminent friend, the noted Hindi poet Rahim (*i.e.* Abdur Rahim Khankhana, the soldier-statesmen-saint-scholar-poet who was among the Nav-Ratnas of Akbar) also spent some time here, when he had fallen from favour with Akbar's son Emperor Jahangir.

Rama Left Chitrakuta

When Bharata was asked by his ministers to take his seat upon the throne of Ayodhya, he refused and came to Chitrakuta to meet Lord Rama. Here at place called Bharat Milap, Bharata met Lord Rama and requested him to return to Ayodhya and rule; but Lord Rama would not. Then Bharata returned back to Ayodhya and installed the sandals on the throne, and, living in retirement, carried on the government as their minister. Now Lord Rama decided for two reasons to leave Chitrakuta: first, inasmuch as hosts of rakshasas, out of hatred of him, annoyed the hermits of that place; and, secondly, because the host of men from Ayodhya had tampled and defiled the place; and, moreover, it reminded him too sharply of brother's grief and the citizens' and queen-mothers'. He went, therefore, with Sita and Lakshmana toward Dandaka forest.

Puri

Puri pronunciation (help·info) is a city in the east Indian state of Orissa. The city is famous for its Jagannath temple. The temple was built in the late eleventh century. Puri is one of the oldest cities in the eastern part of the country. It is situated on the coast of Bay of Bengal and is a popular beach resort, positioned in a unique place that both sun set and sun rise can be viewed from the beach.

Name

The word "puri" in Sanskrit Language stands for 'Town or City' but, in this case, it is derived from Jagannath Puri. Another belief is that the name Puri is derived from

Purushottama (one of 108 Shatktipeethas,Puroshottama). It is the only shrine in India, where Goddess (Also referred as Durga, Sati,Parvati) abode here with Lord Krishna who is Jagannatha.

History

Puri is the site of the Govardhana matha, one of the four cardinal institutions established by Sri Adi Shankaracharya, the others being those at Sringeri, Dwaraka and Jyotirmath.

Puri is also famous for its annual Ratha Yatra, or "Festival of Chariots", when the deities Jagannath, Baladeva, and Subhadra, are brought out of the temple, and placed in a chariot procession. This festival occurs on various dates of the Gregorian calendar, typically in the month of July.

The town if famous for its many Mathas (monasteries of the various Hindu sects). It also houses the relics of many Hindu saints as traditionally it is seen as a holy place to die in or to get cremated in. As a result, it has had a disproportionate number of widows. Like other old Hindu religious towns it has a lot of character that is difficult to be glimpsed by a casual visitor.

Puri is Holy city in the state of Orissa. Puri is well connected by National Highway No.203 who has started from Rasulgarh of "BHUBANEHSWAR". (State Capital) and Mail/Express Trains By Indian Railways & AIR PORT Near about 57 km. at Bhubanehswar.

"SWARGADWAR" Means Directly Gateway to HEVEN. (Here is a Hindu's Burning Ghat) SWARG Mean HEVEN & DWAR Mean GATE

Why Puri is Important?

- The beautiful sea beach.
- The world famous Jagannath Temple(BADA DEULA).
- The gate way to Heaven(as per Hindu mythology-SWARGA DUAAR).
- One of the four cardinal institutions established by Sri Adi Shankaracharya-PURI DHAM

- Ratha Yatra.
- Gateway to famous Sun temple (from Puri 36 km.) at KONARK from konark Towards North "KURUMA" is Famous for Buddhist place.
- Bada Thakura/Bada Danda/Bada Deula/Bada Raja/ MahaPrasad/MahaDeepa is Puri's Famous Name

Rameswaram

Rameswaram is a town in Ramanathapuram district in the Indian state of Tamil Nadu. It is located on an island separated from mainland India by the Pamban channel and is less than 40 kilometers from the Jaffna Peninsula, Sri Lanka. Together with Kashi, it is considered by Hindus to be one of the holiest places in India to Hindus. Hence, it is a bustling pilgrim centre.

It is situated in the Gulf of Mannar at the very tip of the Indian peninsula. According to legends, this is the place from where Lord Rama, built a bridge Ram Setu(also known as Adam's Bridge) across the sea to Lanka to rescue his consort Sita, from her abductor, Ravana. This is also the place where Rama worshipped Shiva to be absolved of the sin of killing Ravana. Both the Vaishnavites and Shaivites visit this pilgrimage centre which is known as the Varanasi of the south.

Ex-president of India, Dr. Abdul Kalam, hails from a fishing hamlet called Dhanushkodi situated on the island.

Geography

Rameswaram is located at 9.28° N 79.3° E. It has an average elevation of 10 metres (32 feet). The religious island is spread in an area of 61.8 square kilometers and happens to be in the shape of a conch. The Ramanatha Swamy Temple occupies major area of Rameshwaram.

The island is connected to mainland India by the Pamban Bridge.

Demographics

As of 2001 India census, Rameswaram had a population of 38,035. Males constitute 52% of the population and females 48%. Rameswaram has an average literacy rate of 72%, higher than the national average of 59.5%: male literacy is 77%, and female literacy is 66%. In Rameswaram, 13% of the population is under 6 years of age.

Hindu Holy City

Rameshwaram is significant for the Hindus as a pilgrimage to Benaras is incomplete without a Pilgrimage to Rameshwaram. The presiding deity here is in in the form of a Linga with the name Sri Ramanatha Swamy, it also happens to be one of the twelve Jyotirlingas.

The masterpiece of Dravidian architecture boasts of the largest temple corridor in India. Different rulers built the Ramanatha Swamy Temple over a period of time starting from the 12th century. The temple comprises forty wells where the taste of the water of each well is different from the other.

The grandest part of the temple is the 1219 m pillared corridor consisting of 3.6 m high granite pillars, richly carved and well proportioned. The perspective presented by these pillars run uninterruptedly to a length of nearly 230 m.

According to the Puranas, upon the advice of Rishis (sages), Rama along with Sita and Lakshmana, installed and worshipped the Sivalinga here to expiate the sin of Brahmahatya (killing of a Brahmin) (Ravana was a Brahmin the great grandson of Brahma). Rama fixed an auspicious time for the installation and sent Anjaneya to Mount Kailas to bring a lingam. As Anjaneya could not return in time, Sita herself made a linga of sand. When Anjaneya returned with a linga from Mount Kailas the rituals had been over. To comfort the disappointed Anjaneya, Rama had Anjaneya's lingam (Visvalingam) also installed by the side of Ramalinga, and ordained that rituals be performed first to the Visvalingam.

In Rameshwaram Temple, a spiritual "Mani Darshan" happens in early morning everyday. This "Mani" is made of "sphatik"(a precious stone) and in form of "Holy shivling". according to ved this is "Mani" of "sheshnag".

Sethu Karai is a place 22 kms before the island of Rameshwaram from where God Ram built a Floating Stone

Bridge "Ramasethu" till Rameshwaram that further continued from Dhanushkodi in Rameshwaram till Talaimannar in Sri Lanka as mentioned in the great Hindu epic RAMAYAN. The ruins of the Ramasethu are submerged under the sea as shot from Gemini 1 satellite of NASA in 2004.

Somnath

The Somnath Temple located in the Prabhas Kshetra near Veraval in Saurashtra, on the western coast of Gujarat, India is one of the twelve Jyotirlings (lingas of light) symbols of the God Shiva. It is mentioned in the Rig Veda. Somnath means "The Protector of Moon God". The Somnath Temple is known as 'the Shrine Eternal', as although the temple has been destroyed six times it has been rebuilt every single time.

Folklore

It has been said that The Moon God Chandra, being arrogant about his beauty, was cursed by his father-in-law Daksha to wane. The Moon then prayed to Lord Shiva at the Prabhas tirth who then removed the curse partially, thus causing the periodic waning of moon.

It's been said that Somnath Temple was first built with gold by Moon God, with silver by Ravana, with sandalwood by Lord Krishna, and with stone by Bhimdeva (Solanki Ruler of Gujarat)

History

The present temple is the seventh temple reconstructed on the original site. The first temple of Somnath is said to have existed before the beginning of the Christian era. The second temple, built by the Maitraka kings of Vallabhi in Gujarat, replaced the first one on the same site around 649.

In 725 Junayad, the Arab governor of Sind, sent his armies to destroy the second temple. The Pratihara king Nagabhata II constructed the third temple in 815, a large structure of red sandstone.

In 1024, Mahmud Ghazni raided the temple from across the Thar Desert. During his campaign, Mahmud was challenged by Ghogha Rana, who at the ripe age of 90, sacrificed his own clan fighting against this iconoclast. The temple and citadel were ransacked, and more than 50,000 defenders were massacred; Mahmud personally hammered the temple's gilded lingam to pieces and the stone fragments were carted back to Ghazni, where they were incorporated into the steps of the city's new Jamiah Masjid (Friday mosque).

The fourth temple was built by the Paramara King Bhoj of Malwa and the Solanki king Bhima of Gujarat (Anhilwara) between 1026 and 1042. The wooden structure was replaced by Kumarpal who built the temple of stone.

The temple was razed in 1297 when the Sultanate of Delhi conquered Gujarat, and again in 1394. The Mughal Emperor Aurangzeb destroyed the temple again in 1706.

Sardar Vallabhbhai Patel, then Home Minister & the first Deputy Prime Minister of India took a pledge on November 13, 1947 for its reconstruction for the seventh time. A mosque present at that site was shifted few miles away. It was completed on December 1, 1995 and President of India, Dr. Shankar Dayal Sharma dedicated it in the service of the nation. The present temple was built by the Shree Somnath Trust which looks after the entire complex of Shree Somnath and its environs.

Architecture

The Present temple, Kailash Mahameru Prasada, is built in the Chalukya style of temple architecture and reflects the skill of the Sompuras, Gujarat's master masons.

The temple is situated at such a place that there is no land in between from Somnath seashore to Antarctica. Such an inscription in Sanskrit is found on the ARROW-PILLAR erected on the sea-protection wall at the Somnath Temple.

In 1951 Dr. Rajendra Prasad, the first President of India, who performed the Jyotirling-Pratishthapan ceremony of the new Temple said, "The Somnath Temple signifies that the power of creation is always greater than the power of destruction."

2

Port Cities in India

Bharuch

Bharuch today is a large seaport city of more than a million inhabitants and a municipality in Bharuch district in the state of Gujarat, India. As a trading depot, the limitations of coastal shipping made it a regular terminus via several mixed trade routes of the fabled spice and silk trading between East and West, so that it became known to history by various names such as Bharakuccha, Bhrigu Kaksha (the domain of Bhrigu, an ancient Indian sage), Bhroach, as well as Bhrauch.

History

Bharuch was once but a small village on the banks of the Narmada River but that rivers inland access to central and northern India and with a location in the sheltered Gulf of Khambat in the era of coastal sea travel grew and prospered as a trading transshipment centre and ship building port. Until very modern times the only effective way to move goods was by water transport, and Baruch had sheltered waters in a era without weather forecasting, compasses, and when shipping was necessarily limited to coastal navigation, and the general East-West course of the Narmada gave access to the rich inland empires at the upper reaches of the Narmada, including easy caravan access to the Ganges valley and Delhi plain.

Certainly by the 500s BC, the city was known (at least by reputation, via land-sea routes reaching the Levant) to the Arab and Ethiopian traders feeding goods westwards to the Egyptians, Greeks, Persians, Western Romans, Carthaginians, and eventually, the Eastern Roman Empires, and the Republic of Venice. It is likely even the Phonecians knew of it and so it has acted since antiquity as a link port to the luxury goods trade from the Far East and the interior of the Indian subcontinent to the civilizations of South-west Asia, the Middle-East, the Mediterranean basin including Northern Africa and Europe.

Mythological History

It was considered to be sacred among sages, and they would come to Bharuch and pray. In Bharuch, the celebrated Asura king Mahabali, conducted a great sacrifice. In this sacrifice, came a Bhrahmin boy named Vamana, who interfered with the king's sacrifice and put an end to his reign. A sage named Guru Shukracharya, in the lineage of Bhrigu, was the priest of king Mahabali.

Archeological History

Excavations near the banks of the river Narmada in Bharuch have revealed many archeological and architectural wonders, mostly temples. Later Bharuch was part of the Mauryas (322-185 BC), the Western Satraps and the Guptas. As part of the Sultanate of Gujarat, it was subsequently annexed by the Mughals, and finally by the British. It is also situated near a small village called halderva where two islamic priests were found performing miricles.

It was known to Europeans as Barigaza (Greek) and probably had a settlement of Greek traders. It is mentioned extensively as a major trading partner of the Roman world, in the 1st century Periplus of the Erythraean Sea. The Periplus describes numerous Greek buildings and fortifications in Bharuch, although mistakenly attributing them to Alexander the Great (who never went this far south), as well as the circulation of Indo-Greek coinage in the region:

"The metropolis of this country is Minnagara, from which much cotton cloth is brought down to Barygaza. In these places there remain even to the present time signs of the expedition of Alexander, such as ancient shrines, walls of forts and great wells." Periplus, Chap. 41.

Geography

Bharuch is located at 21.7° N 72.97° E. It has an average elevation of 15 metres (49 feet).

Commerce

Bharuch has always been prosperous because of its location on the Narmada River. Although water tends to be scarce in Gujarat, one never finds difficulty in getting water in Bharuch. As a result of this, agriculture and other linked commercial activities have flourished in Bharuch.

Bharuch is also a central stopping point for many villages spread around its boundaries such as Palej, Valan, Vareydiya, Kamboli e.t.c. People from these small villages come to Bharuch when they want to shop for new clothes, or make a major purchase. Lately a lot of retiring expatriates have been returning to Bharuch and building new houses giving the economy a boost. Modern Bharuch is one of the most heavily industrialized areas, not only in Gujarat but in India as a whole, with many large chemical plants producing fertilizers, paints, dyes, cotton, textiles, and dairy products. Bharuch has also advantage of Gujarat's biggest Liquid cargo terminal A very large plant of fertilizers, chemicals and IT Services-GNFC Ltd. Company is also located in Narmada nagar,Bharuch City since 1976.

Large multinationals like Guardian corp, videocon, China light & power, BASF, Johnson mathey, Reliance, Tata's, Aditya Birla group, Welspun Stahl,aventis,wockhardt,rallis,pfizer,ciba, L&T,bayer,glenmark,UPL, Lupin, J B Chemicals, Gujarat Fluorochmicals Ltd. Dahej (a largest manf. unit for PTFE in India) etc. have set up Mfg. Units in and around Bharuch. Preferrably the most dense district of india in industrial terms.

Demographics

As of 2001 India census, Bharuch had a population of 148,391. Males constitute 52% of the population and females 48%. Bharuch has an average literacy rate of 78%, higher than the national average of 59.5%; with male literacy of 82% and female literacy of 73%. 10% of the population is under 6 years of age.

Culture

There are many religions being followed by the people of this town. Usually there is a sense of harmony and co-existence without incident. However, there have been situations in the past in which this delicate social fabric has broken down. Today the city is considered to be a great example of communal equality.

There are various avenues for leisure time activities in Bharuch, and there are a few very good parks maintained by the municipal commission. There are river banks where people go for walks and strolls, as well as a couple of libraries and a few auditoriums. The auditoriums along with movie halls make the theatrical entertainment available in the city.

Of late there has been a boom in the retail sector in the city and there are new shopping malls and multiplexes opening up all over the place.

Wonders

- The 150-year-old Golden Bridge connects Bharuch to Ankleshwar across the Narmada River.
- The crowded but fascinating bazar of bharuch

Trivia

Bharuch is one of the Indian cities which has a Martian crater named after it. The other cities/towns are Amet, Bhor, Kakori, Poona (Pune), Rayadurg, Sandila and Wer. The Salty Peanuts of Bharuch are world famous.

Kochi

Kochi formerly known as Cochin) is a city in the Indian state of Kerala and is the commercial capital of kerala. The city is one of the principal seaports of the country and is located in the district of Ernakulam, about 220 kilometres (137 mi) north of the state capital, Thiruvananthapuram. It has an estimated population of 600,000, with an extended metropolitan population of about 1.5 million, making it the largest city in Kerala.

Since 1102 CE, Kochi was the seat of the Kingdom of Cochin, a princely state which traces its lineage to the Kulasekhara empire. Heralded as the Queen of the Arabian Sea, Kochi was an important spice trading centre on the Arabian Sea coast from the 14th century onwards. Ancient travellers and tradesmen referred to Kochi in their writings, variously alluding to it as Cocym, Cochym, Cochin, and Cochi. Occupied by the Portuguese in 1503, Kochi was the site of the first European colonial settlement in India. It remained the capital of Portuguese India until 1530, when Goa became the capital. The city was later occupied by the Dutch, the Mysore and the British. Kochi was the first princely state to willingly join the Indian Union, when India gained independence in 1947.

Kochi experienced decades of economic stagnation from independence until 2003, when it entered a period of economic growth, leading to a spurt in the city's development. A growing centre of information technology, tourism and international trade, Kochi is the commercial hub of Kerala, and one of the fastest growing second-tier metros in India. Like other large cities in the developing world, Kochi continues to struggle with urbanisation problems such as traffic congestion and environmental degradation.

Successive waves of migration over the course of several millennia have made Kochi a cultural melting pot. Despite the risk of overdevelopment, the city retains its distinct colonial heritage and a blend of tradition and modernity.

Name

Theories regarding the etymology of the name "Kochi" are disputed. One suggests that the city's modern name is derived from the Malayalam word koch azhi, meaning 'small lagoon'. Another version mentions the name as derivative of the Sanskrit word Go shree which means 'prosperous with cows'. Certain ancient texts refer to the city Balapuri (Sanskrit for 'small town'), which became Cochin in course of time. According to some accounts, traders from the court of the Chinese ruler Khubilai Khan gave Cochin the name of their homeland. Yet another theory is that Kochi is derived from the word Kaci meaning 'harbour'. Certain scholars claim that Cochin is derived from the term Cocha, which is a transfiguration of the Biblical term Cohen. Accounts by Italian explorers Nicolo Conti (15th century), and Fra Paoline in the 17th century say that it was called Kochchi, named after the river connecting the backwaters to the sea.

After the arrival of the Portuguese, and later the British, the name Cochin stuck as the official appellation. The city reverted to a closer anglicisation of its original Malayalam name, Kochi, in 1996. However, it is still widely referred to as Cochin.

History

Kochi was the centre of Indian spice trade for many centuries, and was known to the Yavanas (Greeks) as well as Romans, Jews, Arabs, and Chinese since ancient times. Kochi rose to significance as a trading centre after the port at Kodungallur (Cranganore) was destroyed by massive flooding of the river Periyar in 1341. The earliest documented references to Kochi occur in books written by Chinese voyager Ma Huan during his visit to Kochi in the 15th century as part of Admiral Zheng He's treasure fleet. There are also references to Kochi in accounts written by Italian traveller Niccolò Da Conti, who visited Kochi in 1440.

The Kingdom of Kochi came into existence in 1102, after the fall of the Kulasekhara empire. The King of Kochi had authority over the region encompassing the present city of Kochi and adjoining areas. The reign was hereditary, and the family that ruled over Kochi was known as the Cochin Royal Family (Perumpadappu Swaroopam in the local vernacular). The mainland Kochi remained the capital of the princely state since the 18th century. However, during much of this time, the kingdom was under foreign rule, and the King often only had titular privileges.

Fort Kochi in Kochi was the first European colonial settlement in India. From 1503 to 1663, Fort Kochi was ruled by Portugal. This Portuguese period was difficult for the Jews installed in the region, since the Inquisition was active in

Portuguese India. Kochi hosted the grave of Vasco da Gama, the first European explorer to set sail for India, who was buried at St. Francis Church until his remains were returned to Portugal in 1539. The Portuguese rule was followed by that of the Dutch, who had allied with the Zamorins in order to conquer Kochi. By 1773, the Mysore King Hyder Ali extended his conquest in the Malabar region to Kochi forcing it to become a tributary of Mysore. The hereditary Prime Ministership of Kochi held by the Paliath Achans came to an end during this period.

Meanwhile, the Dutch, fearing an outbreak of war on the United Provinces signed a treaty with the United Kingdom, under which Kochi was ceded to the United Kingdom in exchange for the island of Bangka. However, there are evidences of English habitation in the region even prior to the signing of the treaty. In 1866, Fort Kochi became a municipality, and its first Municipal Council election was conducted in 1883. The Maharaja of Cochin, who ruled under the British, in 1896 initiated local administration by forming town councils in Mattancherry and Ernakulam. In 1925, Kochi legislative assembly was constituted due to public pressure on the state.

Towards the early 20th century, trade at the port had increased substantially, and the need to develop the port was greatly felt. Harbour engineer Robert Bristow was brought to Kochi in 1920 under the direction of Lord Willingdon, then the Governor of Madras. In a span of 21 years, he transformed Kochi as one of the safest harbours in the peninsula, where ships berthed alongside the newly reclaimed inner harbour equipped with a long array of steam cranes.

In 1947, India gained independence from the British colonial rule. Cochin was the first princely state to join the Indian Union willingly. In 1949, Travancore-Cochin state came into being with the merger of Cochin and Travancore. The King of Travancore was the Rajpramukh of the Travancore-Cochin Union from 1949 to 1956. Travancore-Cochin, was in turn merged with the Malabar district of the Madras State. Finally, the Government of India's States Reorganisation Act (1956) inaugurated a new state-Kerala-incorporating Travancore-

Cochin (excluding the four southern Taluks which were merged with Tamil Nadu), Malabar District, and the taluk of Kasargod, South Kanara. On 9 July 1960, the Mattancherry council passed a resolution-which was forwarded to the government-requesting the formation of a municipal corporation by combining the existing municipalities of Fort Kochi, Mattancherry, and Ernakulam.

The government appointed a commission to study the feasibility of the suggested merger. Based on its report, the Kerala Legislative Assembly approved the corporation's formation. On 1 November 1967, exactly eleven years since the establishment of the state of Kerala, the corporation of Cochin came into existence.

The merger leading to the establishment of the corporation, was between the municipalities of Ernakulam, Mattancherry and Fort Kochi, along with that of the Willingdon Island, four panchayats (Palluruthy, Vennala, Vyttila and Edappally), and the small islands of Gundu and Ramanthuruth.

Kochi witnessed economic stagnation in the years following India's independence. The city's economic recovery gathered momentum after economic reforms in India introduced by the central government in the mid-1990s. Since 2000, the service sector has revitalised the city's stagnant economy. The establishment of several industrial parks based on Information technology (IT) triggered a construction and realty boom in the city. Over the years, Kochi has witnessed rapid commercialisation, and has today grown into the commercial capital of Kerala.

Geography and Climate

Kochi is located on the southwest coast of India at 9°58'N, 76°13'E, spanning an area of 94.88 square kilometres (36.63 sq. mi). The city is situated at the northern end of a peninsula, about 19 kilometres (12 mi) long and less than one mile (1.6 km) wide. To the west lies the Arabian Sea, and to the east are estuaries drained by perennial rivers originating in the Western Ghats. Much of Kochi lies at sea level, with a coastline of 48 km.

The current metropolitan limits of Kochi include the mainland Ernakulam, old Kochi, the suburbs of Edapally, Kalamassery and Kakkanad to the northeast; Tripunithura to the south east; and a group of islands closely scattered in the Vembanad Lake. Most of these islands are very small, varying in extent from six square kilometre to less than a square kilometre (1,500 to less than 250 acres).

Soil consists of sediments such as alluvium, teri's, brown sands etc. Hydromorphic saline soils are also found in the areas surrounding the backwaters. Predominant rock types found here are Archaean-basic dykes, Charnockites and Gneisses. An ecologically sensitive area, the Mangalavanam Bird Sanctuary is located in the central part of the city. It has a wide range of mangrove species and is nesting ground for a vast variety of migratóry birds. Certain species of dolphins are also present in the backwaters.

Kochi's proximity to the equator along with its coastal location results in little seasonal temperature variation, with moderate to high levels of humidity. Annual temperatures range between 20 to 35 °C (68-95 °F) with the record high being 38 °C (100 °F), and record low 17 °C (63 °F). From June through September, the south-west monsoon brings in heavy rains as Kochi lies on the windward side of the Western Ghats. From October to December, Kochi receives light rain from the northwest monsoon, as it lies on the leeward side. Average annual rainfall is 3,500 millimetres (138 in), with an annual average of 132 rainy days.

Civic Administration

The city is administered by the Kochi Corporation, headed by a mayor. For administrative purposes, the city is divided into 70 wards, from which the members of the corporation council are elected for a period of five years. The Corporation has its headquarters in Ernakulam, and zonal offices at Fort Kochi, Mattancherry, Palluruthy, Edappally, Vaduthala and Vyttila. The general administration of the city is handled by the Personnel Department and the Council Section. Other departments include that of town planning, health, engineering, revenue and accounts. The corporation is also responsible for waste disposal, sewage management and the supply of potable water, sourced from the Periyar River. Electricity is provided by the Kerala State Electricity Board.

The Greater Cochin Development Authority (GCDA) is the government agency overseeing the development of Kochi. The Kochi City Police is headed by a Police Commissioner, an Indian Police Service (IPS) officer. It comprises the traffic police, Narcotics Cell, Armed Reserve Camps, District Crime Records Bureau, Senior citizen's Cell, and a Women's Cell. It operates 19 police stations functioning under the Home Ministry of State Government. An anti-corruption branch of the Central Bureau of Investigation also operates out of the city. Kochi is the seat of the High Court of Kerala, the highest judicial body in the state. The High Court also has jurisdiction over the Union Territory of Lakshadweep.

Kochi contributes five seats to the State Assembly, and a seat to the Lok Sabha, the Lower House of the Indian Parliament.

Economy

Kochi is the economic capital of Kerala by volume of trade; though, unlike other South Indian cities, Kochi has been slow to industrialise. In recent years the city has rejuvenated from its economic stagnation and has witnessed heavy investment, thus making it one of the fastest-growing second-tier metro cities in India. The economy of the city can be classified as a business economy with emphasis on the service sector. Major business sectors include gold and textile retailing, seafood and spices exports, information technology (IT), tourism, health services, banking, shipbuilding, and the fishing industry. The economy is mostly dependent on trade and retail activities. As in most of Kerala, remittances from non-resident Indians (NRI)s is a major source of income. The city also houses Kerala's only bourse-the Cochin Stock Exchange.

Kochi is a major destination for IT and ITES companies, ranked by NASSCOM as the second-most attractive city in India for IT-based services. Availability of cheap bandwidth through undersea cables and lower operational costs compared to other major cities in India, has been to its advantage. Various technology and industrial campuses including the government promoted InfoPark, Cochin Special Economic Zone and KINFRA Export Promotion Industrial Park operate in the outskirts of the city. Several new industrial campuses for research, trade and development in biotechnology, electronic hardware and information technology are in various stages of construction in the suburbs of the city. Prominent among them are the Sobha Hi-tech city at Maradu and the SmartCity at Kakkanad, which on completion, would rank among the largest such ventures in the country. The Cochin International Airport is also in the process of setting up an aerotropolis at Nedumbasserry.

Eloor, situated 17 kilometres (10.5 mi) north of the city, is the largest industrial belt in Kerala, with more than 250 industries manufacturing a range of products including chemical and petrochemical products, pesticides, rare earth elements, rubber processing chemicals, fertilisers, zinc and chromium compounds, and leather products.

The Chinese Fishing Net-bridge in Kochi

Kochi is the headquarters of the Southern Naval Command, the primary training centre of the Indian Navy. The Cochin Shipyard in Kochi is the largest shipbuilding facility in India. The Cochin fishing harbour, located at Thoppumpady is a major fishing port in the state and supplies fish to local and export markets. To further tap the potential of the all-season deep-water harbour at Kochi, an international cruise terminal and several marinas are being constructed.

Exports and allied activities are also important contributors to the city's economy. The Cochin Port currently handles export and import of container cargo at its terminal at Willington Island. A new international container transshipment terminal-the first in the country-is being commissioned at Vallarpadam. Kochi's historical reliance on trade continues into modern times, as the city is a major exporter of spices and is home to the International Pepper Exchange, where black pepper is globally traded. The Spices Board of India is also headquartered in

Kochi. Kochi also has an oil refinery-the Kochi Refineries Limited (KRL) at Ambalamugal. Central Government establishments like the Coconut Development Board, the Coir Board and the Marine Products Export Development Authority (MPEDA) have head offices located in the city.

Transport

Public transport in the city is largely dependent on private buses. Taxis and autorickshaws (called autos) are available for hire throughout the day. Narrow roads and the mix of vastly differing types of vehicles have made traffic congestion a major problem in the city. A metro rapid transit service, intended to considerably ease congestion, is planned for the city.

Because it is one of the safest harbours in the Indian Ocean, Kochi ranks among India's major seaports. The port, administered by a statutory autonomous body known as the Cochin Port Trust, offers facilities for bunkering, handling cargo and passenger ships and storage accommodation. It also operates passenger ships to Colombo and Lakshadweep. Boat services operated by Kerala Shipping and Inland Navigation Corporation, the State Water Transport Department, and of private ownership are available from various boat jetties in the city. The junkar ferry for the transshipment of vehicles and passengers between the islands are operated between Ernakulam and Vypin, and between Vypin and Fort Kochi. However, with the construction of the Goshree bridges (which links Kochi's islands), ferry transport has become less essential.

The Cochin International Airport, which is about 25 kilometres (15 mi) north of the city, handles both domestic and international flights. It is the largest airport of Kerala, and one of the busiest in India. It is the first international airport in India to be built without Central Government funds. An airport run by the Navy also operates in the city. A third airport, for use by the Indian Coast Guard, is under construction in the suburbs.

There is no intra-city rail transport system in Kochi. The inter-city rail transport system in the city is administered by the Southern Railway division of the Indian Railways. There are two main railway stations-the Ernakulam Junction and the Ernakulam Town (locally known as the 'South' and 'North' railway stations respectively). The railway line connecting these two stations cuts the city longitudinally in two, with two narrow bridges connecting the two halves.

Demographics

As of 2001, Kochi had a population of 596,473, with a density of 6850.7 persons per square kilometre. Scheduled castes and tribes comprise 14.3% of the city's population. The female-to-male ratio is 1,024:1,000, significantly higher than the all-India average of 933:1,000. Kochi's literacy rate is 94.3%. The female literacy rate lags that of males by 1.1%, amongst the lowest such gaps in India.

Kochi's major religions are Hinduism, Christianity, and Islam; Jainism, Judaism, Sikhism, and Buddhism have smaller followings. Though 47% practise Hinduism, Christianity's large following (35%) makes Kochi a city with one of the largest Christian populations in India. The majority of residents are Malayalis; however, there are significant ethnic minority communities including Tamils, Gujaratis, Jews, Sikkimese, Anglo-Indians, Konkanis, and Tulus. Malayalam is the main language of communication and medium of instruction, although English is more commonly used in business circles. Hindi and Tamil are widely understood-albeit rarely spoken.

Like other fast-growing cities in the developing world, Kochi suffers from major urbanisation problems, poor sanitation, and unemployment. The city registered an increase of 9.7% in its unemployment rate from 14.8% in 1998 to 24.5% in 2003. Shortage of potable water is a major concern in the city. The situation is aggravated by the threat posed by pollution in industrial areas. The city also has a growing slum-dwelling population. Kochi has a high suicide rate with 32 suicides per lakh, which is three times higher than the national average of 11.2 per lakh. According to the National Crime Records Bureau, Kochi has one of highest rates of crime in India-498.6, against the national average of 287.3. However, a survey conducted by The Week, found Kochi to be the safest city in India for women.

Culture

As a result of successive waves of migration over the course of several centuries, the population of the city is a mix of people from all parts of Kerala and most of India. The pan-Indian nature is highlighted by the substantial presence of various ethnic communities from different parts of the country. Kochi has a diverse, multicultural, and secular community consisting of Hindus, Christians, Muslims, Jains, Sikhs, and Buddhists among other denominations, all living in peaceful co-existence.

The city once had a large Jewish community, known as the Malabar Yehuden-and now increasingly as Cochin Jews-that figured prominently in Kochi's business and economic strata. The Syro-Malabar Church, one of the 22 sui iuris Eastern Catholic Churches, has its seat at Ernakulam. Appropriate to its multi-ethnic composition, Kochi celebrates traditional Kerala festivals like Onam and Vishu along with North Indian Hindu festivals like Holi and Diwali with great fervour. Christian and Islamic festivals like Christmas, Easter, Eid ul-Fitr and Milad-e-sherif are also celebrated. A merry making fest called the Cochin Carnival is celebrated at Fort Kochi during the last ten days of December.

Residents of Kochi are known as Kochiites; they are an important part of the South Indian weltanschauung. However, the city's culture is rapidly evolving, with Kochiites generally becoming more cosmopolitan in their outlook. The people are also increasingly fashion-conscious, often deviating from the traditional Kerala wear to western clothing.

Kochiites generally partake of Keralite cuisine, which is generally characterised by an abundance of coconut and spices. Other South Indian cuisines, as well as Chinese and North Indian cuisines are popular. Fast food culture is also very prominent.

Kochi was home to some of the most influential figures in Malayalam literature, including Changampuzha Krishna Pillai, Kesari Balakrishna Pillai, G. Sankara Kurup, and Vyloppilli Sreedhara Menon. Prominent social reformers such as Sahodaran Ayyappan and Pandit Karuppan also are from Kochi.

Kochiites are known for their enthusiasm in sports, especially cricket and football. The Jawaharlal Nehru International Stadium in Kochi is one of the largest multi-use stadiums in India. The Regional Sports Centre is an important centre of sporting activity in the city.

Education

Schools and colleges in the city are either run by the government or by private trusts and individuals. The schools are each affiliated with either the Indian Certificate of Secondary Education (ICSE), the Central Board for Secondary Education (CBSE), or the Kerala State Education Board. English is the medium of instruction in most private schools; though government run schools offer both English and Malayalam. After completing their secondary education, which involves ten years of schooling, students typically enrol at Higher Secondary School in one of the three streams-Arts, Commerce or Science. Upon completing the required coursework, the student can enroll in general or professional degree programmes.

The Cochin University is situated in the city. Most of the colleges offering tertiary education are affiliated either with the Mahatma Gandhi University or the Cochin University. Other national educational institutes include the Central Institute of Fisheries Nautical and Engineering Training, the National University of Advanced Legal Studies, the National Institute of Oceanography and the Central Marine Fisheries Research Institute.

Lothal

Lothal was one of the most prominent cities of the ancient Indus valley civilization. Located in the modern state of Gujarat and dating from 2400 BC, it is one of India's most important archaeological site that dates from that era. Discovered in 1954, Lothal was excavated from February 13, 1955 to May 19, 1960 by the Archaeological Survey of India (ASI).

Lothal's dock-the world's earliest-connected the city to an ancient course of the Sabarmati river on the trade route between Harappan cities in Sindh and the peninsula of Saurashtra when the surrounding Kutch desert of today was a part of the Arabian Sea. It was a vital and thriving trade centre in ancient times, with its trade of beads, gems and valuable ornaments reaching the far corners of West Asia and Africa. Lothal's people were responsible for the earliest-known portrayals of realism in art and sculpture, telling some of the most well-known fables of today.

Its scientists used a shell compass and divided the horizon and sky into 8-12 whole parts, possibly pioneering the study of stars and advanced navigation-2000 years before the Greeks. The techniques and tools they pioneered for bead-making and in metallurgy have stood the test of time for over 4000 years.

Lothal is situated near the village of Saragwala in the Dholka taluka of Ahmedabad district. It is at a distance of six kilometres (south-east) from the Lothal-Bhurkhi railway station on the Ahmedabad-Bhavnagar railway line. It is also connected by all-weather roads to the cities of Ahmedabad (85 km/53 mi), Bhavnagar, Rajkot and Dholka. Nearest cities are Dholka and Bagodara. Resuming excavation in 1961, archaeologists unearthed trenches sunk on the northern, eastern and western flanks of the mound, bringing to light the inlet channels and nullah ("ravine", or "gully") connecting the dock with the river. The findings consist of a mound, a township, a marketplace and the dock. Adjacent to the excavated areas stands the Archaeological Museum, where some of the most prominent collections of Indus-era antiquities in modern India are displayed.

Archaeology

The meaning of Lothal (a combination of Loth and (s) thal) in Gujarati to be the "the mound of the dead" is not unusual, as the name of the city of Mohanjodaro in Sindhi means the same. People in villages neighbouring to Lothal had known of the presence of an ancient town and human remains. As recently as 1850, boats sailed up to the mound, and timber was shipped in 1942 from Broach to Saragwala via the mound. A silted creek connecting modern Bholad with Lothal and Saragwala represents the ancient flow channel of a river or creek. When

India was partitioned in 1947, most of the sites, including Mohanjodaro and Harappa, came to be located in the state of Pakistan. The Archaeological Survey of India undertook a new programme of exploration, and excavated many sites across Gujarat. Between 1954 and 1958, more than 50 sites were excavated in the Kutch (see also Dholavira), and Saurashtra peninsulas, extending the limits of Harappan civilization by 500 kilometres (310 mi) to the river Kim, where the Bhagatrav site accesses the valley of the rivers Narmada and Tapti. Lothal stands 270 kilometres (170 mi) from Mohanjodaro, which is in Sindh.

It has also been speculated that owing to the comparatively small dimensions of the main city, Lothal was not a large settlement at all, and its "dock" was perhaps an irrigation tank. However, the ASI and other contemporary archaeologists assert that the city was a part of a major river system on the trade route of the ancient peoples from Sindh to Saurashtra in Gujarat. Cemeteries have been found which indicate that its people were probably of Dravidian, Proto-Australoid or Mediterranean physiques. Lothal provides with the largest collection of antiquities in the archaeology of modern India. It is essentially a single culture site-the Harappan culture in all its variances is evidenced. An indigenous micaceous Red Ware culture also existed, which is believed to be autochthonous and pre-Harappan. Two sub-periods of Harappan culture are distinguished: the same period (between 2400 and 1900 BC) is identical to the exuberant culture of Harappa and Mohanjodaro.

To the northwest of Lothal lies the Kutch { see also Dholavira}peninsula, which was a part of the Arabian Sea until very recently in history. Owing to this, and the proximity of the Gulf of Khambat, Lothal's river provided direct access to sea routes. Although now sealed off from the sea, Lothal's topography and geology reflects its maritime past.

After the core of the Indus civilization had decayed in Mohanjodaro and Harappa, Lothal seems not only to have survived but to have thrived for many years. But its constant threats, tropical storms and floods, caused immense destruction, which destabilised the culture and ultimately caused its end.

Topographical analysis also shows signs that at about the time of its demise, the region suffered from aridity or weakened monsoon rainfall.

Thus the cause for the abandonment of the city may have been changes in the climate as well as natural disasters, as suggested by environmental magnetic records. Lothal is based upon a mound that was a salt marsh inundated by tide. Remote sensing and topographical studies published by Indian scientists in the Journal of the Indian Geophysicists Union in 2004 revealed an ancient, meandering river adjacent to Lothal, 30 kilometres (19 mi) in length according to satellite imagery-an ancient extension of the northern river channel bed of a tributary of the Bhogavo river.

Small channel widths (10-300 m/30-1000 ft) when compared to the lower reaches (1.2-1.6 km/0.75-1.0 mi) suggest the presence of a strong tidal influence upon the city-tidal waters ingressed up to and beyond the city. Upstream elements of this river provided a suitable source of freshwater for the inhabitants.

History

Before the arrival of Harappan people (c. 2400 BC), Lothal was a small village next to the river providing access to the mainland from the Gulf of Khambhat. The indigenous peoples maintained a prosperous economy, attested by the discovery of copper objects, beads and semi-precious stones. Ceramic wares were of fine clay and smooth, micaceous red surface. A new technique of firing pottery under partly-oxidising and reducing conditions was improved by them-designated black-and-red ware, to the micaceous Red Ware. Harappans were attracted to Lothal for its sheltered harbour, rich cotton and rice-growing environment and bead-making industry.

The beads and gems of Lothal were in great demand in the west. The settlers lived peacefully with the Red Ware people, who adopted their lifestyle-evidenced from the flourishing trade and changing working techniques-Harappans began producing the indigenous ceramic goods, adopting the manner from the natives.

Town Planning

A flood destroyed village foundations and settlements (c. 2350 BC). Harappans based around Lothal and from Sindh took this opportunity to expand their settlement and create a planned township on the lines of greater cities in the Indus valley. Lothal planners engaged themselves to protect the area from consistent floods. The town was divided into blocks of 1-2-metre-high (3-6 ft) platforms of sun-dried bricks, each serving 20-30 houses of thick mud and brick walls.

The city was divided into a citadel, or acropolis and a lower town. The rulers of the town lived in the acropolis, which featured paved baths, underground and surface drains (built of kiln-fired bricks) and a potable water well. The lower town was subdivided into two sectors-the north-south arterial street was the main commercial area-flanked by shops of rich and ordinary merchants and craftsmen. The residential area was located to either side of the marketplace. The lower town was also periodically enlarged during Lothal's years of prosperity.

Lothal engineers accorded high priority to the creation of a dockyard and a warehouse to serve the purposes of naval trade. While the consensus view amongst archaeologists identifies this structure as a "dockyard," it has also been suggested that owing to small dimensions, this basin may have been an irrigation tank and canal.

The dock was built on the eastern flank of the town, and is regarded by archaeologists as an engineering feat of the highest order. It was located away from the main current of the river to avoid silting, but provided access to ships in high tide as well. The warehouse was built close to the acropolis on a 3.5-metre-high (10.5 ft) podium of mud bricks.

The rulers could thus supervise the activity on the dock and warehouse simultaneously. Facilitating the movement of cargo was a mud-brick wharf, 220 metres (720 ft) long, built on the western arm of the dock, with a ramp leading to the warehouse. There was an important public building opposite to the warehouse whose superstructure has completely disappeared. Throughout their time, the city had to brace itself through multiple floods and storms. Dock and city peripheral walls were maintained efficiently. The town's zealous rebuilding ensured the growth and prosperity of the trade. However, with rising prosperity, Lothal's people failed to upkeep their walls and dock facilities, possibly as a result of over-confidence in their systems. A flood of moderate intensity in 2050 BC exposed some serious weaknesses in the structure, but the problems were not addressed properly.

Economy and Urban Culture

The uniform organization of the town and its institutions give evidence that the Harappans were a very disciplined people. Commerce and administrative duties were performed according to standards laid out. Municipal administration was strict-the width of most streets remained the same over a long time, and no encroached structures were built. Householders possessed a sump, or collection chamber to deposit solid waste in order to prevent the clogging of city drains.

Drains, manholes and cesspools kept the city clean and deposited the waste in the river, which was washed out during high tide. A new provincial style of Harappan art and painting was pioneered-new approaches included realistic portrayals of animals in their natural surroundings, including the portrayal of stories and folklore. Fire-altars were built in public places. Metalware, gold and jewellery and tastefully decorated ornaments attest to the culture and prosperity of the people of Lothal.

Most of their equipment-metal tools, weights, measures, seals, earthenware and ornaments-were of the uniform standard and quality found across the Indus civilization. Lothal was a major trade centre, importing en masse raw materials like copper, chert and semi-precious stones from Mohenjo-daro and Harappa, and mass distributing to inner villages and towns. It also produced large quantities of bronze celts, fish-hooks, chisels, spears and ornaments. Lothal exported its beads, gemstones, ivory and shells.

The stone blade industry catered to domestic needs-fine chert was imported from the Sukkur valley or from Bijapur in modern Karnataka. Bhagatrav supplied semi-precious stones while chank shell came from Dholavira and Bet Dwarka. An intensive trade network gave the inhabitants great prosperity-it stretched across the frontiers to Egypt, Bahrain and Sumer.

Declining Years

While the wider debate over the end of Indus civilization continues, archaeological evidence gathered by the ASI appears to point to natural catastrophes, specifically floods and storms as the source of Lothal's downfall. A powerful flood submerged the town and destroyed most of the houses, with the walls and platforms heavily damaged. The acropolis and the residence of the ruler were levelled (2000-1900 BC), and inhabited by common tradesmen and newly built makeshift houses. The worst consequence was the shift in the course of the river, cutting off access to the ships and dock. Despite the ruler leaving the city, the leaderless people built a new but shallow inlet to connect the flow channel to the dock for sluicing small ships into the basin.

Large ships were moored away. Houses were rebuilt, yet without removal of flood debris, which made them poor-quality and susceptible to further damage. Public drains were replaced by soakage jars. The citizens did not undertake encroachments, and rebuilt public baths and maintained fire worship. However, with a poorly organised government, and no outside agency or central government, the public works could not be properly repaired or maintained. The heavily damaged warehouse was never repaired properly, and stocks were stored in wooden canopies, exposed to floods and fire.

The economy of the city was transformed. Trade volumes reduced greatly, though not catastrophically, and resources were available in lesser quantities. Independent businesses caved, allowing a merchant-centric system of factories to develop where hundreds of craftsmen worked for the same supplier and financier.

The bead factory had ten living rooms and a large workplace courtyard. The coppersmith's workshop had five furnaces and paved sinks to enable multiple artisans to work.

The declining prosperity of the town, paucity of resources and poor administration increased the woes of a people pressured by consistent floods and storms. Increased salinity of soil made the land inhospitable to life, including crops. This is evidenced in adjacent cities of Rangpur, Rojdi, Rupar and Harappa in Punjab, Mohenjo-daro and Chanhudaro in Sindh. A massive flood (c. 1900 BC) completely destroyed the flagging township in a single stroke. Archaeological analysis shows that the basin and dock were sealed with silt and debris, and the buildings razed to the ground. The flood affected the entire region of Saurashtra, Sindh and south Gujarat, and affected the upper reaches of the Indus and Sutlej, where scores of villages and townships were washed away. The population fled to inner regions.

Later Harappan Culture

Archaeological evidence shows that the site continued to be inhabited, albeit by a much smaller population devoid of urban influences. The few people who returned to Lothal could not reconstruct and repair their city, but surprisingly continued to stay and preserved religious traditions, living in poorly-built houses and reed huts. That they were the Harappan peoples is evidenced by the analyses of their remains in the cemetery. While the trade and resources of the city were almost entirely gone, the people retained several Harappan ways in writing, pottery and utensils.

About this time ASI archaeologists record a mass movement of refugees from Punjab and Sindh into Saurashtra and to the valley of Saraswati (1900-1700 BC). Hundreds of ill-equipped settlements have been attributed to this people as Late Harappans-a completely de-urbanised culture characterised by rising illiteracy, undiversified economy, unsophisticated administration and poverty.

Though Indus seals went out of use, the system of weights with an 8.573 gram (0.3024 oz) unit was retained. Between 1700 and 1600 BC, trade would revive again. In Lothal, Harappan ceramic works of bowls, dishes and jars were mass-produced. Merchants used local materials such as chalcedony instead of chert for stone blades. Truncated sandstone weights replaced hexahedron chert weights. The sophisticated writing was simplified by exempting pictorial symbols, and the painting style reduced itself to wavy lines, loops and fronds.

Civilisation

The people of Lothal made significant and often unique contributions to human civilization in the Indus era, in the fields of city planning, art, architecture, science, engineering and religion. Their work in metallurgy, seals, beads and jewellery was the basis of their prosperity.

Science and Engineering

A thick ring-like shell object found with four slits each in two margins served as a compass to measure angles on plane surfaces or in the horizon in multiples of 40 degrees, up to 360 degrees. Such shell instruments were probably invented to measure 8-12 whole sections of the horizon and sky, explaining the slits on the lower and upper margins. Archaeologists consider this as evidence that the Lothal experts had achieved something 2,000 years before the Greeks: an 8-12 fold division of horizon and sky, as well as an instrument for measuring angles and perhaps the position of stars, and for navigation.

Lothal contributes one of three measurement scales that are integrated and linear (others found in Harappa and Mohanjodaro). An ivory scale from Lothal has the smallest-known decimal divisions in Indus civilization. The scale is 6 millimetres (0.2 inches) thick, 15 mm (0.6 inches) broad and the available length is 128 mm (5.0 inches), but only 27 graduations are visible over 46 mm (1.8 inches), the distance between graduation lines being 1.70 mm (0.067 inches) (the small size indicates use for fine purposes). The sum total of ten graduations from Lothal is approximate to the angula in the Arthashastra. The Lothal craftsmen took care to ensure durability and accuracy of stone weights by blunting edges before polishing.

For their renowned draining system, Lothal engineers provided corbelled roofs, and an apron of kiln-fired bricks over the brick face of the platform where the sewerage entered the cesspool. Wooden screens inserted in grooves in the side drain walls held back solid waste. The well is built of radial bricks, 2.4 metres (7.9 ft) in diameter and 6.7 metres (22 ft) deep. It had an immaculate network of underground drains, silting chambers and cesspools, and inspection chambers for solid waste.

The extent of drains provided archaeologists with many clues regarding the layout of streets, organization of housing and baths. On average, the main sewer is 20-46 cm (7.8-18.1 inches) in depth, with outer dimensions of 86 × 68 × 33 cm (34 × 27 × 13 in). Lothal brick-makers used a logical approach in manufacture of bricks, designed with care in regards to thickness of structures. They were used as headers and stretchers in same and alternate layers. Archaeologists estimate that in most cases, the bricks were in ratio 1:0.5:0.25 on three sides, in dimensions which were integral multiples of large graduations of Lothal scale of 25 mm (1.0 in).

Religion and Disposal of the Dead

The people of Lothal worshipped a fire god, speculated to be the horned deity depicted on seals named Atha (Athar) and Arka, which is also evidenced by the presence of private and public fire-altars where sacrifices of animals and cattle were apparently conducted. Archaeologists have discovered gold pendants, charred ashes of terra-cotta cakes and pottery, bovine remains, beads and other signs that may indicate the practice of the Gavamayana sacrifice, associated with the ancient Vedic religion. Animal worship is also evidenced, but not the worship of the Mother Goddess that is evidenced in other Harappan cities-experts consider this a sign of the existence of diversity in religious traditions.

However, it is believed that a sea goddess, perhaps cognate with the general Indus-era Mother Goddess, was worshipped. Today, the local villagers likewise worship a sea goddess, Vanuvati Sikotarimata, suggesting a connection with the ancient port's traditions and historical past as an access to the sea. But the archaeologists also discovered that the practice had been given up by 2000 BC (determined by the difference in burial times of the carbon-dated remains). It is suggested that the practice occurred only on occasion. It is also considered that given the small number of graves discovered-only 17 in an estimated population of 15,000-the citizens of Lothal also practised cremation of the dead. Post-cremation burials have been noted in other Indus sites like Harappa, Mehi and Damb-Bhuti. The mummified remains of an Assyrian and an Egyptian corpse were also discovered at the mound.

Metallurgy and Jewellery

Lothali copper is unusually pure, lacking the arsenic typically used by coppersmiths across the rest of the Indus valley. The city imported ingots from probable sources in the Arabian peninsula. Workers mixed tin with copper for the manufacture of celts, arrowheads, fishhooks, chisels, bangles, rings, drills and spearheads, although weapon manufacturing was minor. They also employed advanced metallurgy in following the cire perdue technique of casting, and used more than one-piece moulds for casting birds and animals. They also invented new tools such as curved saws and twisted drills unknown to other civilizations at the time.

Lothal was one of the most important centres of production for shell-working, owing to the abundance of chank shell of high quality found in the Gulf of Kutch and near the Kathiawar coast Gamesmen, beads, unguent vessels, chank shells, ladles and inlays were made for export and local consumption. Components of stringed musical instruments like the plectrum and the bridge were made of shell. An ivory workshop was operated under strict official supervision, and the domestication of elephants has been suggested.

An ivory seal, and sawn pieces for boxes, combs, rods, inlays and ear-studs were found during excavations. Lothal produced a large quantity of gold ornaments-the most attractive item being microbeads of gold in five strands in necklaces, unique for being less than 0.25 millimetres (0.010 inches) in diameter. Cylindrical, globular and jasper beads of gold with edges at right angles resemble modern pendants used by women in Gujarat in plaits of hair. A large disc with holes recovered from a sacrificial altar is compared to the rukma worn by Vedic priests. Studs, cogwheel and heart-shaped ornaments of fainence and steatite were popular in Lothal. A ring of thin copper wire turned into double spirals resembles the gold-wire rings used by modern Hindus for weddings.

Art

The discovery of etched carnelian beads and non-etched barrel beads in Kish and Ur (modern Iraq), Jalalabad (Afghanistan) and Susa (Iran) attest to the popularity of the Lothal-centric bead industry across West Asia. The lapidaries show a refined taste in selecting stones of variegated colours, producing beads of different shapes and sizes. The methods of Lothal bead-makers were so advanced that no improvements have been noted over 4,000 years-modern makers in the Khambhat area follow the same technique. Double-eye beads of agate and collared or gold-capped beads of jasper and carnelian beads are among those attributed as uniquely from Lothal. It was very famous for micro-cylindrical beads of steatite (chlorite).

Lothal has yielded 213 seals, third in importance amongst all Indus sites, considered masterpieces of glyptic art and calligraphy. Seal-cutters preferred short-horned bulls, mountain goats, tigers and composite animals like the elephant-bull for engravings. There is a short inscription of intaglio in almost every seal. Stamp seals with copper rings inserted in a perforated button were used to sealing cargo, with impressions of packing materials like mats, twisted cloth and cords-a fact verified only at Lothal. Quantitative descriptions, seals of rulers and owners were stamped on goods. A unique seal found here is from Bahrain-circular, with motif of a dragon flanked by jumping gazelles.

Lothal offers two new types of potter work-a convex bowl with or without stud handle, and a small jar with flaring rim, both in the micaceous Red Ware period-not found in contemporary Indus cultures. Lothal artists introduced a new form of painting closely linked to modern realism. Paintings depict animals in their natural surroundings. Indeed, upon one large vessel, the artist depicts birds-with fish in their beaks-resting in a tree, while a fox-like animal stands below. This scene bears resemblance to the story of the crow and cunning fox in Panchatantra. Artistic imagination is also suggested via careful portrayals-for example, several birds with legs aloft in the sky suggest flight, while half-opened wings suggest imminent flight.

On a miniature jar, the story of the thirsty crow and deer is depicted-of how the deer could not drink from the narrow-mouth of the jar, while the crow succeeded by dropping stones in the jar. The features of the animals are clear and graceful. Movements and emotions are suggested by the positioning of limbs and facial features-in a 15 × 5 cm (6 × 2 in) jar without overcrowding.

A complete set of terra-cotta gamesmen, comparable to modern chessmen, has been found in Lothal-animal figures, pyramids with ivory handles and castle-like objects (similar to the chess set of Queen Hatshepsut in Egypt). The realistic portrayal of human beings and animals suggests a careful study of anatomical and natural features. The bust of a male with slit eyes, sharp nose and square-cut beard is reminiscent of Sumerian figures, especially stone sculptures from Mari. In images of men and women, muscular and physical features are sharp, prominently marked. Terra-cotta models also identify the differences between species of dogs and bulls, including those of horses. Animal figures with wheels and a movable head were used as toys.

Excavated Lothal

On plan, Lothal stands 285 metres (935 ft) north-to-south and 228 metres (748 ft) east-to-west. At the height of its habitation, it covered a wider area since remains have been found 300 metres (1000 ft) south of the mound. Due to the fragile nature of unbaked bricks and frequent floods, the superstructures of all buildings have receded. Dwarfed walls, platforms, wells, drains, baths and paved floors are visible. But thanks to the loam deposited by persistent floods, the dock walls were preserved beyond the great deluge (c. 1900 BC). The absence of standing high walls is attributed to erosion and brick robbery. The ancient nullah, the inlet channel and riverbed have been similarly covered up. The flood-damaged peripheral wall of mud-bricks is visible near the warehouse area. The remnants of the north-south sewer are burnt bricks in the cesspool. Cubical blocks of the warehouse on a high platform are also visible.

The ASI has covered the peripheral walls, the wharf and many houses of the early phase with earth to protect from natural phenomena, but the entire archaeological site is nevertheless facing grave concerns about necessary preservation. Salinity ingress and prolonged exposure to the rain and sun are gradually eating away the remains of the site. But there are no barricades to prevent the stream of visitors from trudging on the delicate brick and mud work. Stray dogs throng the mound unhindered.

Heavy rain in the region has damaged the remains of the sun-dried mud brick constructions. Stagnant rain water has lathered the brick and mud work with layers of moss. Due to siltation, the dockyard's draft has been reduced by 3-4 metres (10-13 ft) and saline deposits are decaying the bricks. Officials blame the salinity on capillary action and point out that cracks are emerging and foundations weakening even as restoration work slowly progresses.

Dock and Warehouse

The dock was located away from the main current to avoid deposition of silt. Modern oceanographers have observed that the Harappans must have possessed great knowledge relating to tides in order to build such a dock on the ever-shifting course of the Sabarmati, as well as exemplary hydrography and maritime engineering. This was the earliest known dock found in the world, equipped to berth and service ships. It is speculated that Lothal engineers studied tidal movements, and their effects on brick-built structures, since the walls are of kiln-burnt bricks.

This knowledge also enabled them to select Lothal's location in the first place, as the Gulf of Khambhat has the highest tidal amplitude and ships can be sluiced through flow tides in the river estuary. The engineers built a trapezoidal structure, with north-south arms of average 21.8 metres (71.5 ft), and east-west arms of 37 metres (121 ft). Another assessment is that the basin could have served as an irrigation tank, for the estimated original dimensions of the "dock" are not large enough, by modern standards, to house ships and conduct much traffic.

The original height of the embankments was 4.26 metres (13.98 ft). (Now it is 3.35 metres (10.99 ft).) The main inlet is 12.8 metres (42.0 ft) wide, and another is provided on the opposite side. To counter the thrust of water, offsets were provided on the outer wall faces. When the river changed its course in 2000 BC, a smaller inlet, 7 metres (23 ft) wide was made in the longer arm, connected to the river by a 2 kilometre (3.2 mi) channel. At high tide a flow of 2.1-2.4 metres (6.9-7.9 ft) of water would have allowed ships to enter. Provision was made for the escape of excess water through the outlet channel, 96.5 metres (317 ft) wide and 1.7 metres (5.6 ft) high in the southern arm.

The dock also possessed a lock-gate system-a wooden door could be lowered at the mouth of the outlet to retain a minimum column of water in the basin so as to ensure floatation at low tides. Central to the city's economy, the warehouse was originally built on sixty-four cubical blocks, 3.6 metres (11.8 ft) square, with 1.2-metre (3.9-ft) passages, and based on a 3.5-metre-high (11.5 ft) mud-brick podium. The pedestal was very high to provide maximum protection from floods. Brick-paved passages between blocks served as vents, and a direct ramp led to the dock to facilitate loading. The warehouse was located close to the acropolis, to allow tight supervision by ruling authorities. Despite elaborate precautions, the major floods that brought the city's decline destroyed all but twelve blocks, which became the make-shift storehouse.

Acropolis and Lower Town

Lothal's acropolis was the town centre, its political and commercial heart, measuring 127.4 metres (418 ft) east-to-west by 60.9 metres (200 ft) north-to-south. Apart from the warehouse, it was the residence of the ruling class. There were three streets and two lanes running east-west, and two streets running north-south. The four sides of the rectangular platform on which houses were built are formed by mud-brick structures of 12.2-24.4 metre (40-80 ft) thickness and 2.1-3.6 metres (6.9-11.8 ft) high. The baths were primarily located in the acropolis-mostly two-roomed houses with open courtyards. The bricks used for paving baths were polished to prevent seepage. The pavements were lime-plastered and edges were wainscoted (wooden panels) by thin walls.

The ruler's residence is 43.92 square metres (472.8 sq. ft) in area with a 1.8-square-meter-bath (19 sq. ft) equipped with an outlet and inlet. The remains of this house give evidence to a sophisticated drainage system. The Lower town marketplace was on the main north-south street 6-8 metres (20-26 ft) wide. Built in straight rows on either side of the street are residences and workshops, although brick-built drains and early period housing has disappeared. The street maintained a uniform width and did not undergo encroachment during the reconstructive periods after deluges. There are multiple two-roomed shops and workplaces of coppersmiths and blacksmiths.

The bead factory, which performs a very important economic function, possesses a central courtyard and eleven rooms, a store and a guardhouse. There is a cinder dump, as well as a double-chambered circular kiln, with stoke-holes for fuel supply. Four flues are connected with each other, the upper chamber and the stoke hold. The mud plaster of the floors and walls are vitrified owing to intense heat during work.

The remnants of raw materials such as reed, cow dung, sawdust and agate are found, giving archaeologists hints of how the kiln was operated. A large mud-brick building faces the factory, and its significance is noted by its plan. Four large rooms and a hall, with an overall measurement of 17.1 × 12.8 metres (56 × 42 ft). The hall has a large doorway, and a fire-altar is posed on a raised floor in the southern corner of the building. A square terra-cotta stump in the centre is associated with the place of worship found in the sister site of Kalibangan (in Rajasthan), making this a primary centre of worship for Lothal's people.

Machilipatnam

Machilipatnam pronunciation (help·info), also known as Masulipatnam or Bandar or Masula (for short among Finnish mission workers), is a city and a special grade municipality in Krishna district in the Indian state of Andhra Pradesh. The town existed since 3rd century BC(Satavahana period) when it was known as 'Maisolos' (Ptolemy) and as 'Masalia' (Periplus). Flourishing sea trade was carried out from Masula port. The port is located on the southeastern or Coromandel Coast of India. Situated on one of the mouths of the river Krishna at the Bay of Bengal, Machilipatnam is the administrative centre of Krishna District in the state of Andhra Pradesh. It was a 17th century port for French, British and Dutch trade. It has a medium fishing harbour which can accommodate 350 fishing vessels; has a carpet-weaving industry; other products include rice, oilseeds and scientific instruments. This town is a railway terminus and an educational centre. Machilipatnam is known for its Kalamkari textiles and paintings created using vegetable dyes. As a kalam (pen) is used in the technique of painting, it was named "Kalamkari Painting". During the 17th century, western traders were attracted by this art. The city is also well-known for its sweet dish called Bandar Laddu.

The Andhra Pradesh coast between Ongole and Machilipatnam is most vulnerable to high surges due to cyclones. Andhra Cyclone of 14-20 November, 1977 that crossed the coast near Nizampatnam took a toll of about 10,000 lives. As the storm approached the coast, gale winds reaching 200 km/h lashed Prakasam, Guntur, Krishna, East Godavari and West Godavari districts. Storm surge, 5 meters high, inundated Krishna estuary and the coast south of Machilipatnam. The 2004 Tsunami affected many fishing villages around Machilipatnam. The Government and the NGOs are involved in rebuilding and reconstruction of the devastated villages.

History

Machilipatnam was a flourishing seaport on the east coast during the time of the Satavahanas. Periplus mentioned that a great quantity of muslins are made in Masalia. The word 'muslin' originated from the name 'Masalia'. In the 17th century CE, the port was a centre of French, British and Dutch trade. It is one of the earliest known British settlements in the subcontinent of India, its importance being due to the fact that it was the major port of Golconda kingdom. It was the British East India Company's first trading post on the coromandel coast. An agency was established there in 1611 CE.

During the wars of the Carnatic, the English were temporarily expelled from the town, which was held by the French for some years. In 1759 CE the town and fort were captured by Colonel Forde, an achievement followed by the acquisition of the Northern Circars (q.v.). In 1864 a great storm-wave swept over the entire town and is said to have destroyed 30,000 lives. Machilipatnam is well known for its Kalamkari painting.

The art flourished during the reign of Qutub Shahis. Weavers form a large portion of the inhabitants, though their trade has greatly declined since the beginning of the 19th century. Their operations, besides weaving, include printing, bleaching, washing and dressing. In former days the chintzes of Masulipatam had a great reputation abroad for the freshness and permanency of their dyes.

The port is only a roadstead, where vessels anchor 5 m. out. A branch line from Vijayawada on the Southern Mahratta railway was opened in 1908. The port of Machilipatnam today is in desperate need for modernization. It has not seen any ships in the last decade.

In its heyday, the port used to handle export of different items weighing more than 2.7 lakh tonnes and imports of 37,000 tonnes. Much needs to be done to bring the city back to its glory. In January 2006, Government of Andhra Pradesh revealed plans for reviving the Machilipatnam port at a cost of Rs. 1200 crores. It has allocated 6000 acres (24 km²) of land for the project.

Geography

Machilipatnam is located at 16.17° N 81.13° E on the southeast coast of India and in the east corner of Andhra

Pradesh. The city has an average elevation of 14 meters (45 feet).

Climate

A family waits to be evacuated outside their half-submerged hut in Machilipatnam

Machilipatnam gets annual rainfall due to the southwest monsoon. The climate is tropical in nature with hot summers and moderate winters. The hottest months are between April and June. The average normal rainfall in the district is 102 cm.

Machilipatnam is frequently hit by cyclones due to low pressure created by the southwest monsoon. On 8 December 2004, a high capacity S-Band Doppler radar meant for cyclone warning was installed, commissioned and operationalized at the city. It was purchased from a German manufacturer, Gematronik.

With the installation of the radar, the state will be better equipped to track down cyclones by the onset of monsoon, according to an official from the State Met Office talking to the The Hindu newspaper. This facility will monitor 960 km long coastline of the state.

The radar's information is posted real-time on the Indian Meteorological Department website. Similar radars were installed in other coastal cities forming a S-Band Cyclone Detection Radar Network.

Layout

For administrative purposes, Machilipatnam falls into Bandar revenue division of the Krishna District. It is a special grade municipality with 34 panchayats and 28 villages. The city area covers an area of 27 kilometers (10 miles).

Administration

It is governed by the Collector and the District Magistrate of the Krishna district.

Economy

Machilipatnam has many small scale industries.

- o Fashion Gold (also called rolled gold) ornaments are made here,famous gold covering companys are National gold,Uma gold Raja gold and etc. are the pillar of fashion gold industries in Machilipatnam.
- o Agriculture is the most important occupation, paddy being the main food crop produced.
- o Bharat Electronics Limited (BEL), a unit of the Union Defence Ministry, of Government of India, has a manufacturing unit here. BEL is involved in design, development and manufacture of sophisticated, state-of-the art electronic equipments that are used by Indian Defence Services and para military organisations.

Arts and Crafts

The Kalamkari fabrics of Machilipatnam and Kalahasti with their intricate designs, are used in clothing and wall hangings. Kalamkari refers to dye-painted cloths and the technique used to create them.

Their name derives from kalam, the Persian word for a pen-like tool used to draw outlines on the cloth, and kari (work). Fabrics are outlined with a cotton-tipped bamboo stick and dyed in vegetable or mineral colours. The process involves washing, rinsing, soaking and bleaching muslin, and applying mordants and dyes using natural substances like indigo for blue, madder for red, mango bark and dried myrobalan fruit for yellow, palm sugar and rusted iron for black.

The dyeing process is very elaborate and can take several days to complete. While some pieces are hand-drawn, large canvas and sheets are block-printed. Kalahasti is noted for its wall hangings depicting mythological tales and characters, while Machilipatnam for the block-painted large prints used for sarees.

The work done in Machilipatnam, often using block printing in conjunction with hand painting, features more decorative floral and vegetal designs that appealed to local kingdoms and to an extraordinary export trade. This culminated in European demand for Machilipatnam chintz, which derives its name from the Hindi word chint (spotted).

Kalahasti, is known for the distinctive temple hangings, chariot decorations and canopies of typically feature Hindu stories, and the images are often identified with text in Telugu, the regional language.

Demographics

As of 2001 India census, Machilipatnam had a population of 183,370.Present population(2007) rose to 205,043. Males constitute 50% of the population and females 50%. Machilipatnam has an average literacy rate of 69%, higher than the national average of 59.5%: male literacy is 73%, and female literacy is 65%. In Machilipatnam, 10% of the population is under 6 years of age.

Culture

People in Machilipatnam practice Hinduism, Islam. Hindus speak Telugu and the Muslims tend to speak Urdu. Women of all cultures and faith communities in Machilipatnam typically wear the traditional Indian dress, the sari-sometimes Shalwar Qamis.

Kuchipudi

Kuchipudi, a popular Indian Classical Dance form originated at Kuchipudi, 25 kilometers from Machilipatnam. The dance form is in practice in Machilipatnam.

Tourism

Machilipatnam is a city with a rich history of foreign conquests, business and trade. The beaches in Machilipatnam are long, broad, pristine, with pale blonde sands.

- HAZARAT SHAH SHARIF KHALANDAR RAHMATULLAH ALLAI durguh is located on kenedy road at Machilipatnam (jabbar pet),is famous in krishna dist and all Muslims & Hindus togeather celebrate sandal of HAZARAT SHAH SHARIF KHALANDAR RAHMATULLAH ALLAI on RAJJAB 19th,DURGUH has the history of 200 years & so on.
- RAHOLIA MOSQ is oldest mosq located on kenedy road at Machilipatnam (jabbar pet) is well known for

its acient beauty and also as a history of 500 years.this is the first mosq in krishna dist,Machilipatnam.

- Manginapudi Beach, a beach side fishing hamlet, located at a distance of 11 km from Machilipatnam, is well known for its scenic beauty and also as a historic port city. During its heydays this port served as a gateway to India. The beach has a natural bay with shallow waters. The unique feature of this beach is that instead of sand it contains black soil.
  - o Thousands of pilgrims take a holy dip in the sea, at the beach, during an annual Hindu festival called Khartika poornima.
  - o A full fledged dance school at the beach, offers courses that train students in the Kuchipudi, popular dance form.
  - o Carting the visitors with the old lighthouse, Dattashram on the banks of sea coast is a pilgrimage site. Dattashram has an ancient Shiva temple and Datta temple that was recently built. Manginapudi is popularly known as "Datta Rameswaram" due to the consecration of 9 wells to bath, as in Rameswaram.
- Panduranga Swamy temple at Chilakalapudi, near the city, close to the Manginapudi Beach, is a famous piligrimage site. It is a temple of Lord Vishnu, said to be similar to the temple at Pandaripur.
- Ghantasala, 21 km from Machilipatnam, it has the remains of an old Buddhist stupa.
- Agastheeswara Temple, 36 km from Machilipatnam, is a temple of Lord Shiva, a piligrimage site. Lord Shiva at this temple is called by the name, Ekaratri Mallikarjunaswamy. An annual festival is celebrated at this temple when the deities are taken out in procession.
- Gudivada, North west of Machilipatnam, visitors are attracted by the old ruins of the stupas.

Further up the coast of Machilipatnam there are five

temples dedicated to Lord Shiva. These ancient temples are located at Amravati, Samalkot, Bhimavaram, Draksharama and Chebrolu.

- Shivaganga temple is one of the oldest temples located on the Avanigadda road attracts tourists and devotees all through the year. On Shivratri major celebrations are carried out by the temple trustees.

Transport

Road Transport: Another important city in Krishna district is Vijayawada which is 65 k.m. away but because of traffic congestion it takes 2 hours by road. Even after 50 yrs of independence Machilipatnam internal roads didnt see improvement.Main Roads are Broadened in to four lanes.

Rail Transport: Machilipatnam is connected to Vijayawada,south central railway important railway station and junction that connects allover india. There are Eleven passenger trains to Vijayawada,One fast passenger to Visakhapatnam, Two Express trians to Secunderabad and Tirupathi.

Sea Transport

Development: The main problem with the town's development is the lack of it! The main reason for the backwardness of this great city could be that the next city Vijayawada became a parallal administrative centre for Krishna district and the politicians remember Machilipatnam only during elections. The people have not been given an opportunity to see and experience what the modern life has got to offer. Unfortunately the representatives (MLA, MP) chose to rule the people rather than to serve and represent them both in parliament and assembly.

Second major thrust area is shifting all the auto repair units to a centralised locality so that the main roads and other smaller roads are decongested. This because of the fact that most (99%) of these units have no garage facility to repair the automobiles brought in by the clients. Thus more often than not, the roads are used as open air garages to park, repair and to clean the vehicles. This in turn causes tremendous inconvenience to the general public and school children. Although there was an effort by Late Shri Puppala Lakshmana Rao and others to develop an Autonagar in Machilipatnam area, this had run into bad weather due to the apathy of the people's representatives.

Almost 100 acres of land had been bought and been given to APIIC (Andhra Pradesh Industrial Infrastructure Corporation). But until now, there is no development in this area.

Media

The city receives television and radio transmissions from Hyderabad and the rest of country.

All major print media are in circulation here. The major Telugu dailies include the Eenadu, Vaartha, Andhra Jyoti, Andhra Bhoomi, and Andhra Prabha. The major English dailies are The Deccan Chronicle, Business Standard, The Hindu, The Times of India, The Indian Express and The Economic Times.

The town also receives numerous channels transmitted from Bombay, Hyderabad and elsewhere. One local channels citicable also broadcasts songs and movies. However there is a pressing need for a channels which can bring awareness to the population about the problems of the town.

Education

Machilipatnam has a high literacy rate. It has public (state-run) and private-run schools.

- St. Fancis English Medicum High School-Christian missionary run school provides education from kindergarten to the higher secondary level affiliated with ICSE, New Delhi.
- HYNY High School and Elementary School, an aided school and run by missionaries from Finland. Miss A.E.Hyny is the founder of this school.
- Sri Venkateswara Public School, an affiliated institute to the Hindu College, Machilipatnam, is the only CBSE

school in the city until the Kendriya Vidyalaya came up. The School has set high standards for education by providing NCERT (central) syllabus.

- Sharon High School, provides education from kindergarten to the higher secondary level, Mrs Indira Deenabandu was the founder of this school.
- Nirmala High School, a Christian missionary run school provides education from kindergarten to the higher secondary level.
- Noble College, founded in 1843 is University Grants Commission (UGC) approved and offers graduation studies.
- Andhra Jaateeya Kalasala founded in 1910 by local freedom fighters, is University Grants Commission (UGC) approved and offers graduation studies.
- Hindu College was established in 1928. It is affiliated to Nagarjuna University and offers graduation studies. It is a University Grants Commission (UGC) approved college.
- Sri Venkateswara Hindu College Of Engineering was established in 1980. It offers engineering degrees in civil, electrical and electronics, elctronics and communication and mechanical engineering divisions and business studies.
- Viswabharati vidyalama is the oldest Telugu medium school.
- Jaihind Hind High school founded on 15 August 1947 is a famous school situated near Inugudurupet having two branches
- St. Mary's A.A.M.M High school (short for Adi Andhra Madana Mohana and also known as 'RATNA HIGH SCHOOL') is one of the oldest schools located in Machavaram area.
- Gandhi Vidyalaya is a famous school situated at Balaramunipet, Its a government aided public school.
- Anniebesant Sisu Vidya Mandiram is a famous telugu medium school situated at Edepally.

Maikala

Maikala is one of the ancient names of Mangalore, India. The Bearys of the Tulunadu refer Maikala to the city of Mangalore, which is their cultural and economical capital. The word Maikala is derived from the word Mayadevi which is a Budhist goddess.

According to historian Dr. B.A. Salethur, Maikala was an area in the southern part of Mangalore. It got its name through the Kadri Manjunath Temple, which earlier was a Buddhist temple. The Buddhist goddess Tara Bhagavathi was also known as Mayadevi. In course of time it came to be called Maikala, or Maikal. Historians conclude that Maikala is one of the ancient names of Mangalore.

Other Names

Mangalore (English), Kudla (Tulu), Kodial (Konkani), Mangalapuram (Malayalam), Mangaluru (Proposed by state government).

Porbandar

City

The name "Porbandar" came from the combination of two words: "Porai", the name of a local goddess, and "Bandar" means port or harbour. Thus, 'Porbandar' translates to 'Porai's harbour'. Several sources refer to the area as 'Pauravelakul', a name known to have been in use during the 10th century; this ancient name may possibly translate to 'land of Porai's clan' or to that effect.

The town finds mention in the Hindu epics as the hometown of Sudama, a beloved friend and class-fellow of lord Krishna; the town has also often been referred to as 'Sudamapuri' on that account.

Located in the extreme west of India, Porbandar is an important all-weather port on the Arabian sea. It supports a population (c.2001 CE) of over 150,000. Given its association with Mahatma Gandhi, Porbandar is today something of a tourist centre and is served by an airport and train line. Its deep sea port was built during the last quarter of the 20th century.

Places of Interest

- Kirti Mandir (Birthplace of Mahatma Gandhi)
- Sudama Mandir
- Nehru Planetarium
- Bharat Mandir
- Gita Mandir
- Gaytri Mandir
- Rokhadia Hanuman temple
- Sandipani Vidyaniketan
- Bird Sanctuary
- Rana Bapu's Mahal
- Chowpati
- Satyanarayan's Mandir
- Kamla Nehru park
- Sai Baba's Mandir
- Shri Hari Mandir (Courtesy: Bhaishri Rameshbhai Oza)
- Many Vandis(Community Centres)

Educational Institutions

- Arya Kanya Gurukul at Porbandar is among the most reputed educational organizations dedicated to female education in India. Unique in its way, the education system here is a blend of the rich ancient Vedic heritage and the modern educational system. It was established by Shri Nanjibhai Kalidas Mehta.
- Victoria Jubilee Madressa Boys' & Girls' High School, Porbandar... 120 years old leading educational institution was founded by Sheth Haji Abdullaha Jhaveri,(a Legendary person of Memon History) who was the founder President of Natal Indian Congress and who called Mahatma Gandhi for the first time to South Africa.(Courtesy: Faruq Suria-Hon. Secretary, V. J. Madressa Managing Committee, Porbandar)

History

Harappan Settlement (1600-1400 BC)

Onshore explorations in and around Porbandar brought to light for the first time the remains of a late Harappan settlement dating back to the 16th-14th century BC, which is similar to that from Bet Dwarka. This is another evidence to suggest that the Harappan legacy of maritime activity continued till the late Harappan period on the Saurashtra coast.

The discovery of ancient jetties along the Porbandar creek signifies the importance of Porbandar as an active centre of maritime activities in the past. This is an Darji community.

Princely Porbandar (1600 CE onwards)

Porbandar was formerly the seat of the eponymous princely state in British India. The ruling family of the state belonged to the Jethwa clan of rajputs and had been established in the area since at least the mid 16th century. The state was subordinate to the Mughal governor of Gujarat until being overrun by the marathas in the latter half of the 18th century, whereafter they came under the authority of the Gaekwad court at Baroda, and eventually of the Peshwa.

In common with the other states of Kathiawar, the state first came into the ambit of British influence in 1807, when the HEIC guaranteed security in the area in lieu of a fixed annual tribute to be paid to the Peshwa and the Gaekwad. In 1817, the Peshwa ceded his share to the HEIC; in 1820, the Gaekwad agreed to have the HIEC collect his due tributes in Kathiawar and remit the same to his treasury.

During the Raj, the state covered an area of 1,663 sq.km, encompassing 106 villages and a population, in 1921, of over 100,000 people. It enjoyed a revenue of Rs.21,00,000/-. By 1947, the rulers held the style of "Highness" and the title of "Maharaj Rana Sahib"; they were entitled to a salute of 13 guns as a hereditary distinction.

Upon the Independence of India in 1947, the state acceded unto the dominion of India. It was merged with the 'United state of Kathiawar' with effect from February 15, 1948 and eventually came to form part of the present-day state of Gujarat.

Current Situation

Despite being the birthplace of one of the most famous leaders of the world, Porbandar lacks any significant tourism infrastructure, although the area around Mahatma Gandhi's home has been renovated to become a temple of peace.

The major complaint of tourists is that the town is not known well enough, and that the bad traffic scenario means that bus journeys take many hours.

Porbandar has an excellent beach and a brilliant azure sea which could become a tourism hot spot, however the government has failed to assure cleanliness and although the ocean itself is pristine, reconstruction activities were carried on to give the chowpati (Beach) a new look by some collector in around 2003 and now it hold well arranged sitting arrangement for tourist and commuters and there is also a skating platform for children. Although the local civic body is not paying enough attention for cleanliness, their condition can be said to be better than many beaches across the country.

Ratnagiri

Ratnagiri is a city in India, located in the southwestern part of Maharashtra State on the Arabian Sea coast, in the Ratnagiri district. It forms a part of the greater tract known as Konkan. This tract is historically famous for it long coastline and convenient harbours.

The surrounding area is bordered by the Sahyadri Hills on the West; the heavy rainfall results into highly eroded landscape in the coastal region. Fertile alluvial valleys produce rice and coconut as the main crops; fruit and cashew nut cultivation is being promoted.

Ratnagiri is noted for the delicious golden Haapus (Alphonso) mangoes that are produced here.

It is here that the great freedom fighter Bal Gangadhar Tilak was born.

Geography

Ratnagiri is located at 16.98° N 73.3° E. It has an average elevation of 11 metres (36 feet).

- Climate: Tropical
- Clothing: Cotton Clothes
- Food: Rice, fish and wheat are the staple diet of the people.
- Language: The principal language is Marathi
- STD code: 02352

Demographics

As of 2001 India census, Ratnagiri had a population of 70,335. Males constitute 53% of the population and females 47%. Ratnagiri has an average literacy rate of 80%, higher than the national average of 59.5%: male literacy is 84%, and female literacy is 76%. In Ratnagiri, 11% of the population is under 6 years of age.fishing is main business in ratnagiri.

History

In 1731 it came under the control of Satara kings; in 1818 it was surrendered to the British. A fort was built during the Bijapur dynasty and strengthened in 1670 by the Maratha king Shivaji, which is located on a headland near the harbour. It is one of the ports of the Konkan coast. It has a palace where the last king of Burma, Thibaw, and later Veer Savarkar, were confined.

It is also believed that the Pandavas having performed their pilgrimage on the 13th year had settled in the adjoining territory of the Ratnagiri district and when the Pandavas and the Kauravas had the famous war at Kuruskshetra, the king of this region Veeravat Ray had accompanied then there.

Buddhist Monastery

Ratnagiri was once the site of a mahavihara, or major Buddhist monastery. According to Amit Jha, a lecturer in the Department of History at Sri Aurobindo College, Delhi University, "Ratnagiri comprises two magnificient monasteries, also rebuilt more than once. One of them was double-storeyed and had an extensive courtyard with two-sides of it having a number of cells for habitation of monks.

Besides, we have archaeological remains of six temples, thousands of small stupas, 1386 seals, myriad sculptural relics and architectural pieces of daily use. The largest stupa was 47 feet square and 17 feet high surrounded by four minor stupas. There are hundreds of miniature votive stupas decorated with lotus, petal and beaded tassels."

Prime Attractions

Parashuram Temple near Chiplun, Ganapatipule and Pavas draw many visitors. Caves in the Chiplun, Khed, Dabhol, Sangameshwar, Gauhani Velgaum and Vade Padel are also worth visiting. The Buddhist legend in the Papanch, Sudan and Srath Appakasini record the conversion of Konkan to Buddhism as early as the lifetime of Gautama (BC 560-481). Chiplun, Kol, and Pabol caves indicate that the Sarthawalas or Caravan-men donated some of them. Shivsamarth gad at sawarde near chipalun is also worth visiting with all sculptures from Shivaji Maharaj era.

The "Ganga (Ganges) of Rajapur" is a natural phenomenon believed by many locals to be a miracle. Nearly every 3 years the well forms 14 small pools of water of different temperatures about 3 ft apart. It is believed that the holy Ganga Mata appears to the devotees there. Geologists have theorized that this is a rare case of a large natural syphon from a nearby mountain.

Thebaw Palace: Constructed in 1910-1l, the Thebaw Palace was built for the exiled king and queen of Burma (now Myanmar). They lived in this palace from 1911 till their death in 1916. The five years of their stay are now immortalised in stone with their tombs. In future, this palace might be converted into a regional museum or a heritage hotel

Malgund: Birthplace of the famous Marathi poet, Keshavsut. Itis a small peaceful village about 1 km away from Ganapatipule. The poet's house was recently renovated and converted into a students' hostel. The Marathi Sahitya Parishad (Marathi Literature Society) has constructed a beautiful monument called Keshavsut Smarak in his memory.

Jaigad Fort: Nestled on a cliff, at the entrance of the Sangameshwar river and 35 km from Ganapatipule is the Jaigad Fort.This 17th century fort offers a commanding view of the sea. Jaigad's sea fort is situated at a sheltered bay. Its beach is small and safe.

Pawas: Besides its natural beauty and serenity, Pawas achieved prominence when Swami Swaroopanand (a spiritual leader who influencedan entire generation of Maharashtrians) had made it his abode. The place where he used to reside is now converted into an ashram. A visit there is still like a journey through time.

Velneshwar: 170 km from Ratnagiri is the sleepy, village of Velneshwar. Its adjoining beach is clean and natural and is lined with coconut trees. It is possible to swim there as the beach is free from rocks. There is an old Shiva temple near Velneshwar which is frequently visited by pilgrims; a haven for those in search of quiet mysticism in the ethereal presence of the master mystic-Lord Shiva.

Ratnadurga Fort: Built during the Bahamani rule. Later to become the property of Adilshah. In 1670, Shivaji conquered the fort.1761 saw the fort fall into the hands of a man impersonating Sadashivrao Bhau. In 1790, Dhondu Bhaskar Pratinidhi rebuilt the fort and strengthened its ramparts.The fort has never witnessed any decisive, or historically notable battles.

The fort is horseshoe shaped, with a length of 1300 metres and width of 1000 metres.Surrounded by sea on three sides, with land touching it on the fourth side. On one of the sea facing sides, part of the cliff has collapsed to reveal a cave. One of the fort's bastions, the ' Siddha Buruj ', still has a lighthouse, that has stood here for years. A picturesque temple of The Goddess Bhagwati is one of the important places of worship in the area of the fort. A well near the temple has steps leading down.

Ganpatipule: Ganpatipule is a famous place for clean sea beaches. It is 21 kilometers from Ratnagiri city on the way to Purnagad and 4.5 kilometers from Pawas. It is also famous for Lord Ganesh Temple.

Surat

Surat is a port city in the Indian state of Gujarat and administrative headquarters of the Surat District. As of 2006, Surat and its metropolitan area had a population of approximately 4.9 million. It is the second largest city in Gujarat and ninth largest in India.

The city is situated on the left bank of the Tapti River, 14 miles from its mouth. A moat indicates the dividing-line between the old city, with its narrow streets and handsome houses, and the newer suburbs, but the city wall has almost disappeared. The city is largely recognized for its textile and diamond businesses. 92% of the world's diamonds are cut and polished in Surat.

History

Local traditions fix the establishment of the modern city in the last years of the fifteenth century, and in 1514 the Portuguese traveller Duarte Barbosa described it as an important seaport, frequented by many ships from Malabar and all parts of the world. There still is an irregular picturesque fortress on the banks of the river built in 1540. One particular village in the suburbs of Surat is Barbodhan Village, possibly named after the explorer Duarte Barbosa (it derives from "Bab-ul-Aden"-Doorway to Aden, Yemen-where it has strong cultural and trading links).

Surat eclipsed Cambay as the major port of western India, as Cambay's harbour had begun to silt up by the end of fifteenth century. Subsequently during the reigns of Mughal emperors Akbar, Jahangir and Shah Jahan it rose to be the chief commercial city of India. An Imperial mint was established at Surat during that time. As the major port on the western seaboard of that time, Surat also served as the sailing port for the Hajj to Mecca. At the end of the 16th century the Portuguese were undisputed masters of the Surat sea trade. In 1608, ships from the British East India Company started docking in Surat, which was established as a trade transit point. In 1612, the British Captain Best, and after him Captain Downton, destroyed the Portuguese naval supremacy and obtained an imperial firman establishing a British factory at Surat following the Battle of Swally.

The city was made the seat of a presidency under the British East India Company after the great success of the embassy of Sir Thomas Roe to the court of emperor Jehangir. The Dutch also founded a factory.

In those days Surat was known to be almost the city of Kubera, the God of Wealth. In 1664 the Maratha leader Shivaji sacked and looted Surat. When Shivaji arrived at Surat he demanded tribute from the Mughal commander and the small army stationed with him for port security. The tribute was refused and so after Shivaji took the city, he put it to sack. Surat was under sack for nearly 3 weeks, in which the army looted all possible wealth from Mughal & Portuguese trading centers. All this loot was successfully transported to Maharashtra before the Mughal Empire at Delhi was alerted. This wealth later was used for development & strengthening the Maratha Empire.

The only exception to the looting was the British factory, a fortified warehouse-counting house-hostel, which was successfully defended by Sir George Oxenden. But the prosperity of the factory at Surat received a fatal blow when Bombay was ceded to the British as part of the dowry for Catherine of Braganza's wedding to Charles II in 1662. Shortly afterwards in 1668 another factory was established in Bombay(Mumbai) by the British East India Company. From that date Surat began to decline with the rise of British interests in Bombay, and the city was sacked again by Shivaji in 1670. By 1689 the seat of presidency was moved to Bombay by the British East India Company.

The Surat population had reached an estimated 800,000 in its heyday, but by the middle of the 19th century the number had fallen to 80,000. Surat was again taken by the British in

1759, and the conquerors assumed the undivided government of the city in 1800. Since the introduction of British rule, the city and the surrounding district remained comparatively tranquil; and even during the Revolt of 1857(also known as the first struggle for India's independence) peace was not disturbed, owing in great measure to the loyalty of the leading Muslim families to the British and to the largely mercantile interests of the local population.

A fire and a flood in 1837 destroyed a great number of buildings. Among the interesting monuments still surviving are the tombs of the English and Dutch merchants and their families, dating to the 17th century, especially those of the Oxenden brothers.

By the early 20th century, the population had slowly climbed to 119,306 and Surat remained a centre of trade and manufacturing, although some of its former industries, such as shipbuilding, were extinct. There were cotton mills, factories for ginning and pressing cotton, rice-cleaning mills and paper mills. Fine cotton goods were woven on hand-looms, and there were special manufactures of silk brocade and gold embroidery (known as zari). The chief trades were organized in guilds. The manufacturing and trading brought an eclectic mix of ethnicities to the city, making Surat's culture unique even in modern times.

In 1992, violent riots took place between Hindus and Muslims, the first and worst of their kind in the modern history of Surat. In 1994, a combination of heavy rains and blocked drains led to water logging in the city. A number of dead street animals and public waste were not removed in time and a plague epidemic spread through the city. This brought the world's attention to the city as evinced by the sanctions on travel and goods exchange put up by a number of countries. The municipal commissioner during that time, S. R. Rao and the people of Surat worked hard in the late 1990s to clean the city up after which it was recognized in many circles as the 'second-cleanest city in India'.

In the second week of August, 2006, a massive flood caused severe damage to the city of Surat. In less than three days, at least 120 people died. More than 4,000 animal carcasses were later hauled out of the mud. Two weeks after the floods, Surat's diamond-polishing factories were practically empty of workers, who had fled fearing disease.

An industry group estimated the losses at $60 million. Surat got its domestic airport opened on 29-04-07, which started its operation from 6th day of May 2007.

Geography

Surat is a port city situated on the banks of the Tapti river (though the port has disappeared because of the damming of the river Tapti, the nearest port is now in Hazira which falls in the metropolitan area of Surat). The city is located at 21.17° N 72.83° E. It has an average elevation of 13 metres (42 feet). The Surat district is surrounded by Bharuch, Narmada (North), Navsari and Dang (South) districts. To the west is the Gulf of Cambay. The climate is tropical and the monsoon is abundant (about 2500 mm a year).

- Area: 112.27 km^2

Climate

- Winter Temperature: Max 31 °C, Min 12 °C
- Summer Temperature: Max 42 °C, Min 24 °C
- Rainfall (mid-June to mid-September): 931.9 mm
- Lowest Recorded Temperature: 7 °C
- Highest Recorded Temperature: 44 °C

Economy

Surat is at the heart of India's thriving diamond-polishing industry, which in 2005 cut 92% of the world's diamond pieces and earned India $8 billion in exports. Gujarati diamond cutters emigrating from East Africa established the industry in 1901 and by the 70s Surat-based diamond cutters began exporting stones to the US for the first time. Though a majority of polishing work takes place on small weight stones, Surat's workshops have set their eyes on the lucrative market for finishing larger, pricier stones in the future. It is a major production centre for synthetic textiles in India.

Surat is famous for tasty and delicious foods, especially surti khamam, locho, surti undhayu etc.

Surat has a very good shopping area. It includes all major brands. Mark Pi's Crazy Noodles, Pizza Hut, McDonald's, Subway are some of the major restaurant chains offering fast food to the locals.

Surat is also famous for its saree. 1 out of every 5 sarees manufactured in India is from Surat. During festive season and during marriage season people throng to surat to buy sarees as they get more varieties at cheaper rates.

Surat is also an industrial hub for the production of synthetic fibers and man-made fabrics, contributing almost 28% of India's total synthetic fiber output and 40% of the nation's total man-made fabric production and computrised embroidery work. In addition it is home to several major processing facilities/ manufacturing centers for Reliance Petrochemicals, Essar Steel, Larsen & Toubro, KRIBHCO, ONGC, Shell, ABG Shipyard, Torrent Power.

Government and Politics

The Surat Municipal Corporation is responsible for the city's civic infrastructure as well as carrying out associated administrative duties.

Transport

Now Surat has a City bus service called SMSS Service, which is one of the best City bus service in the country. On the 22nd of August the Bus service has been opend by the Mayore of the City Mr. Kanubhai Mavani. Privately operated auto rickshaws are overall fasility spread in the every part of the city. The city has recently seen the completion of a large number of road engineering projects, particularly the elevated roads, or flyovers in the diamond and textile districts of the city. This has significantly cut down on the commuting time for many commuters travelling to the diamond and textile districts.

Surat has the highest No. of flyovers in Gujarat.

The Golden Quadrilateral highway system will pass through Surat at its expected completion in December of 2006. At present the city is connected to the National Highway 8 through a 16 k.m. connector highway. National Highway 8 corridor is one of the most industrially developed area in the country and Surat is one of the most industrially active cities that connect to it. National highway 6 starts from Hazira and connects the city to Dhule, Nagpur, Raipur, Sambalpur, Kharagpur and Kolkata.

Surat is very well connected with Mumbai and Ahmedabad by fast luxurious train, although by western standards this may not be a true description.

The city is connected to the national railway system through the Western Railways connecting it to Mumbai and beyond to the south as well as New Delhi, Ahmedabad, Vadodara and other cities to the north. The Surat Railway station is in the eastern-central part of the city and is very conveniently located near major hotels and businesses. There is also a connection to the Central Railways through the Udhana Junction and the Tapti line. There are numerous daily trains that travel to the north, south and east during all times of the day. The variety of passenger trains range from local trains that stop at all stations on the way, to super fast express trains (by Indian standards) like the August Kranti Rajdhani Express. In addition there are plenty of goods trains that move the goods produced by the city to the rest of the country and beyond, and bring supplies to the city.

The New Airport became functional with Surat-Delhi IA flight on 6th May 2007. And also going to connect to other major cities in India very soon hopefully and also International airport in future.

Demographics

As of 2001 India census, Surat had a population of 2,433,787. Males constitute 56% of the population and females 44%. Surat has an average literacy rate of 72%, higher than the national average of 59.5%: male literacy is 77%, and female literacy is 66%. In Surat, 13% of the population is under 6 years of age.

Because of presence of unauthorized residential buildings and shanty towns which bring difficulties in counting the residents of these areas, combined with the explosive growth in population (mostly through migration) it is estimated that as of 2006 about 4.5 million people live within the Surat Urban Development Authority(SUDA) area. However, the SUDA also covers a 5k.m. surrounding area in addition to the official city limits and thus covers a lot of villages and towns that lie outside the Municipal area.

Culture

Surat is known throughout India for its unique Surti cuisine. Some special and unique dishes of Surat include Locho, Surti Undhiyu, Rasawala Khaman, Cold coco,Surati Chinese and Surti Ghari. Many of the popular types of food of the state of Gujarat originated in this region. Contrary to popular belief, Surti cuisine is not as sweet as the stereotypical Gujarati food, but rather quite on the spicier side.

The most popular eating spots are roadside standalones, called "laaris" or "rekdis". Come winter and Suratis will emerge at river Tapi's banks to eat Ponk. Ponk is a Roasted Millet variety that is available only in this part of the world.

Surat is also well known for its celebrations of Chandi Padvo which usually comes around October. This is the biggest full moon day of the Hindu calendar year. On this day, Surtis buy almost 100 tons of Ghari and other Surati delicacies, then head to Dumas where they have dinner/late night snack under full moon. Suratis are fond of variety of liquors although prohibition of alcohol in the Gujarat state and they do so to celebrate all occasions.

Most major Indian festivals such as Diwali and Ganesh Chaturthi are celebrated here with great enthusiasm. The kite-flying festival of Makar Sankranti is especially popular in the city. The favourite hangouts are Daman and Goa.

Education

Most of the schools in the area have Gujarati as the medium of instruction, and there are a number of English medium schools as well. St. Xaviers and Lourdes Convent are the two Catholic schools in Surat and are often viewed as elite schools though Sir J.J. English school which was once amongst the best has now degraded due to its poor management. Other private schools like the S.V. Rao New Model School continue to have success and often are recognized by the state and local governments.

Regardless of medium of instruction, most schools are part of the Gujarat State Education Board. The Seventh Day Adventist school in Athwa Lines is part of the national ICSE board and Delhi Public school, Surat is affiliated to CBSE. There is a school in Surat called Lancers Army School. It is a good school to make children physically and mentally strong. It is affiliated to GBSE and CBSE.

Vijaydurg

Vijaydurg (formerly also known as Gheriah) is a seaport 425 km from Bombay on India's West Coast. It boasts a safe harbour with average depths in excess of 100 feet.

From Vijaydurg, Goa is a four-hour drive South along the National Highway 17. The beach facing the Arabian Sea has a historic fort (800 years old) from which the town/seaport derives its name. The region offers a very panoramic view of the creek and the fort. It has a number of virgin beaches close by.

Vijaydurg sports a peace-loving cosmopolitan population. There is a historic temple, a church and mosque. Other locations of Tourist interest include:

- Maratha Admiral Kanhoji Angre's Naval Base and Dry Dock. In 1698, Angre located his first base at the Maratha fort of Vijaydurg ('Victory Fort') (formerly Gheriah) located about 425km from Mumbai. The fort which was originally built by Raja (King)Bhoj in 1208, is located on the coast, and has an entrance hollowed out in it to accommodate entry of a vessel from the sea.
- A vast Mango Research Institute that has developed hybrids like a Ratna, a cross between the Alphonso and Neelam variety, as well as the Kesar hybrid. Vijaydurg also has a large number of coconut palms in addition

to Kokum (Garcinia indica) to boot, and is the home of the famed Alphonsos.

Wildlife

Wildlife including the hyena, red fox, barking deer, sea otter, dolphin, porpoise, whale.

A wide variety of fish including Surmai, ladyfish, Pomfret,sting ray, hammerhead shark, puffer fish, Mullet,Great white sharks, carp, eel, seer fish, swordfish and the seemingly rare sailfish are routinely spotted here. Shellfish like lobster, clam, mussels, periwinkle, oyster, crayfish and many types of crab are abundant. Commonly occurring birds abound like the Barn Owl, kingfisher, kite, cormorant, stork, egret, Red-whiskered Bulbul and cuckoo. Endangered species include the Great Indian Hornbill, vulture, Langur (Black faced Monkey), Giant Squirrel, Red-eyed Pheasant and Tern.

Since the mouth of the estuary opens into the Arabian Sea, the water is clean due to intertidal flushing. Vijaydurg also has a Port Trust, Sea & Land Customs Outposts, and a large State Transport Depot. Up until 1983, Vijaydurg was a port of call for the Konkan Steamer service, which ran two ships: Konkan Sevak and Konkan Shakti, which were later sent to supply the IPKF (Indian Peace Keeping Forces) in Sri Lanka.

Visakhapatnam

Visakhapattanamu, shortened and anglicized: Vizag or Vizagapatnam) is a port city in the Indian state of Andhra Pradesh. It is located on the eastern shore of India, nestled among the hills of the Eastern Ghats and facing the Bay of Bengal to the east. The city is about 650km northeast of Hyderabad. The city is the administrative headquarters of Visakhapatnam District.

Alternatively, it sometimes goes by its now mostly defunct colonial British name, Waltair. During the colonial era, the city had at its hub the Waltair railway station, and that part of the city still goes by the name of Waltair. It is also popularly referred to as "Vizag", a shortening of its full name. It is sometimes also referred to as the "City of Destiny".

The city is home to several state owned heavy industries, one of the most advanced steel plant and has one of the country's largest ports and its oldest shipyard. It has the only natural harbour on the eastern coast of India.

Andhra University, a prominent seat of education in Andhra Pradesh, is located here.

Vizag is primarily an industrial city, apart from being a tourist destination. Tourists are attracted by its unspoilt beaches, nearby scenic Araku Valley and Borra caves, the 11th-century Simhachalam temple and ancient Buddhist sites like Totlakonda & Bavikonda spread across the area.

The city boasts a submarine museum, the first of its kind in South Asia, at Rama Krishna Beach.

Visakhapatnam is also the headquarters of the Eastern Naval Command of the Indian Navy.

History and Culture

This region, formerly part of the great Kalinga empire that stretched up to the river Godavari, has also been mentioned in Hindu and Buddhist texts from the 5th and 6th centuries BC, as well as by Sanskrit grammarians Panini and Katyayana in the 4th century BC.

This city was ruled by several dynasties: the Kalingas during the 7th century, the Chalukyas during the 8th century, the Cholas, the Qutb Shahis of Golconda, the Mughal Empire and the Nizams of Hyderabad.

Local legend says that an Andhra king (9-11th century) on his way to Benares rested there. So enchanted was he with the sheer beauty of the place that he ordered a temple to be built in honour of his family deity, Vishakha. Archaeological sources, however, reveal that the temple was possibly built between the 11th and 12th centuries by the Chola king, Kulottunga Chola I. A shipping merchant, Sankarayya Chetty, built one of the mandapams, or pillared halls, of the temple.

Although it no longer exists (it may have been washed away about a hundred years ago by a cyclonic storm), elderly residents of Vizag talk of visits to the ancient shrine by their grandparents. Noted author Ganapatiraju Atchutarama Raju contradicted this.

In the 18th century, Visakhapatnam was part of the Northern Circars, a region of Coastal Andhra that came first under French control and later that of the British. Visakhapatnam became a district in the Madras Presidency of British India. After India's independence it was the biggest district in the country and was subsequently divided into the three districts of Srikakulam, Vijayanagaram and Visakhapatnam.

Demographics

As of 2001 India census, Visakhapatnam had a population of 1,498,900. Males constitute 50% of the population and females 50%. Visakhapatnam has an average literacy rate of 69%, higher than the national average of 59.5%: male literacy is 74% and female literacy is 63%. In Visakhapatnam, 10% of the population is younger than six.

Language

Visakhapatnam is predominantly Telugu speaking city. The Telugu spoken by the middle classes is a standard dialect with a good dose of English words, while a significant population who have settled down in the city from adjoining villages and neighbouring districts mainly Vizianagaram and Srikakulam speak Uttarandhra (North Coastal) Mandalikam (dialect). But even in Uttarandhra dialect there are subtle differences and in fact Telugu spoken in Srikakulam (Kalinga Andhra) is quite different from Telugu spoken in Visakhapatnam. Historians believe that centuries ago, when Uttarandhra was part of Kalinga empire Buddhist Missionaries and Merchants might have taken Telugu (derived from Brahmi script) script to Southeast Asia from the shores of Uttarandhra where it parented into the scripts of Mon, Burmese, Thai, Khmer, Siam, Javanese and Balinese languages and even Sinhala of Srilanka.

Their similarities to Telugu script can be discerned even today. Vizag is also home to a large Oriya and Bengali communities. One can find Oriya inscriptions in Simhachalam temple and the temple in fact thrives on pilgrims of Orissa. Vizag due to the NAVY and high concentration of public sector industries has good amount of Hindi speaking people. Vizag is also home to a large section of muslim's most of them date back to many generations in Vizag which makes Hindi probably second most popular spoken language in vizag.

The City/Town

From being a small fishing village in the nineteenth century, Vizag has grown into an industrial hub. Its saga began with the quest of British to find a suitable port that connects the rich mineral belt of Central provinces with the East Coast. Unlike western coast of India, East Coast have few undulations to form a natural harbour. Their quest for finding out a harbour ended with Vizag. Vizag is the most protected natural harbour in India. They started building a harbour in 1927 and in 1933 it was opened to traffic. One more important milestone is setting up of Scindia Steam Navigation Co. later known as Hindustan Shipyard Ltd in 1940.

With the construction of KK line connecting iron ore mines of Biladila in MP (present day Chattisgarh) its importance grew. In 1950s and 1960s Government and private sector setting up some largescale Basic industries like Bharat Heavy Plates and Vessels (BHPV), Hindustan Zinc Ltd., Caltex oil refinery (later acquired by Government as HPCL), Coramandel fertilizers, Andhra Polymers (Now LG Polymers), etc. 1980s saw a major development with the setting up of Vizag steelVizag Steel and other major industries.

Economic liberalization in the 1990s brought a modest growth to the city but not as much as it did to the state capital, Hyderabad. However, some industries sprang up like Rain calclining Ltd., Expansion of HPCL, Setting up of Vizag Export Processing zone, Simhadri Thermal Power plant of NTPC, etc. The urban sprawl that characterizes other major cities has yet to be seen in Vizag.

Due to the presence of Eastern Naval Command, Steel Plant, HPCL, the city has been the home to people from different parts of the country and due to this the city has a cosmopolitan texture to it. The city's main commercial and shopping centres are located in the Dwaraka Nagar-RTC Complex area and Jagadamda Junction area. In the recent years since 2000, the Dwaraka Nagar-RTC Complex area has transformed into a commercial hub with new shopping malls and complexes spring up within a radius of 2-3 kilometers.

Vizag is well connected with daily flights from Hyderabad, Chennai, Delhi, Mumbai, Bangalore, Tirupati, and Raipur. With the entry of several new airlines, Air Sahara, Air Deccan, Kingfisher Airlines, and Paramount Airways operating there along with the state-owned airline Indian, there has been a modest increase in frequency of the flights. Vizag Airport has recently received permission to operate night flights, a new runway 10,000 feet long was contructed and became operational to accommodate international flights and larger aircraft. Visakhapatnam has a good network of roads.there are frequent buses to vizianagaram, srikakulam, araku and rajahmundry. There are even bus services to hyderabad, vijaywada and few parts of orissa. The city is home to many five star hotels with the presence of Taj group, ITC Welcomegroup & Park hotels group.

There has been a rise in the real estate prices, mainly attributed to the Telangana movement for a separate Telangana state, some speculate on Vizag becoming the next capital. Satyam Computer Services Limited opened software development centre in 2007. Recently various other software and BPO companies such as Patra Corporation, Encore India, and Tata Consultancy Services Limited have announced their plans for starting development and outsourcing centers in Vizag, which has also contributed to the rise in real estate prises. Inflows from NRIs from Vizag has further added to this rise. Leading Cisco Partner Datasoft Comnet Pvt. Ltd. has setup the Operations of Patra Corp. and a host of other ITES companies etc. and also provide LAN and WAN consultancy to the Various BPOs and ITES companies in Vizag.

The city has the Indira Gandhi Zoological Park setup in the year 1972 at the city outskirts. The Zoo Park features some of the rarest species in India.

Educational Facilities

Visakhapatnam is also considered as one of the main centres of education in the state of Andhra Pradesh. The Mrs.A.V.N. College is one of the oldest and premier educational institutions established in 1878. It is the home of the renowned Andhra University (established in 1926). Prof S. Radhakrishnan, before he became the President of India, worked as the Vice Chancellor of this university between 1931 to 1936. The university and its affiliated colleges provide high quality and affordable education to thousands of students not only from the northern region of Andhra Pradesh but of the entire state. Post Graduate and Graduate courses are offered in various branches like Arts, Commerce, Science & Technology, Engineering, IT, Business Management,Law and Pharmacy.

Another important landmark in the education map of Visakhapatnam is the Andhra Medical College (established 1902). The college has ushered in an era of Medical Education in Visakhapatnam and continues to uphold the prestigious tradition of engendering the finest doctors from its aisles.

Coming down to the primary, high school and college level,Visakhapatnam has several good institutions, providing quality education. Apart from state run schools for the poor, there are many private institutions and missionary schools and colleges all of which provide quality education. Few of these schools have been running since more than 75 years whereas St. Aloysius Anglo-Indian High School was established in 1847 and is one of the oldest in India.

Georgia Institute of Technology (GA Tech) will establish its campus in Vizag. Making it the first foreign university to establish a campus in India.

Visakhapatnam has now become a preferred destination for students after Hyderabad. The city now has a large number of engineering colleges. The prominent institutions are:

- Gandhi Institute of Technology & Management (GITAM) now a Deemed University.
- Gayatri Vidya Parishad College of Engineering
- Pydah College of Engineering & Technology

- Al-Ameer college of engineering and Information technology
- Raghu Engineering College (REC)
- Vignan's Institute of Information Technology
- Anil Neerukonda Institute of Technology & Sciences (ANITS)
- Sanketika Vidya Parishad Engineering College
- Chaitanya College of Engineering
- Viswanadha Institute of Technology and Management
- Maharaj Vijayaram Gajapathi Raj College of Engineering (MVGR)

There is one famous polytechnic college in Visakhapatnam:

- Government Polytechnic-VSKP

One more famous educational institution in Vizag is St. Frances De Sales (SFS) situated in Seethammadhara.

Economy

The city's growth has mostly been due to its heavy industries (both state-owned and private), such as:

- HPCL-Oil Refinery (Hindustan Petroleum Corporation Limited)
- Vizag Steel Plant
- Hindustan Zinc Limited
- Bharat Heavy Plate and Vessels Ltd (BHPV).
- Hindustan Shipyard Limited
- Visakhapatnam Port Trust
- Coromandel Fertilizers
- National Thermal Power Corporation
- Dredging Corporation of India Limited
- Rain Calcining Limited
- Essar Pelletization Plant (Recently a major expansion occurred. The iron ore now used by this plant comes via a pipeline 267km long from Bailadila, helping reduce transportation costs substantially.)
- HSBC

- Synergies Castings Ltd. is a Major Alloy Wheel Manufacturer in India with manufacturing base in Visakhapatam/Vizag.

Total Logistics India Pvt Ltd

Its traditional importance in shipbuilding is confirmed by the fact that India's first ship, the "Jala Usha", was launched in Vizag.

Vizag is also one of India's main fishing ports, has a dedicated harbour for the fishing industry and handles a large percentage of India's seafood exports.

The Vizag Special Economic Zone plays a vital role in the industrial growth of the city.

The Andhra Pradesh government has confirmed deals with Satyam and Wipro to set up a presence in the city. Satyam's office has already been built and started working. Wipro's office is coming up on the site of the old TB hospital. The Bhabha Atomic Research Centre has also expressed interest in setting up a research centre and a nuclear power plant here.

Vijayanagara

Vijayanagara is in Bellary District, northern Karnataka. It is the name of the now-ruined capital city, located at 15°19'N 76°28'E, of the historic Vijayanagara empire which extended over the southern part of India.

Location and Surroundings

Most of the city lies on the south bank of the Tungabhadra River. The city was built around the original religious centre of the Virupaksha temple at Hampi. Other holy places lie within its extents, including the site of what is said to be Kishkinda where a Hanuman temple, the cave home of Anjani, Kesari and Shabari, a holy pond named the Pampasarovar are located. It also contains the cave home of Sugriva, the monkey king of the Ramayana.

The central areas of the city, which include what are now called the Royal Centre and the Sacred Centre, extend over an area of at least 40 km^2. It includes the modern village of Hampi. Another village, Kamalapuram, lies just outside the old walled city, but is also surrounded by ruins and monuments. The nearest town and railhead is the town of Hospet, about 13 km away by road. Hospet also lies within the original extents of the old city, though most of the items of interest are within walking distance of Hampi and Kamalapuram.

The natural setting for the city is a hilly landscape, dotted with numerous granite boulders. The Tungabhadra river runs through it, and provides protection from the north. Beyond the hills on the south bank on which the city was built, a plain extended further the south. Large scale walls and fortifications of hewn granite defended the centre of the city.

The City

The name translates as 'City of Victory', from vijaya (victory) and nagara (city). As the prosperous capital of the largest and most powerful kingdom of its time in all of India, Vijayanagara attracted people from all around the world. Pandit Nehru, in his book, "The Discovery of India" writes:

After Timur's sack of Delhi, North India remained weak and divided up. South India was better off, and the largest and most powerful of the southern kingdoms was Vijayanagar. This state and city attracted many of the Hindu refugees from the north. From contemporary accounts, it appears that the city was rich and very beautiful—The city is such that eye has not seen nor ear heard of any place resembling it upon earth", says Abdur-Razzak from Central Asia.

There were arcades and magnificent galleries for the bazaars, and rising above them all was the palace of the king surrounded by "many rivulets and streams flowing through channels of cut stone, polished and even." The whole city was full of gardens, and because of them, as an Italian visitor in 1420, Nicolo Conti, writes, the circumference of the city was sixty miles. A later visitor was Paes, a Portuguese who came in 1522 after having visited the Italian cities of the Renaissance. The city of Vijayanagar, he says, is as "large as Rome and very beautiful to the sight"; it is full of charm and wonder with its innumerable lakes and waterways and fruit gardens. It is "the best-provided city in the world" and "everything abounds." The chambers of the palace were a mass of ivory, with roses and lotuses carved in ivory at the top—"it is so rich and beautiful that you would hardly find anywhere, another such."

The ruined city is a UNESCO World Heritage Site, (where it is called the Ruins of Hampi). In recent years there have been concerns regarding damage to the site at Hampi from heavy vehicular traffic and the construction of road bridges in the vicinity. Hampi is now listed as a "threatened" World Heritage Site, and is included in the 'UNESCO List of World Heritage in Danger: 1999'.

It is widely believed that Vijaynagar was the largest city in India and the second largest city in the world at the end of 15th century with 500,000 inhabitants.

History

The Vijayanagara empire was founded by Hakka (Harihara) and Bukka, also called the Sangama brothers. The empire consolidated under Harihara I and began to expand and prosper under Bukka Raya. Some time after its original establishment, the capital was established at the more defensible and secure location of Vijayanagara, on the south side of the river.

Contemporary descriptions depict a very large and highly-developed metropolitan area: recent commentators say,

"The massive walls, which can still be traced, enclosed an area of more than sixty square miles, much of which was occupied by fields and gardens watered by canals from the river. The population cannot be estimated with precision, but it was certainly very large when judged by the standards of the fifteenth century. The great majority of the houses were naturally small and undistinguished, but among them were scattered palaces, temples, public buildings, wide streets of shops shaded by trees, busy markets, and all the equipment of a great and wealthy city.

The principal buildings were constructed in the regular Hindu style, covered with ornamental carving, and the fragments which have survived suffice to give point to the enthusiastic admiration of the men who saw the city in the days of its magnificence."

The city flourished between the 14th century and 16th century, during the height of the power of the Vijayanagar empire. During this time, the empire was often in conflict with the Muslim kingdoms which had become established in the northern Deccan, and which are often collectively termed the Deccan sultanates. In 1565, the empire's armies suffered a massive and catastrophic defeat at the hands of an alliance of the sultanates, and the capital was taken.

The victorious armies then proceeded to raze, depopulate, and destroy the city over a period of several months. Despite the empire continuing to exist thereafter during a slow decline, the original capital was not reoccupied or rebuilt. It has not been occupied since.

The buildings in the city are mostly built in the original native traditions of southern India, associated with the Hindu religion. Some of them show a certain amount of Islamic influence due the interaction with the Islamic kingdoms.

The Sacred Centre

This title has been given by historians to the areas extending from Hampi village to Matanga Hill to its east. It is sometimes extended further northeast to the Vitthala Temple. It consists of a hilly region immediately to the south of the Tungabhadra.

Virupaksha Temple

This surviving temple and temple complex is the core of the village of Hampi. Also known as the Pampapati temple, it predated the empire, and was extended between the 13th and 17th centuries. It has two courts with entrance gopurams. The main entrance with a 50 meter gopuram faces east into a ceremonial and colonnaded street, that exends for about 1 km to a monolithic statue of Nandi.

The temple is still in use now. It is dedicated to Virupaksha, an aspect of Shiva and his consort Pampa, a local deity.

Hemakuta Hill

The hill is situated to the south of Hampi village. It bears several small temples that predate the construction of Vijayanagara as the capital of the empire, some being as early as the 10th century. The hill was fortified when the main city was constructed, and a number of more recent temples, tanks, entrances, and gopurams exist on the hill, some of which were never completed.

Krishna Temple

This is a ruined temple, south of Hampi and Hemakuta hill. It was built by the emperor Krishnadevaraya after military campaigns in Orissa. The temple is contained in twin enclosures. Parts of the temple and its compound have collapsed, and while some restoration has been carried out, it is generally in poor condition. There is now no image in the inner sanctuary.

Ugra Narasimha

Also to the south of Hampi is this massive rock cut idol of Narasimha, the fierce aspect of Vishnu, 6.7 m high. Originally the idol bore a smaller image of Lakshmi on one knee; this had fallen off, probably due to vandalism. The Lakshmi statue is now in the museum at Kamalapuram. Narasimha is depicted seated on the coils of Shesha. Shesha is shown here in a form with seven heads, the heads arching over Narasimha to form a canopy. The statue has recently been restored. The granite strap binding between his knees is a recent addition to stabilise it. The donation of this work is ascribed to either Krishnadeva Raya, or to a wealthy merchant during his reign.

Sugriva's Cave

This is a natural cave, said to be the original home of the monkey king Sugriva, where Rama is said to have met him and Hanuman on his travels. The cave is marked by coloured markings, and the attentions of pilgrims.

Kodandarama Temple

This is situated to the east of Hampi, near the end of the colonnaded street that leads out from the Virupaksha temple.

It is in the sacred centre of the city, and by a narrow point of the Tungabhadra river. This temple marks the spot where Rama crowned Sugriva. The temple is still in use, and the garbha grha contains statues of Rama, Lakshmana and Sita all carved out a single boulder.

Vittala Temple

Situated northeast of Hampi, opposite the village of Anegondi, this is one of the principal monuments of the city. It is dedicated to Vittala, an aspect of Vishnu worshipped in the Maratha country. It is believed to date from the 16th century.

In the front of the temple is the famous stone chariot or ratha. This is itself a miniature temple, carved out of a single rock, to resemble the temple chariots or rathas in which temple idols are traditionally taken out in procession.

One of the notable features of the Vittala Temple is the musical pillars. Each of the pillars that support the roof of the main temple is supported by a pillar representing a musical instrument, and is constructed as 7 minor pillars arranged around a main pillar. These 7 pillars, when struck, emanate the 7 notes from the representative instrument, varying in sound quality based on whether it represents a wind, string or percussion instrument. The temple is the venue of the annual Purandaradasa festival.

The King's Balance

This structure, the Tulapurushandana, stands to the southwest of the Vittala temple. consists of two carved granite pillars, spanned by a carved horizontal granite transom. This was used on ceremonial days, when scales were hung from the transom, and the Raya (the emperor) was ceremonially weighed against gold or jewels. The treasure was then distributed, to Brahmins or others in the city.

The Royal Centre

This extensive area consists of a small plateau, which starts about 2 km to the southeast of Hampi, and extends southeast, almost to the village of Kamalapuram. It is separated from the Sacred Centre by a small valley, now consisting of agricultural fields, and which carries irrigation canals or streams that join the river opposite Anegondi. A granite platform overlooks the Royal Cenre. The Royal Centre contains the ruins of palaces, administrative buildings, and some temples directly associated with royalty. Little remains of the palaces except the foundations, as they were largely timber structures, for comfort. The temples and some of the other stone structures survive however, as do many of the surrounding city walls.

An aqueduct runs through much of the Royal Enclosure and into the Great Tank where water was brought for special events. The west end of the tank is overlooked by a platform shrine. The aqueduct also runs into the large stepped tank, lined in green diorite, with a geometric design that has not required restoration.

Ramachandra Temple

The temple stands in a rectangular courtyard, with entrances facing to the east. Reliefs showing daily life and festival scenes occur on the outer walls of the courtyard. Scenes from the Ramayana occur on the inner courtyard walls, and on the temple itself. There is a well-relief of baby Krishna on the walls.

The temple may have been exclusively for royal use. It is believed to be constructed at the site of Vaali's killing in the hands of Rama. It may have been a private shrine for royalty. It is unusual in that it has four black basalt columns in the mandapa (columned hall). The inner sanctuary of the temple is now empty.

This is also known as the Hazara Rama temple (temple of a thousand Ramas), due to the recurrence of images of Rama on the walls. Sometimes it is called the Hajara Rama temple (the Rama temple in the courtyard).

Underground Shiva Temple

Also known as the Virupaksha Temple (not to be confused with the temple of the same name at Hampi), this extensive temple stands in an excavation in the ground, and is surrounded by earth embankments. At times the base of the temple is flooded and may be inaccessible. When it is accessible, masses of small insect bats may be found in the temple.

Lotus Mahal

A palace for the queen that has, among other things, pipes with running water. A construction of the later Vijayanagara period, this structure shows Islamic influence in its arched gateways and vaulted ceilings; its construction entirely in stone is a clear deviation from conventional Vijayanagara palace and house construction that used wooden structures on stone platforms.

Pushkarani

Also called the Stepped Bath, or the Queen's bath, this is a stepped well designed for bathing. Such sunken wells were created to provide relief from daytime heat. It would have been covered when the city was occupied.

Elephant Stables

A set of large stables, to house the ceremonial elephants of the royal household. The area in front of them was a parade ground for the elephants, and for troops. This is another structure that shows Islamic influence in its domes and arched gateways. The guards' barracks are located right next to the elephant stables.

Bibliography

Ashish, Bose : *India's Urbanization, 1901-2001*, McGraw Hill, New Delhi, 1978.

Ashish, Bose : *Studies in India's Urbanization 1901-1971,* Tata McGraw-Hill Publishing Co., Bombay & New Delhi, 1973.

Ballhatchet, Kenneth and Harrison, John : *The City in South Asia: Pre-Modern and Modern*, Curzon Press; London, 1980.

Banga, Indu : *The City in Indian History*, Urban Demography, Society, and Politics, Manohar for Urban History Association of India, Delhi, 1991.

Basu, D. K. : *The Rise of the Colonial Port City in Asia*, Center for South and Southeast Asian Studies, Santa Cruz and Berkeley, 1979.

Bhatia, Gautam : *Punjabi Baroque and Other Memories of Architecture*, Penguin, New Delhi, 1994.

Chaudhuri, Nirad : *Thy Hand, Great Anarch! India: 1921-1952*, Chatto & Windus, London, 1987.

Choudhury, Ranabira Ray : *Calcutta: A Hundred Years Ago*, Nachiketa Publications, Bombay, 1988.

Eck, Diana L. : *Banaras : City of Light*, Princeton UP, Princeton, 1983.

Fanshawe, H.C. : *Delhi: Past and Present*, John Murray, London, 1902.

Forrest, G. W. : *Cities of India,* Archibald Constable & Co., Westminster, 1903.

Fox, Richard : *Urban India : Society, Space and Image*, Program in Comparative Studies on Southern Asia, Duke University, 1969.

Freitag, Sandria B. : *Culture and Power in Benares : Community, Performance, and Environment, 1800-1980.* University of California Press, Berkeley, 1989.

Ghosh, A. : *Calcutta, The Primate City*, Ministry of Home Affairs, Office of the Registrar General, New Delhi, 1966.

Gillion, Kenneth L. : *Ahmedabad : A Study in Indian Urban History*, University of California Press, Berkeley, 1968.

Greaves, Edwin : *Kashi the City Illustrious or Benares*, The Indian Press, Allahabad, 1909.

Grewal, J.S. : *In the by-lanes of History : Some Persian Documents from a Punjab Town*, Indian Institute of Advanced Study, Shimla, 1975.

Gupta, I. P. : *Urban Glimpses of Mughal India : Agra, the Imperial Capital (16th & 17th Centuries)*, Discovery Publishing House, Delhi, 1986.

Hansen, Thomas Blom : *Wages of Violence : Naming and Identity in Postcolonial Bombay*, Princeton UP, Princeton, 2001.

Havell, E. B. : *Benares, the Sacred City: Sketches of Hindu Life and Religion*, Blackie & Son, London, 1905.

Heber, Reginald : *Narrative of a Journey Through the Upper Provinces of India,* John Murray, London, 1861.

Heber, Reginald : *Narrative of a Journey Through the Upper Provinces of India from Calcuta to Bombay, 1824-1825*, John Murray, London, 1829.

Indu, Banga : *Studies in Urban History*, Guru Nanak Dev University, Department of History, Amritsar, 1981.

Jyoti, Kanchan : *The City of Jullunder: A Study in Urban History, 1846-1947*, Guru Nanak Dev University, Amritsar, 1988.

Kaarsholm, Preben : *City Flicks : Cinema, Urban Worlds and Modernities in India and Beyond*, Graduate School, International Development Studies, Roskilde University, Roskilde, Denmark, 2002.

Kanwar, Pamela : *Imperial Shimla : The Political Culture of the Raj*, Oxford University Press, Delhi, 1990.

Keyserling, Count Hermann : *Travel Diary of a Philosopher*, Harcourt, Brace & Co., New York, 1969.

Latif, Syed Muhammad : *Lahore: Its History, Architectural Remains, and Antiquities, with an Account of its Modern Institutions, Inhabitants, Their Trade, Customs, & Co,* New Imperial Press, Lahore, 1892.

Manor, James : *Power, Poverty and Poison : Disaster and Response in an Indian City*, Sage Publications, New Delhi, 1993.

Metcalf, Thomas R. : *An Imperial Vision: Indian Architecture and Britain's Raj*, University of California Press, Berkeley, 1989.

Mishra, Pankaj : *Butter Chicken in Ludhiana : Travels in Small Town India*, Penguin, New Delhi, 1995.

Misra, R.P. : *Million Cities of India*, Vikas, New Delhi, 1978.

Naidu, Ratna : *Old Cities, New Predicaments: A study of Hyderabad*, Sage Publications, New Delhi, 1990.

Nair, Thankappan P. : *A History of Calcutta's Streets*, Firma KLM, Calcutta, 1987.

Nandy, Ashis : *An Ambiguous Journey to the City : The Village and Other Odd Ruins of the Self in the Indian Imagination*, Oxford UP, Delhi, 2001.

Nilsson, Sten : *The New Capitals of India, Pakistan and Bangladesh*, Studentlitteratur, Lund, Sweden, 1973.

Parker, Arthur : *A Handbook of Benares*, J. Lazarus & Co., Banaras, 1895.

Parry, Jonathan P. : *Death in Banaras*, Cambridge University Press, Cambridge, 1994.

Poolani, Sunil K. : *Urban Voice : Essays from the Indian Subcontinent*, Frog Books, New Bombay, 2003.

Rao, M. S. A. : *Urban Sociology in India : Reader and Source Book*, Orient Longman, New Delhi, 1974.

Roberts, Emma : *Scenes and Characteristics of Hindostan, with Sketches of Anglo-Indian Society,* Wm. H. Allen & Co., London, 1835.

Rosenthal, Donald B. : *The City in Indian Politics*, Faridabad, 1976.

Roy, Ashim Kumar : *History of the Jaipur City*, Manohar, Delhi, 1978.

Salim, Ahmad, : *Lahore 1947, Introduction by Ian Talbot*, India Research Press, New Delhi, 2001.

Schwartzberg, Joseph E. : *A Historical Atlas of South Asia*, The University of Chicago Press, Chicago, 1978.

Sharp, H. : *Delhi: Its Story and Its Buildings*, Oxford, London, 1921.

Sherring, M.A. : *Hindu Tribes and Castes as Represented in Benaras*, Thacker, Spink & Co., Calcutta, 1872.

Tagore, Rabindranath : *Glimpses of Bengal*, Macmillan, London, 1991

Taneja, Kusum Lata : *Morphology of Indian Cities*, National Geographic Society of India, Varanasi, 1971.

Tavernier, Jean Baptiste : *Travels in India*, Macmillan & Co., London, 1889.

Turner, Roy : *India's Urban Future*, University of California Press, Berkeley, 1962.

Varma, P.K. and S. Shanker : *Mansions at Dusk : The Havelis of Old Delhi*, Spantech, Delhi, 1992.

Venkatarayappa, K.N. : *Bangalore (a socio-ecological study)*, University of Bombay, Bombay, 1957.

Verma, T.K. : *Varanasi Through the Ages*, Bharatiya Itihas Sankalan Samiti, Varanasi, 1986.

Willigen, Van John : *The Indian City: A Bibliographical Guide to the Literature on Urban India*, Human Relations Area Files, New Haven, 1979.

Index

C

D

H

I

J

K

S

T

U

V

❑❑❑